THE DEATH PENALTY IN AFRICA

This study is dedicated to
Almighty God,
my parents,
my stepfamily,
my spouse Jeanne, my son Ange, my daughter Amelia,
Professor Rwigamba Balinda and
all victims of the barbarity of human justice in Africa.

The Death Penalty in Africa

The Path Towards Abolition

AIMÉ MUYOBOKE KARIMUNDA

Supreme Court of the Republic of Rwanda and the University of Rwanda

Routledge
Taylor & Francis Group
LONDON AND NEW YORK

First published 2014 by Ashgate Publishing

Published 2016 by Routledge
2 Park Square, Milton Park, Abingdon, Oxfordshire OX14 4RN
711 Third Avenue, New York, NY 10017, USA

First issued in paperback 2016

Routledge is an imprint of the Taylor & Francis Group, an informa business

British Library Cataloguing in Publication Data
A catalogue record for this book is available from the British Library

The Library of Congress has cataloged the printed edition as follows:
Karimunda, Aimé Muyoboke, author.
The death penalty in Africa / by Aimé Muyoboke Karimunda.
pages cm
Includes bibliographical references and index.
ISBN 978-1-4724-1534-9 (hardback)
1. Capital punishment--Africa. I. Title.

KQC981.4.K37 2014
364.66096--dc23

2014003012

ISBN 13: 978-1-138-27951-3 (pbk)
ISBN 13: 978-1-4724-1534-9 (hbk)

Contents

List of Figures

List of Tables

Preface

William A. Schabas OC MRIA
Professor of International Law, Middlesex University (London)
Professor of International Criminal Law and Human Rights, Leiden University
Emeritus Professor of Human Rights, National University of Ireland Galway

In the celebrated 1995 judgment of the South African Constitutional Court abolishing capital punishment in a country that had seen the worst abuses of the death penalty under the apartheid regime, Justice Albie Sachs advanced the proposition that capital punishment was not necessarily indigenous to Africa. He lamented the relative neglect of traditional African law by judges and academics on the continent. Justice Sachs has sometimes been taken as romanticising the situation in pre-colonial Africa, but a close reading of his judgment shows that this is not necessarily the case: 'I am sure that there are many aspects and values of traditional African law which will also have to be discarded or developed in order to ensure compatibility with the principles of the new constitutional order', he wrote.

On the subject of capital punishment, Justice Sachs insisted upon the contribution of the Europeans, who had implemented the practice in a brutal manner and with the objective of securing their colonial domination rather than enhancing the rule of law, justice and fairness. Precisely because of the dearth of scholarly attention to such matters, Justice Sachs was only in a position to present initial impressions on the subject. It remained for researchers like Muyoboke Aimé Karimunda to explore the subject in detail, something that is largely accomplished in this extraordinary and important study.

To a large extent, Dr Karimunda has confirmed the observation of Justice Sachs that much of pre-colonial African society was inspired by a 'rational and humane adjudicatory approach' that meant capital punishment was not in fact generally used as a punishment for murder. At the same time, the present study also shows that the reality is more complex, and that the apparent generalisation by Justice Sachs needs to be accompanied by more nuanced observations. Perhaps detailed analysis of various aspects of colonialism shows the shortcomings of any simplistic reduction.

This seems particularly true with law and justice, where sophisticated approaches whose ancestry goes back to the Romans and then before, to Hammurabi in what is modern-day Iraq, were imported to the African continent by Europeans about a century ago. In one sense, much benefit resulted, and most of the law studied at universities throughout Africa is indeed of European origin. But

European law of the time had many brutal aspects. The use of capital punishment stands out particularly.

Already, in the heyday of the colonial 'scramble', as it is called, a process of reform was underway in Europe that had brought much change to the practice of capital punishment. In some countries, it had been all but abandoned, while in others the number of crimes for which it might be imposed had been reduced dramatically. It was no longer carried out in public. The methods of execution imposed were allegedly deemed to avoid prolonged suffering as much as possible. Thus, there had been much improvement from the middle ages when criminals were mutilated in public and their body parts displayed prominently.

The gradual process of reform within Europe was to suffer a temporary setback in the early twentieth century as fascist governments took power in a number of States. Then, when the Second World War was over, Europe really began a half-century-long process that has led to total abolition. Many factors have contributed, but probably it is the work of the Council of Europe and the European Court of Human Rights that is entitled to the largest share of credit for this.

But the increasingly liberal European approach did not necessarily extend to African colonies where criminal justice did not seem to follow the same rules. Often, the colonial courts practised a parody of justice, and criminal law was essentially an instrument of control and repression rather than one of social protection and reform. Probably the great excesses in the death penalty within colonised Africa actually increased as the struggle for independence gained momentum. In Africa, the turning point in the abolition of capital punishment was not the influence of European reform so much as liberation from colonial domination.

Nevertheless, it was to take several decades for the traditional African principles of justice and fairness, upon which Justice Sachs based his analysis, to take hold. Beginning sometime in the 1980s, Africa went through a process of transformation with respect to capital punishment that was even more rapid and determined than what occurred in Europe. There were some especially dramatic developments, like the judgment of the South African Constitutional Court in 1995 and, more recently, the decision to turn its back on capital punishment in Dr Karimunda's native Rwanda, in 2007.

Today, only a handful of African states continue to carry out executions. A reform process is underway that appears both inexorable and irreversible. In many respects, Africa stands as a model for other parts of the world where the death penalty lingers. China, for example, insists that while it is on a path towards abolition, the process will take many decades because it is linked to economic development. Pointing to Europe, Chinese specialists sometimes explain that only when China has become a developed country will it be able to adopt the most progressive views towards criminal justice, including suppression of the death penalty. Instead, they should be looking to the African model, where progressive attitudes to punishment rooted in both traditional and modern concepts of human dignity have meant that that change need not await great prosperity. Human development is not simply about wealth and economic well-being. It is also dependent upon shared values that cherish the sanctity of human life. The story of the decline of capital punishment in Africa, told so ably in this book, is rich with lessons that go well beyond the continent itself.

Acknowledgements

The completion of this book has required more than personal efforts. I am greatly indebted to Professor William A. Schabas who guided my insights on the discovery of the unexplored field of the death penalty in Africa. The combination of his expertise, wisdom and love towards his disciples makes inestimable his contribution to the finalisation of this work.

However, without the financial support of both the Centre for International Legal Cooperation (CILC) and the Kigali Independent University, which unconditionally continued to pay my wages when on research leave, my dream would have been an illusion. Particular members of these institutions have been understanding and supportive at times of low morale. They are, in no particular order, Ingrid de Haer Douma, Tamara Van Vliet, Alexandre Kayiranga, Karin Huis, Gustave Tombola and Didace Kayihura. Furthermore, the encouragement of Professors Rwigamba Balinda, Vinodh Jaichand, Yolandi Le Roux, Jean Marie Kamatali and Drs Roelof Haveman, Nadia Bernaz and Justice David Majanja has provided the energy that enabled me to cross the Rubicon.

Words fail me in thanking Patient Gumiliza, Kris Depont, Hadidja Mukazure, Desire Kana, Gabriel Tchimanga, Moise Mwacha and Nogugu Mafu, who welcomed me into their homes during my stays in the Netherlands, Belgium, United Kingdom and Ireland. Of the long list of colleagues that made working in Ireland such a pleasant experience, I especially thank James Nyawo, Kenny Izhevuwa, Kyra Hild Naomi and Drs Maria Varaki, Michelle Farell and Andrea Breslin.

My deep gratitude is expressed as well to the staff of the James Hardman Library in Galway, the libraries of the Institute of Advanced Legal Studies and the School of Oriental and African Studies in London, the libraries of Utrecht University in the Netherlands and the Irish Embassy in Kampala. Without their prompt assistance, the process of writing this work would have been seriously hampered.

Last but not least, there are no appropriate words to acknowledge the support of my family, friends and colleagues in Rwanda and abroad and especially my grandmother. My wife's love and encouragement and the patience of my son and daughter have been priceless contributing factors to the completion of this book.

Table of Cases

International Court of Justice

North Sea Continental Shelf Cases (Federal Republic of Germany v. Denmark and v. The Netherlands), Judgment [1969] ICJ Reports 1969, 3–375.

International Criminal Tribunal for Rwanda

Prosecutor v. Jean Uwinkindi, ICTR-2001-75-R11bis, 51.
Prosecutor v. Yussuf Munyakazi, ICTR-97-36-R11bis, 22–32.

African Commission on Human and People's Rights

Constitutional Rights Project v. Nigeria, African Commission on Human and Peoples' Rights, Comm. No. 60/91 (1995).
ACHPR /Res.11 (XVI) 94: Resolution on Nigeria (1994).
ACHPR /Res.16 (XVII) 95: Resolution on Nigeria (1995).

Democratic Republic of Congo

Military Prosecutor v. Bongi Massaba, RP No. 018/2006, ILCD 387 (CD2006), 61, 66–68 and 117.
Military Prosecutor v. Khawa Panga Mandro, RMP N0227/PEN/2006, ILDC 524 (CD), Elisabethville, 4 February 1943.

East Africa (Kenya, Tanganyika and Uganda)

Rex v. Hassan wa Saleh and Another (1908) 3 K.L.R. 105.
Rex v. Kichingeri and others (1908) 3 E.A.P.L.R. 1, 2, 4 and 5.
Rex v. Weer S/O Muga (1911) 5 E.A.P.L.R. 62, 62–63.
Kasan wa Muiga and others v. Rex (1912) 4 E.A.P.L.R. 103.
Rex v. Karoga wa Kithengi and 53 others (1913) 5 E.A.P.L.R. 50, 53.
Rex v. Odar Odeyu (1918) 7 E.A.P.L.R. 108, 109.
Rex v. Tromoi and Another (1919) 8–9 K.L.R. 6.

Rex v. Opiri (1927) K.L.R. 90.
Rex v. Mwandamere s/o Sefula (1931) 8 K.L.R. 58, 58–59.
Rex v. Kumwaka wa Mulumbi (1932) 14 K.L.R. 137.
Kimno Arap Kipturji v. Rex (1934) 1 E.A.C.A. 190.
Rex v. Farasisiko Sheshaho (1938) 5 E.A.C.A. 110.
R v. Komen Arap Chelal and 43 others (1938) 5 E.A.C.A. 150.
Rex v. Mohamed Shah s/o Lal Shah (1939) 5 E.A.P.L.R. 103, 104.
Rex v. Kamau s/o Njeroge (1939) 6 E.A.C.A. 133, 133–135.
Rex v. Kinanda Bin Mwaisumo (1939) 6 E.A.C.A. 105.
Rex v. Kibiegon Arap Bargutwa (1939) 6 E.A.C.A. 142, 143–144.
Rex v. Kichanjele s/o Ndamungu (1941) 8 E.A.C.A. 65.
Rex v. Gerevazi s/o Lutabingwa (1941) 9 K.L.R. 56, 56–57.
Rex v. Mvula s/o Irove (1944) 11 E.A.C.A. 112, 112–113.
Rex v. Petero Mukasa and Katabazi Yamumbi (1944) 11 E.A.P.L.R. 115.
Rex v. James Adekanmi (1946) 17 E.A.C.A. 99, 101.
Rex v. Kulabirawo (1947) 14 E.A.C.A. 116.
Mawji and another v. R (1957) J.C. 126, 130 and 133.
CC 317/1952 'Kamau Ndirangu and Githuka Kagwe' at Nairobi, 10 April 1953, KNA MLA I/464.
CC40/1953 'Karaya Njonji and three others' at Nairobi, 23 April 1953, KNA.

France

Cour de Cassation (Chambre Criminelle) 12 juillet 1946.
Cour de Cassation (Chambre Criminelle) 6 octobre 1955.

Gold Coast (Ghana)

Rex v. Kwamina Afferi (1926) G.C.L.R. 197, 201.

Namibia

R. v. Goseb 1956 (2) S.A. 696 (S.W.A.).

Nigeria

Rex v. Francis Ojifo (1942) 16 N.L.R. 63, 63 and 66.
Rex v. Lamidi Balugon (1942) 16 N.L.R. 75, 75–80.
Rex v. James Ojifo (1944) 17 N.L.R. 99, 102.
Rex v. Nwonwu Nshi (1944) 17 N.LR. 103, 107.

Rex v. Uko and Another (1951) 20 N.L.R. 16.
Regina v. Ibrahim and two others (1954) 20 N.L.R. 137.
Queen v. Kadiri (1958) S.C.N.L.R. 25, 26–27.
Queen v. Amoo (1959) S.C.N.L.R. 272, 278.
DPP v. Obi (1961) 1 All N.L.R. 182.
Onuoha v. The State (1998) 13 N.W.L.R. 531, 587–588.
Abacha v. Fuwehinmi (2000) 6 N.W.L.R. 228.

Rwanda

Re Tubarimo Aloys, RS/Inconst/Pén.0002/08/CS of 29 August 2008.

Sierra Leone

Kanu, Seisay and Koroma v. Regina (1959) A.L.R. 331, 336.
Rex v. Sard (1935) A.L.R. 395, 400 and 401.
Yebema v. Regina (1959) A.L.R. 235, 237.

South Africa

R v. Nonosi (1882) 1 Buch AC 154, 155 and 156.
Rex v. Bodenstein (30 September, 2 October 1901), reprinted (1901) 18 *South African Law Journal* 425–426.
R v. Mazibuko 1958 (4) SA 353 (A.D.).
S v. Makwanyane and Another 1995 (3) SA 391 (CC).
The State v Lionel Phillips and Sixty-Three Others, 1896, reprinted (1900) 17 *South African Law Journal* 21 and 28.

Southern Rhodesia (Zimbabwe)

Rex v. Sanka [1923] R&N 20 (SR).
Rex v. Sales [1936] R&N 55 (SR), 55 and 56.
Rex v. Sikonia [1937] R&N 54 (SR), 54 and 56.
R v. Longone [1938] R&N 131 (SR).
Rex v. Chikokonya [1938] R&N 122 (SR), 122 and 125.
Rex v. Van Biljon [1938] R&N 180 (SR).
Rex v. Mahoko [1949] R&N 6 (SR), 6 and 7.
Rex v. Gideon [1951] R&N 11 (SR), 11 and 12.

United Kingdom

R v. Joykissen Mookerjee (1862) 1 Moo PC (N.S.) 172, 190 and 191.
Ex parte Deeming (1892) A.C. 422, 426.
Mondihar Sigh v. R.I. (1950) A.C. 345.
Kuruma v. R. (1955) A.C. 197, 200.
Hardtmann v. R (1963) A.C. 746, 758.

United States of America

Olmstead v. United States (1928) 277 U.S. 438.

Table of Legislation

International and Regional Instruments

Charter of the United Nations (1945) AJIL Supp.190 (1945) CTS7.
Chapters XII and XIII
European Convention on the Protection of Human Rights and Fundamental Freedoms, Rome 4 November 1950, E.T.S. No 5.
Articles 2–3
International Covenant on Civil and Political Rights (1966) entered into force 23 March 1976, 999 UNTS 171.
Rome Statute of the International Criminal Court of 17 July 1998, UN Doc A/CONF. 183/9, 17 July 1998.
Article 12 (1)
Second Optional Protocol to the International Covenant on Civil and Political Rights, aiming at the abolition of the death penalty, 15 December 1989, GA Res.44/128 (1990) 29 *ILM* 1464.
Statute of the International Court of Justice, 26 June 1945, 59 Stat. 1031, T.S. No 993, 3 Bevans 1179.
Article 38 (1) (b)

Algeria

Decree of 25 June 1831.
Article 2
Décret du 28 février 1841.
Article 49
Arrêté de Bageaud of 6 March 1841.
Article 8, para 3

Angola

Constitutional Law of the Republic of Angola of 2010.
Article 30

Belgium

Loi du 8 juin 1867, *Moniteur Belge* du 9 juin 1867.
Articles 7–11
Article 52
Article 69
Article 77
Articles 101–103
Articles 113–115
Article 118
Article 120
Articles 394–397
Article 475

Botswana

Proclamation Act no 40 of 1912.
Section 1 (1)
Proclamation Act no 11 of 1928.

Cape Verde

Constitution of the Republic of Cape Verde of 1992 as amended in November 1999.
Article 26 (2)

Democratic Republic of Congo

Code Pénal du Congo-Belge tel que promulgué par le Décret du 26 mai 1888.
Article 87 ter
Décret du 22 décembre 1888.
Article 21
Décret du 24 novembre 1890.
Arrêté du Gouverneur General du 9 avril 1898.
Articles 1–2
Décret du Gouverneur Général du 9 avril 1898.
Article 2
Circulaire du 14 mai 1898.
Décret du 3 août 1936.
Code Pénal du 30 janvier 1940 in Léon Strouvens and Pierre Piron, *Codes et lois du Congo-Belge* (Larcier 1948) 111–146.
Article 4, para 2

Articles 5–6
Article 23, para 3
Articles 44–45
Article 49
Article 85
Article 108
Article 171
Articles 181–182

Décret du 12 mai 1943.

Décret du 29 avril 1944.

Ordonnance no 11/37 du 24 janvier 1948.
Articles 2–3

Ordonnance no 66/338 du 30 mai 1966 portant création du tribunal militaire d'exception.

Ordonnance-loi no 68/193 du 3 mai 1968, M.C. no 14 du 15 juillet 1968, 1324.
Article 1

Ordonnance-loi no 72/60 du 25 septembre 1972 portant code de justice militaire, *Journal Officiel*, no 6, 25 septembre 1972.

Ordonnance no 79/238 du 13 octobre 1979 portant grâce présidentielle.

Loi no 024/2002 du 18 novembre 2002 portant code pénal militaire, *Journal Officiel*, no spéciale, 20 mars 2003.
Articles 26–28
Article 161

Décret du 30 janvier 1940 portant code pénal congolais tel que modifié à ce jour (Mis à jour au 30 novembre 2004), *Journal Officiel*, 45ème année, no spéciale, 30 novembre 2004.
Articles 5–6
Article 18
Article 35

Constitution de la République Démocratique du Congo du 18 février 2006 telle que révisée par la loi no 11/002 du 2 janvier 2011, *Journal Officiel de la République Démocratique du Congo*, no 3, 1 février 2011.
Article 16
Article 61
Article 149, para 3

France

Code Pénal Français (Loi décrétée le 12 février 1810 et promulguée le 22 février 1810) in Hyppolyte F. Rivière, *Codes français et lois usuelles* (A. Maresq Aine 1970).
Article 2
Article 7

Articles 12–13
Article 27
Article 56, para 7
Article 59
Article 64
Articles 75–79
Article 82
Article 86
Articles 91–97
Article 132
Article 296
Articles 302–304
Article 381
Loi du 28 Avril 1832.
Decree of 26 September 1842.
Article 39
Decree of 1 June 1878, *Bulletin des Lois* (12 Ser), pt. II at 553.
Article 14
Decree of 11 May 1892, PENANT (1892).
Article 23
Decree of 26 July 1894, PENANT (1894).
Article 23, para 3
Decree of 16 December 1896, PENANT III, 17 (1897).
Article 23, para 6
Decree of 6 August 1901, PENANT III, 117 (1901).
Article 17, para 10
Decree of 15 April 1902, PENANT III, 122 (1902).
Article 17, para 11
Decree of 17 March 1903 PENANT III, 118 (1903).
Article 17
Decree of 30 April 1946, *Journal Officiel*, 1 mai 1946, at p. 3680.

Gabon

Loi no 3/2010 du 15 février 2010 portant Abolition de la Peine de Mort, *Journal Officiel de la République Gabonaise*, 51ème année, no 3, 30 mars 2010.

Gold Coast (Ghana)

Protectorate Courts Jurisdiction Ordinance, no 16 of 1932.
Section 36

Guinea

Constitution of the Republic of Guinea of 1984 as amended in 1991, *Sabado*, 11 May 1991.
Article 32

India

Indian Penal Code Act XLV of 1860.
Section 121
Section 132
Sections 302–303
Section 305
Section 396

Kenya

Model Penal Code for the East African Dependencies Act, 1929, in *The Gazette of the Colony and Protectorate of Kenya*, no 40, 1 August 1929.
Section 2
Section 4
Kenya Penal Code, cap. 24, Uganda Protectorate, *The Penal Code, 1950 and the Criminal Procedure Code, 1950* (Government Printer 1950) 17.
Section 40

Liberia

Declaration of Independence in Convention of the Commonwealth Republic of Liberia, 26 July 1847, 5. Available at www.digital.library.cornell.edu (accessed 23 August 2009).
Constitution of the Republic of Liberia of 6 January 1986, ICL Doc status, 6 January 1986.
Section 2 (2)

Mozambique

Constitution of the Republic of Mozambique of 16 November 2004, *Mozlegal, Lda* 2004.
Article 40

Namibia

Namibian Constitution Second Amendment Act, 2010.
Section 6

Nigeria

Charter of the Royal Niger Company of 10 July 1886.
Protectorate Courts Proclamation of 1900.
Section 34
Protectorate Courts Proclamation of 1900.
Supreme Court Proclamation of 1902.
Provincial Courts Proclamation of 1902.
Nigeria (Constitution Amendment no 3) Order in Council, 1959 (S.I. 1959 No 1772, p. 3229, s. 69 and Sch).
Nigeria Independence Act, 1960 (8 and 9 Eliz, 2 Ch. 55).
Section 3
Constitution of the Federation of Nigeria Act no 20, 1963.
Sections 18–19
Decree no 1 of 1966 (Nigeria).
Decree no 17 of 1966.
Section 3 (1)
Robbery and Firearms (Special Provision) Act of 1970.
Constitution of the Federal Republic of Nigeria of 1 October 1979.
Sections 30–31
Robbery and Firearms (Special Provision) Decree No 5 of 1984.
Section 11 (4)
Exchange Control (Anti-Sabotage) Act of 1990, Cap. 114.
Recovery of Public Property (Special Military Tribunal) Act of 1990, Cap. 389.
Robbery and Firearms (Special Provision) Act of 1990, Cap. 398.
Special Tribunal (Miscellaneous Offences) Act of 1990, Cap. 410.
Constitution of the Federal Republic of Nigeria (Decree no 24 of 1999).
Sections 33–34
Shari'a Courts (Administration of Justice and Certain Consequential Changes) Law, No 5 of 1999.
Section 127 (b)
Section 129 (b)
Section 131 (b)
Section 136 (b)
Section 153 (d)
Section 200

Northern Rhodesia (Zambia)

Native Courts Ordinance of 1 October 1937.
Section 11 (1) (a), (b)

Nyasaland (Malawi)

Native Courts Ordinance of 1 October 1937.
Section 11 (1) (a), (b)

Queensland

Queensland Criminal Code Act, 1899 (68 Vic no 9, 1899).
Sections 37–53
Sections 79–82
Section 305

Ruanda-Urundi

Exécution de l'article 22 du Traité de Versailles du 28 juin 1919 à travers la Décision de la Société des Nations du 31 août 1923 confirmant à S.M. le Roi des Belges le mandat sur le territoire de l'Est Africain, *Bulletin Officiel du Ruanda-Urundi (B.O.R.U.)*, 2ème année, no 1, p. 1.

Loi du 21 août 1925 portant union du territoire du Ruanda-Urundi et de la colonie du Congo Belge, *Bulletin Officiel du Ruanda-Urundi (B.O.R.U.)*, 3ème année, no 1, p. 10/178.

Ordonnance du Ruanda-Urundi no 43/Just du 18 mai 1940, *Bulletin Officiel du Ruanda-Urundi (B.O.R.U.)*, 1940, p. 86.

Rwanda

The Décret-loi no 21/77 du 18 août 1977 portant Code Pénal Rwandais, *Journal Officiel*, no 13 bis, 1978.
Article 26
Articles 28–33
Articles 151–200
Article 209
Article 238
Article 240
Article 282

Articles 312–317
Article 324
Article 349
Article 359
Article 360
Article 388
Article 403
Article 404 ter
Article 442
Article 444
Articles 459–487

Organic Law no 31/2007 of 25 July 2007 relating to the abolition of the death penalty, *Official Gazette*, no special of 25 July 2007.
Article 2

Organic Law no 32/2010 of 22 September 2010 relating to Serving Life Imprisonment with Special Provisions, *Official Gazette*, no special of 14 October 2010.

Organic Law no 66/2008 of 21 November 2008 modifying and completing the Organic Law no 31/2007 of 25 July 2007 relating to the Abolition of the Death Penalty, *Official Gazette*, no 23, 1 December 2008.
Article 1

Organic Law no 01/2012/OL of 2 May 2012 instituting the Penal Code, *Official Gazette*, no special of 14 June 2012.

São Tomé and Príncipe

Law no 1/2003 establishing the Constitution of the Democratic Republic of São Tomé and Príncipe of 2003.
Article 22

Seychelles

Constitution of the Republic of Seychelles of 18 June 1993 as amended by Constitutional Act no 14 of 1996.
Article 15 (2)

Sierra Leone

Sierra Leone Offences Act, 1861 (24 and 25 V. c. 31).
Section 1

South Africa

South African Offences Act, 1863 (26 and 27 V. c. 35).
Passes for Natives Act 22 of 1867.
Native Territories Penal Code Act 24 of 1886.
Section 135
Law no 27 of 1887 (N).
Section 1
Native Dance Act 16 of 1891.
Article 1
Sale to Native Act 28 of 1898.
Immigration Act 47 of 1902.
Section 2 (a)
Criminal Procedure Code (Transvaal) Ordinance 1 of 1903.
Chapter 18
Criminal Procedure Code (Transvaal) Ordinance 1 of 1903.
Section 259
First Offenders (The Cap) Act 10 of 1906.
Administration of Justice (Orange Free State) Supplementary Ordinance 1 of 1906.
Criminal Law Amendment (Transvaal) Act 38 of 1909.
Criminal Law Amendment (Natal) Act 10 of 1910.
Criminal Procedure Act 31 of 1917.
Section 338
General Law Amendment Act 46 of 1935.
Section 61 (a)
Native Courts Ordinance of 1 October 1937.
Section 11 (1) (a), (b)
Internal Security Act 44 of 1950 for communism and advocating social change.
Section 11
Criminal Law Amendment Act 16 of 1959.
Section 25
General Law Amendment Act 76 of 1962 for sabotage.
Section 21
Terrorism Act 83 of 1967 sm.
Section 2 (1)
Criminal Procedure Act 51 of 1977.
Section 1 (1) (i)
Section 227

South West Africa (Namibia)

Proclamation no 21 of 1919 (South West Africa).
Section 1 (1)

Southern Rhodesia (Zimbabwe)

High Court Act, 1891, cap. 8 (Southern Rhodesia).
Article 13

Swaziland

Swaziland Criminal Procedure and Evidence Act, no 4 of 1907.
Section 2

Tunisia

Décret du 26 septembre 1842.
Article 42

Uganda

Uganda penal code, cap. 22, in Uganda Protectorate, *The Penal Code, 1950 and The Criminal Procedure Code, 1950* (Government Printer 1950) 17.
Section 53
Penal Code Amendment Act, 1966.
Section 25 (a) and (b)

United Kingdom

Murders Abroad Act, 1817 (57 Geo. 8, c. 58).
Section 1
Admiralty Offences (colonial) Act, 1860 (23 and 24 V. c. 123).
Colonial Laws Validity Act, 1865 (28 and 29 V. c. 63).
Section 2
West Africa Offence Act, 1871 (34 and 35 V. c. 8).
Fugitive Offenders Act, 1881 (44 and 45 V. c. 69).
Sections 20–21

Chapter 1
General Introduction

The eighth United Nations' quinquennial report on capital punishment indicates that attitudes in Africa as regards the death penalty have improved. Thirty-eight out of 54 African countries (70 per cent) are now either *de jure* or *de facto* abolitionists, and retentionist countries have become reluctant to carry out executions or are moving towards minimal resort to the death penalty.[1] The progress is significant, as just two decades ago Africa was depicted as the most troubled continent, where the abundance of human rights abuses (including but not limited to courts lacking independence and impartiality, and politically motivated executions) overwhelmed the few examples of good practices.[2]

The classic arguments for retention of the death penalty are retribution and deterrence.[3] Retribution is built on the justifiability of the death penalty as deserved punishment for serious crimes. Deterrence is based on the utilitarian approach that considers the imposition and more likely the execution of the death penalty a warning to potential criminals. As early as 1764, Cesaria Beccaria disclosed the weaknesses in these arguments.[4] Abolitionists have since upheld Beccaria's thesis and framed new arguments that systematically weaken any new grounds justifying the retention of the death penalty.

Thus, judicial errors leading to wrongful convictions and the execution of innocents, the danger of politicising criminal justice by resorting to capital punishment as a mechanism of crime control – particularly during periods of high criminality rates or mass crime – and the subjective and versatile nature of public

---

1 Gambia, which was the thirty-ninth, resumed executions in August 2012. See UN Doc E/2010/10, para 38 and annex, tables 2 and 4. See also UN Doc A/HRC/24/18, 1 July 2013 and Zainabo Sylvie Kayitesi, *Report of the African Commission on Human and People's Rights Working Group on the Death Penalty in Africa: Viewed in 25 Years of Existence of the ACHPR*, Yamoussoukro, October 2012, at pp. 10–11, available at www.achpr.org (accessed 5 January 2013).

2 William A Schabas, 'African Perspectives on Abolition of the Death Penalty' in William A Schabas (ed), *The International Sourcebook on Capital Punishment* (Northeastern University Press, Boston 1997) 30.

3 For a recent debate on 'The Question of Deterrence' see Roger Hood and Carolyn Hoyle, *The Death Penalty: A Worldwide Perspective* (4th edn, Oxford University Press, New York 2008) 317–349.

4 Cesaria Beccaria, *On Crimes and Punishments* (Richard Bellamy ed, Cambridge University Press, Cambridge 1995).

opinion in both retentionist and abolitionist countries[5] are a few of the additional arguments that have strengthened the abolitionist movement. Today, consequently, it is impossible to execute the death penalty without violating human rights.[6]

Even if these arguments have justified abolition elsewhere, Africa's dynamism towards repeal of the death penalty corresponds to social changes, periods of national unity and reconciliation, divorce from totalitarian regimes and the realisation that since colonial times, resorting to the death penalty has been linked with a political agenda of oppression and repression.[7] Tyrannical regimes have continued the colonial policy of suppressing people's freedom and fundamental human rights. The death penalty is undemocratic.[8] Therefore, capital punishment not only violates the fundamental right to life, it also constitutes an antithesis of 'the right to be free from excessive, repressive, and tortuous punishments'.[9]

Today, it is strongly voiced that the death penalty was introduced in Africa as a part of foreign laws for the purpose of colonial domination. Michello Hansugule argues that traditional African societies were characterised by democracy and egalitarianism. Indigenous justice condemned offenders without destroying their dignity.[10] In the *Makwanyane* case, Justice Sachs confirmed in a concurring opinion that prior to the Western invasion, the death penalty was unknown in Africa, at least for murder.[11] Prominent African lawyers tend to corroborate the view that capital punishment is a colonial legacy. Ross Kinemo, a Tanzanian lawyer, maintains that

> [B]efore the coming of colonialism, Africa had never witnessed a hangman. The most severe form of punishment was ostracism ... the fear of ostracism was one of the chief factors preventing people from committing crime. So hanging was handed down to us through colonialism. We have retained it but it is a great contradiction since the African by nature is a humanitarian.[12]

Although seductive as an argument, the foreign origin of the death penalty in Africa does not enjoy unanimity. Retentionists even consider abolition is rather

---

5 Roger Hood and Carolyn Hoyle, 'Abolishing the Death Penalty Worldwide: The Impact of a "New Dynamic"' (2009) 38 *Crime and Justice* 1, 17–18.

6 ibid 7.

7 Schabas (n 2) 30–32.

8 Robert Badinter, 'Moving towards Universal Abolition of the Death Penalty' in *Death Penalty: Beyond Abolition* (Council of Europe Publishing, Strasbourg 2004) 10.

9 Hood and Hoyle (n 5) 17.

10 Michello Hansungule, 'The Historical Development of International Human Rights' in Azizur Rahman Chowdhury and Jahid Hossain Bhuiyan (eds), *An Introduction to International Human Rights Law* (Martinus Nijhoff Publishers, The Hague 2010) 20.

11 *S v. Makwanyane and Another* 1995 (3) SA 391 (CC), at para 377D–E.

12 Ross EJ Kinemo, *Contemporary Tanzanian Penal Policy: A Critical Analysis* (British Institute in East Africa) http://www.tzonline.org/pdf/contemporarytanzanianpenalpolicy.pdf (accessed 18 April 2007).

un-African.[13] Abolition is perceived as an attempt by former colonial powers to impose their views on independent countries 'to override their sovereign rights to fashion their justice system according to their own judgment of the needs and culture of their country'.[14] Taking advantage of cultural relativism, African Muslim countries further argue that the death penalty is un-abolishable because it is prescribed by sacred texts.[15] This cultural argument is one of the barriers to the spread of abolition among current retentionist countries in Africa. It carries two messages: the death penalty is rooted in African culture and, even if it was not, states have sovereign rights in criminal matters.

Cultural relativism considers that cultural traditions, social customs and religious beliefs are so radically diverse that common human rights standards are inconceivable.[16] Therefore, if the death penalty is rooted in the cultures and customs of Africans, abolishing the death penalty would mean abolishing a part of those cultures or customs. The state sovereignty argument holds that the question of the death penalty must be addressed locally.[17] It emphasises the rejection of a universal and intangible human rights provision envisaging the abolition of the death penalty outside the national legal system and equates such initiatives with cultural imperialism.[18] In other words, if the death penalty was not a colonial legacy then it should be retained until the people change their law.

Universal abolitionists, who are more concerned with the emerging international human rights norms that universalise the abolition of the death penalty,[19] hold that cultural relativists and nationalists are merely nostalgic and intend to idealise their indigenous laws such that 'the colonisers could be blamed for everything that deviated from the ideal'.[20] Universalists maintain that traditional African societies had no human rights, but rather had established concepts and practices of human dignity.[21] Africans perceive this position as an insult to African pride and a denial of any kind of civilisation attributed to Africa and retort that human rights are no more than a means to the goal of human dignity.[22]

---

13 Dirk Van Zyl Smit, 'The Death Penalty in Africa' (2004) 4 *African Human Rights Law Journal* 1, 15.

14 Hood and Hoyle (n 5) 39.

15 Schabas (n 2) 30–31.

16 Roberto Toscano, 'The United Nations and the Abolition of the Death Penalty' in *The Death Penalty: Abolition in Europe* (Council of Europe Publishing, Strasbourg 1999) 96.

17 Schabas (n 2) 34.

18 ibid 35; Toscano (n 16); and Nadia Bernaz, *Le droit international et la peine de mort* (La Documentation Française, Paris 2008) 23–27.

19 William A Schabas, *The Abolition of the Death Penalty in International Law* (3rd edn, Cambridge University Press, Cambridge 2002) 42–43.

20 Eva Brems, *Human Rights: Universality and Diversity* (Martinus Nijhoff Publishers, The Hague 2001) 156.

21 Jack Donnelly, *Universal Human Rights in Theory and Practice* (Cornell University Press, London 2003) 78–79.

22 Brems (n 20) 151 and 155. See also Hansungule (n 10) 19–21.

Addressing the nature and scope of the death penalty prior to foreign legal influences is our primary concern. What was the status of the death penalty in Africa prior to foreign legal influences? The inference that the death penalty was not part of African indigenous laws would confirm that traditional laws were imbued with more human values than the laws that influenced them. The establishment of this fact is expected to strengthen the abolitionist movement in Africa. There is no reason to retain the death penalty if it was originally introduced by imperialist laws.

Yet, the most recent research on the death penalty in Africa is conflicting. The death penalty was an exception rather than an institutionalised punishment. As predicted, blame is apportioned to the coloniser, who introduced retributive and deterrent sentencing policies.[23] Later it was found that 'there is no concrete evidence to show … that a murderer, for example was confined in a place (or prison) awaiting execution'.[24]

The statement does not question the existence of the death penalty, but rather the process of execution. Apparently, the punishment existed under indigenous laws, regardless of whether the offender was executed immediately or otherwise. What foreign influences introduced into Africa was the method of execution, rather than the punishment itself: 'the death penalty as practiced today is not in the African tradition', writes Lilian Chenwi in her study of capital punishment in Africa, explaining further that 'the present death penalty system is not as it was practiced in traditional African societies'.[25] In fact, four years after the *Makwanyane* case, Professor Terblanche argued that the concept that was foreign to Africa was imprisonment rather than the death penalty.[26]

Furthermore, no general conclusion can be applied to the whole of Africa. Diversity is found even among peoples who occupy a large territory and generally share common values, such as the Bantu. African people whose laws were free of the death penalty prior to colonisation obviously took on the practice under foreign legal influences. Nevertheless, the existence of the death penalty under indigenous law is not an excuse to retain it. African states are the result of arbitrary frontiers. Retaining the death penalty because some tribes were or are still viscerally attached to it violates the rights of other compatriots who had historically realised the uselessness and atrocious effects of capital punishment. In the modern world, it is unthinkable to claim an historic or cultural right to kill. *A contrario*, any human being has the right not to be killed irrespective of whether it is an indigenous right or not.

---

23 Lilian Chenwi, *Towards the Abolition of the Death Penalty in Africa: A Human Rights Perspective* (Pretoria University Law Press, Pretoria 2007) 18–20.

24 ibid 19.

25 ibid.

26 Stephane S Terblanche, *The Guide to Sentencing in South Africa* (Butterworths, Durban 1999) 507. See also James S Read, 'Kenya, Tanzania and Uganda' in Alan Milner (ed), *African Penal Systems* (Routledge and Kegan Paul, London 1969) 103.

Moreover, there is no question that European and Asian laws contained the death penalty. The issue, rather is what was the scope of death penalty provisions introduced by foreign laws in Africa? Foreign laws do not necessarily mean colonial laws. Anglo-American, Roman Dutch, Islamic and Coptic laws were the first external legal influences in Africa. Although limited to small territories and likely to few people, they all contained death penalty provisions. Originally, the Roman Dutch law was limited to Dutch settlers at the Cape, Anglo-American law applied to former slaves in Liberia, Coptic law's jurisdiction applied in Ethiopian cities, *Shari'a* applied to Muslims and rural areas remained under the influence of indigenous laws.

Colonial laws accommodated or suppressed pre-colonial laws. Only Ethiopia and Liberia escaped colonisation. Across Africa, pre-existing laws and their mechanisms for resolving conflicts were disregarded. The colonisers despised indigenous laws, declaring them savage, primitive or even non-existent,[27] but simultaneously failed to set up legal systems that respected elementary human rights.[28] Westernisation built discriminatory, racist legal systems, which created a maladjusted society with a permanent resort to exceptional and harsh punitive measures.[29] The death penalty was believed to be an effective means of forcing local people into submission.

There was no uniformity in colonial attitudes. Each coloniser introduced its own colonial policies. Sometimes, the same law was applied differently. Often the politics of the death penalty betrayed the true nature of the policy. Colonial domination was the major reason for the export of the death penalty to French, British, Belgian, Italian and Spanish colonies. Portugal never introduced the death penalty in its African colonies.[30] If we succeed in demonstrating that the use of the death penalty during colonial times had atrocious consequences for African civilisation, we will have sent a message to the current political leadership in African retentionist states that the use of the death penalty today perpetuates colonial ideologies.

There can be no doubt that by the time of independence, the death penalty had been normalised in many countries. This raises the question to what extent modern

27 Sandra Fullerton Joireman, 'Inherited Legal Systems and Effective Rule of Law: Africa and the Colonial Legacy' (2001) 4 *Journal of Modern African Studies* 571, 571 and 578.

28 Olivier Le Cour Grandmaison, 'The Exception and the Rule: On French Colonial Law' (2006) 212 *Diogenes* 34, 43.

29 ibid; Frank Furedi, *Colonial Wars and the Politics of the Third World Nationalism* (I.B. Tauris, London and New York 1994) 123–124 and Kristin Mann and Richard Roberts (eds), *Law in Colonial Africa* (Heinmann and James Currey, Portsmouth and London 1991) 35.

30 Fernando O Gouveia Da Veiga, 'Portuguese Africa' in Alan Milner (ed), *African Penal Systems* (Routledge and Kegan Paul, London 1969) 217.

law in Africa is imbued with colonial legacy or if there is any correlation between current death penalty practices and the legacy of colonial state killing policies?

African leaders either kept or introduced the death penalty for the same reason: to protect the fragile political regime. African countries where the death penalty had been applied during colonial times continued to apply it for the same crimes. Countries where the coloniser had become reluctant to impose or execute the death penalty began following through with it, for example in Benin, Togo and the Ivory Coast. Countries where the coloniser had restricted the death penalty to only a few crimes extended the list of capital crimes, for example in the Democratic Republic of Congo, Rwanda and Burundi. Lastly, countries that did not have the death penalty under colonial rule (Angola, Cape Verde, Guinea, Mozambique) eventually learnt from their neighbours that the death penalty was unavoidable in the quest for stability.

Thus, instead of taking abolition of the death penalty as a neo-colonial dictate, African leaders should consider it another step towards complete political independence. It is the rejection of totalitarian regimes and the need for social cohesion that has made the continent the most dynamic as far abolition is concerned. We expect capital punishment will not be reinstated in abolitionist states. We also expect retentionist countries to follow the path of abolitionists in becoming *de facto* abolitionists before complete legal abolition. In Africa, *de facto* abolition has established itself as a transitional phase to *de jure* abolition.

This book explores the historical and cultural background of the death penalty in Africa, analyses the law and practice with regards to the death penalty under European and Asian laws in Africa before independence, assesses the grounds on which the death penalty is retained today and balances arguments on contemporaneous developments on the death penalty in Africa. We expect this broad picture to constitute a humble basis for developing new strategies towards the complete abolition of the death penalty on the continent.

Different approaches have enabled us to reach our conclusions. To begin with, the exegetic and comparative methods engaged keep this work within its legal framework. Furthermore, archival research (content analysis) has filled the gaps left by the documentary technique, which was unavoidable in a documented research like this. Lastly, quantitative findings have been referred to in order to assist in expressing the richness of our conclusions.[31] We should caution that this is not a statistical analysis of the death penalty in Africa. Statistics on the death penalty are often inconsistent and incomplete,[32] and finding a complete picture of criminal cases, death sentences, executions and commutations is impossible. We have also followed the advice that 'statistics cannot really be decisive in

31 Lee Cuba and John Cocking, *How to Write about the Social Sciences* (Longman, Harlow 1997) 93.

32 Ellison Kahn, 'Crime and Punishment 1910–1960: Reflections on Changes since Union in the Law of Criminal Punishment and its Application' (1960) 191 *Acta Juridica* 191, 202.

determining whether one should opt for the abolition or the retention of capital punishment … they can measure attitudes and dispositions, but they cannot really account for deeply rooted human convictions, beliefs and emotions'.[33]

33 Lourens M Du Plessis, 'Capital Punishment: A Legal Philosophical Appraisal' (1989) 2 *South African Journal of Criminal Justice* 181, 184.

Chapter 2
The Death Penalty: Ideas and Practice in Pre-colonial Africa

Introduction

In establishing whether the death penalty existed in African customary laws or not, it is important to outline the grounds on which it was imposed before exploring what justified its exclusion. Both require an inquiry into the practice of those laws. However, there is no consensus among scientists on the existence of customary law, be it local, national[1] or African.[2] Even where a consensus exists, disagreements on its criminal law component and arguments regarding the nature of criminal responsibility prevail.

Lawyers and sociologists have been unable to find a mutually acceptable definition of customary law. Both have employed the definition that has best suited their own purposes.[3] Customary law is not a set of commands or legislated rules. It consists of conventions and enforceable rules repeatedly recognised as rules of law by the community and its courts; these have emerged spontaneously and are agreed upon by people as they go about their daily business and try to solve problems threatening social peace.[4] Furthermore, it must be distinguished from customary international law, which is traditionally defined as a consistent practice among states that has evolved over a period of time to the extent that states believe that the practice has created legal obligations.[5] The International Court of Justice

1 Aberra Jembere argues that depending on whether it is acknowledged all over a particular country or limited to a certain area, tribe or profession, legal custom may take two forms, namely national or local. See Aberra Jembere, 'Legal History of Ethiopia 1434–1974: Some Aspects of Substantive and Procedural Laws' (PhD Thesis, Erasmus Universiteit, Rotterdam 1997) 40.

2 Elias T Olewale, *The Nature of African Customary Law* (Manchester University Press, London 1954) 25.

3 Gordon R Woodman, 'Some Realism About Customary Law: The West African Experience' in Gordon R Woodman and Akintunde O Obilade (eds), *African Law and Legal Theory* (Dartmouth, Aldershot, Singapore and Sidney 1995) 145.

4 Georges BN Ayittey, *Indigenous African Institutions* (Transnational Publisher, New York 2006) 69.

5 Article 38 (1) (b) of the Statute of the International Court of Justice, 26 June 1945, 59 Stat. 1031, T.S. No 993, 3 Bevans 1179. See also Brian D Lepard, *Customary International Law: A New Theory with Practical Applications* (Cambridge University Press, New York 2010) 6.

insists that the practices that form customary international norms are those that are 'settled' and which prove the belief that they have become legally obligatory.[6]

In Africa, customary law has also been referred to as native law[7] or indigenous law,[8] sometimes to dissociate its nature and characteristics from the so-called *ius commune* of the metropolis.[9] Difficulties in defining African customary law have resulted in the use of the expression indigenous law,[10] which is defined as a set of rules of conduct that regulate the behaviour of individuals and communities and which, by maintaining the society's equilibrium, are necessary for its survival as a corporate whole. Its main objective is to maintain equilibrium between interests and forces interacting within one human society and to ensure that nothing threatens to destroy the intergroup equilibrium.[11] Life-threatening sanctions that subject individuals to harsh and inhuman treatments were not necessarily required. Bearing in mind that the reception of foreign laws was made on different dates and certainly in various ways, we will consider data on indigenous law as having been reported before foreign legal influences.

In addressing the issue of the death penalty, however, it is worth bearing in mind that traditional Africa did not apply an indigenous law identical in form and content. Nevertheless, this does not imply the nonexistence of law, let alone criminal law. Sometimes, it is inaccurately thought that because of its restorative nature, the law applied in certain areas of Africa did not differentiate between criminal law and civil law.[12] Some have gone so far as to state that if there is no difference between criminal law and civil law, then there is no law at all.[13] This view overlooks the fact that tort law as a branch of private law is a recent development. African primitive societies, like other ancient societies, classified crimes on the basis of their severity. Only serious crimes called for public

---

6 *North Sea Continental Shelf, Judgment*, ICJ Reports 1969, para 77.

7 Diana Jeater, '"Their Idea of Justice is so Peculiar": Southern Rhodesia 1890–1910' in Peter Coss (ed), *The Moral World of the Law* (Cambridge University Press, London 2000) 178–195.

8 Ebo Chukwuemeka, 'Indigenous Law and Justice: Some Major Concepts and Practices' in Gordon R Woodman and Akintunde O Obilade (eds), *African Law and Legal Theory* (Dartmouth, Aldershot, Singapore and Sidney 1995) 34–42.

9 Paul Hyams, 'Due Process versus the Maintenance of Order in European Law: The Contribution of the *Ius Commune*' in Peter Coss (ed), *The Moral World of the Law* (Cambridge University Press, New York 2000) 63.

10 Kenneth Roberts-Wray, *Commonwealth and Colonial Law* (Stevens and Sons, London 1966) 534.

11 Chukwuemeka (n 8).

12 ibid 36; Ayittey (n 4) 72; Eugene Cotran, 'The Position of Customary Criminal Law in African Countries' in Akilagpa Sawyerr (ed), *East African Law and Social Change* (The East African Institute of Social and Cultural Affairs, Nairobi 1967) 14.

13 Johan F Holleman, 'An Anthropological Approach to Bantu Law (with Special Reference to Shona Law)' in Gordon R Woodman and Akintunde O Obilade (eds), *African Law and Legal Theory* (Dartmouth, Aldershot, Singapore and Sidney 1995) 16.

intervention.[14] Furthermore, the idea of retribution overwhelmingly present in modern criminal law, specifically in today's punishments, has led to the wrongful assumption that in its absence, criminal law would not exist.

Consequently, making any assertion about the death penalty requires that one bears in mind the legal disparities based on the area or people concerned. Moreover, the death penalty has to be distinguished from, among other things, summary executions, poison ordeals, vengeance and ritual murders.

The Death Penalty in African Indigenous Laws

There cannot be punishment unless there are prohibited conducts against which that punishment is effectively applied. The effectiveness of the death penalty in African indigenous laws requires that analysis first be based on facts.

The need to establish whether or not society distinguished crimes from civil wrongs, individual criminal responsibility from collective criminal responsibility and capital crimes from ordinary crimes requires taking into account the numerous indigenous practices that threatened human life without meeting the criterion of a legal punishment. Indeed, Egypt is the only country where knowledge of the existence of the death penalty before foreign legal influences remains unchallenged. However, the methods of execution employed in Egypt might lead to confusion between the death penalty and ritual murders.

Evidence of the Death Penalty in African Indigenous Laws

Once we establish that there existed crimes that outraged society to the extent that they justified public intervention, the next issue will be to find evidence that, before foreign legal influences, Africans resorted to the death penalty to punish those crimes.

Capital crimes

The nonexistence of crimes in indigenous laws is based on a wrongful comparison between modern European law and African indigenous laws that suggests that European law has always categorised crimes, their definitions and punishments, while African indigenous laws aimed at the diametrically opposite purpose of maintaining the social equilibrium.[15] However, like other ancient laws, African indigenous laws distinguished between those acts that disturbed the social equilibrium and fell within the scope of private law and those that negatively

14 Ditlev Tamm, *Roman Law and European Legal History* (Djof Publishing, Copenhagen 1997) 157.

15 Primitive European law made no difference between civil law and criminal law. Ditlev Tamm, ibid.

affected the conditions that made possible the maintenance of that equilibrium and which were part of public law.[16]

Private law embraces all kinds of misconducts that are corrected without community intervention. Here the law of compensation is unavoidable. Theft of another's property is an example of private law because the offender only bears the responsibility of repairing the breach of equilibrium. Public law deals with grave misdeeds deemed anti-social due to their nature and cumulative effects. There is more to this than disturbing the social equilibrium. The whole community is interested. Offences affect the relationships between different groups or individuals or they endanger human life. Poisoning, for example, is a public offence because it threatens the security interests of the entire community.[17]

The problem with this categorisation is still that African indigenous laws are only judged on the basis of the social equilibrium that the law aims to maintain by any means. It seems as if the lack of distinction between criminal law and civil law in African indigenous laws implies confusion between crimes and civil wrongs.[18] However, this simplistic view overlooks the fact that before 1800, 'the modern distinction between the criminal and civil aspects of a wrongful act, and thus between punishment and compensation, was foreign to almost all European legal systems'.[19] In England, for example, the principle of justice was restitution rather than retribution.

> Compensation was the most proper remedy for most wrongs committed and there was no police and no prisons. A criminal, however, caught red-handed was sentenced at once. Sentences of imprisonment were unknown; the punishment for theft was mutilation or the payment of compensation, while murder was avenged by death and in other homicides by compensation.[20]

It is evident that crimes and their punishments have preceded their definitions. Previously, society did not define principles of criminal law before dealing with the daily misbehaviour threatening its existence and the peaceful coexistence of its members.[21] Therefore what matters is not the nomenclature of the crimes but the extent to which they are recognised and punished as crimes. The recognition

16 Chukwuemeka (n 8).

17 ibid.

18 Olewale (n 2) 110–114.

19 Bruce Lenman and Geoffrey Parker, 'The State, the Community and the Criminal Law in Early Modern Europe' in VAC Gatrell et al. (eds), *Crime and the Law: The Social History of Crime in Western Europe since 1500* (Europa Publications Limited, London 1980) 12.

20 Herbert R Hone, 'The Native of Uganda and the Criminal Law' (1939) 21 *Journal of Comparative Legislation and International Law* 179, 186.

21 Nyabirungu Mwene Songa, *Droit pénal général Zaïrois* (DES, Kinshasa 1995) 21.

and the sanction of prohibited conduct ultimately imply a classificatory criterion within a particular society.[22]

By the mid-nineteenth century many African states had catalogued crimes and punishments.[23] Crimes were acts whose nature and cumulative effects threatened the collective sentiment and menaced the security interest of the entire community.[24] In Nigeria, these were witchcraft, incest, divulging the secrets of some religions and political organisations, pronouncing a curse, manslaughter, malicious wounding and poisoning.[25] In Ghana, the list of capital crimes varied from place to place and there was much difference in the degree to which the death penalty was applied. These crimes primarily included referring to the death of the king, not giving way to the wives of the king, witchcraft and sorcery. Other conducts that were sometimes punishable by death were growing one's hair long (except for priests), the mishandling of knives and public statement of the refusal to eat.[26]

Among the AmaXosa of South Africa, crimes were listed as follows: political offences, sorcery and crimes against tribesmen.[27] In general, the Bantu recognised five serious crimes: homicide, witchcraft, theft, adultery and incest, to which in Uganda they added sexual offences against nature.[28] Somali customary law provides the most comprehensive list of offences: homicide, assault, torture, rape, accidental wounding, kidnapping, abduction, robbery, burglary, theft, arson, extortion and fraud.[29] Jan Vansina lists Kuba violent crimes: involuntary homicide, suicide (including involuntary homicide by relatives), simple injuries, injuries inflicted by a weapon of war and murder.[30]

Depending on their nature and seriousness, these offences fall into one of five categories:

- political offences: treason, divulging religious secrets or political secrets;
- offences committed with preternatural powers: witchcraft, sorcery, poisoning and pronouncing a curse;
- offences against human life: homicides;
- offences against bodily integrity: malicious injury;

22 Olewale (n 2) 121.

23 Hone (n 20).

24 Chukwuemeka (n 8).

25 ibid.

26 Clifford Williams, 'Asante: Human Sacrifice or Capital Punishment? An Assessment of the Period 1807–1874' (1988) 21 *International Journal of African Historical Studies* 433, 440.

27 Olewale (n 2) 113.

28 ibid 113–116.

29 Ayittey (n 4) 78.

30 Jan Vansina, 'A Traditional Legal System: The Kuba' in Hilda Kuper and Leo Kuper (eds), *African Law: Adaptation and Development* (University of California Press, Berkeley 1965) 112.

- sexual offences: adultery, incest and sexual offences against nature (bestiality).

The reality of the death penalty in African indigenous laws

There is no consensus as to whether the death penalty existed and if it did, whether it was imposed for these offences. Regional disparities have led researchers to equate some tribal laws with African law. Ross Kinemo describes 'African' indigenous law as the most humanitarian ever because the offender's misbehaviour was redressed without crushing his sense of humanity. Inhuman and degrading punishments were not used. After reviewing the errors, cruelty and barbaric attitudes accompanying the imposition and execution of the death penalty, Kinemo submits, 'Dr Junod ... said ... that in Africa the idea of an executioner appointed by the State and paid for the job, is traditionally unknown ...'.[31] The finding was that hanging was brought to Africa through colonisation. The African is humanitarian by nature; he had therefore never witnessed hanging.[32]

Justice Sachs dilutes this absolutism by stating that African indigenous law did not encompass the death penalty for murder so long it was not provoked by witchcraft or related to military offences. He recalls also that in cases of witchcraft and assault on the king's wives, summary executions were carried out as a result of spontaneous and irrational forms of a frenzied crowd's behaviour.[33] Death sentences were therefore non-existent in the kingdoms of Tsonga, Zulu, Sotho and Barolong. It is further stated that among the Zulu, in murder cases the white ruler replaced cattle fines with the death penalty.[34]

Both Ross Kinemo and Justice Sachs have pointed to 'African' indigenous law. Justice Sachs' research dealt with southern (mainly South African) Bantu tribes whereas Ross Kinemo quoted Jomo Kenyatta's *Facing Mount Kenya* and Junod's 1966 conference paper on penal problems in East Africa. Undoubtedly, the two were speaking on behalf of Bantu law in their respective areas. To equate Bantu indigenous law with African indigenous law would be misleading.

It is submitted that in South Africa, 'not all the Bantu tribes treat murder and culpable homicide in the same way ...'.[35] The death penalty existed among the Tswana and the Venda.[36] Among the Zulu a murderer was in a grave danger of

31 Ross EJ Kinemo, *Contemporary Tanzanian Penal Policy: A Critical Analysis* (British Institute in East Africa) 23, http://www.tzonline.org/pdf/contemporarytanzanianpenalpolicy.pdf (accessed 18 April 2007).

32 ibid.

33 *S v. Makwanyane and Another* 1995 (3) SA 391 (CC) para 381B per Justice Sachs.

34 ibid para 378F per Justice Sachs.

35 Isaac Schapera, *The Bantu-Speaking Tribes of South Africa* (George Routledge and Sons, London 1937) 209.

36 ibid.

receiving a death sentence.[37] The Nguni, Venda and Tswana punished culpable homicide with a fine that amounted to a girl, or the payment of *lobola* (dowry) among the Shangana-Tonga. The Venda imposed ostracism as an alternative to the death penalty.[38] The Tswana imposed no punishment for accidental homicide.[39]

Many Bantu tribes that made a distinction between intent in homicides did so to distinguish between punishments for deliberate murder and accidental homicide based on the offender's moral blameworthiness. This may be the reason that has led some to associate the death penalty with the development of indigenous criminal laws.[40] There is no record of whether or not Dr Junod had changed his views in 1966. He had stated in 1962 that among the Tsonga, a Bantu tribe of the south-eastern Africa coast, 'if the murder was deliberate, it is punished by death. At least such was the law in former times, when Natives still possessed the power of condemning to death.'[41]

It follows that the death penalty was a reality in a large part of Africa prior to foreign legal influences.

> Traditionally a variety of punishments were used for various crimes. In ascending order of severity, they can be listed as a reprimand, removal from home, restriction to an area, a fine, corporal punishment, confiscation or destruction of property, banishment and death. Imprisonment or other form of taking away liberty was unknown. The *talio* principle was an important principle ….[42]

This sentence was applied for redressing the injury suffered by the society at large; its application corresponded to both retributive justice and restorative justice. While deterrence is the most powerful modern argument for retaining the death penalty, Hone stresses that

> [w]here it [the death penalty] was exacted in pursuance of primitive native law, the fundamental justification was retribution and the restoration of balance, rather than that the public conscience was shocked into infliction of the extreme penalty as a warning and deterrent to lawless persons and as a protection to society at large.[43]

---

37 Ellen Jensen Krige, *The Social System of the Zulus* (Shuter and Shooter, Pietermaritzburg 1936) 228.

38 Schapera (n 35).

39 ibid 210.

40 Olewale (n 2) 116. See also Hone (n 20) 180.

41 Henri A Junod, *The Life of a South African Tribe* (University Book Inc, New York 1962) 442.

42 Stephane S Terblanche, *The Guide to Sentencing in South Africa* (Butterworths, Durban 1999) 507. See also James S Read, 'Kenya, Tanzania and Uganda' in Alan Milner (ed), *African Penal Systems* (Routledge and Kegan Paul, London 1969) 103.

43 Hone (n 20) 181.

At times, the death penalty was, however, resorted to as a deterrent or preventive punishment. Speaking for Teso, Basoga, Bagishu, Banyoro and Baganda of Uganda, Hone reminds us that these communities were shocked by witchcraft, incest and sexual offences against nature to the extent that they all exacted the death penalty for such crimes as the only remedy.[44] Kamba of Kenya also resorted to the death penalty for offenders that Olewale calls 'undesirable members of the community'.[45] They were usually executed in a bush, but, by the order of the 'King'ole', they could also be 'hanged by the neck from some tree in a public thoroughfare as a warning to other potential wrong-doers'.[46]

Boasting of the humanitarian nature of Kuba law compared to other Bantu laws, Jan Vansina writes that 'the Kuba have gone further in this respect [of limiting the use of physical force] than many other African states, including even the great lakes kingdoms, where feuds are still allowed provided the kings have given their permission to the lineage of the victim'.[47]

In wondering whether the Kuba law was per se compensatory or retributive, he finds that 'Kuba political structure has to react vigorously [against violent crimes], for the spirit of the feud – the principle of life for life – is not dead'.[48] For most of the Bantu tribes in Uganda, deliberate killing was also dealt with using the death penalty.[49]

Contrary to the opinion that the death penalty was non-existent prior to colonisation,[50] it was an acknowledged sentence beside banishment, compensation, reprimand and the destruction of property.[51] The nonexistence of the death penalty in some areas for some offences cannot, therefore, be used to make a general inference about Africa. It is inaccurate to accuse the coloniser of introducing the death penalty to Africans. In many parts of Africa, the coloniser only legalised and extended an existing practice and introduced new methods of execution.

Thus cases of actual application of the death penalty should be distinguished, on the basis of people's culture and the law in force in their area, from those where there was no death penalty. This allows the identification of the nature of law itself as applied in each area. Bantu law, which was deemed death penalty free is better qualified as a quasi-death penalty free law. In fact many Bantu laws imposed the death penalty. However, not all cases involving death should lead to the conclusion that there was a death sentence in place.

---

44 ibid 182. Critics on this misconception are generally summarised by Olewale (n 2) 110–129.

45 Olewale (n 2) 113.

46 ibid 113.

47 Vansina (n 30).

48 ibid.

49 Hone (n 20). See also Ayittey (n 4) 72.

50 *Makwanyane and Another* (n 33) para 377D–E, per Justice Sachs.

51 Terblanche (n 42) and Read (n 42).

The Practice of the Death Penalty in African Indigenous Laws

The death penalty was a relevant sentence for political offences, offences committed with the aid of supernatural powers, homicides, assault and sexual offences. In most centralised kingdoms, formally settled courts regularly pronounced the death penalty.

Every offence engages the individual offender's criminal responsibility. He is the focus of the sentence and the onus is on him to raise a criminal defence. Group intervention is justified in non-harmful sanctions and only if the offender cannot afford the amount of compensation. The collectiveness of the law, which was so important for social harmony, does not exclude individual obligations. There cannot be a death penalty without individual criminal responsibility. In cases where a death sentence, mutilation or any corporal punishment is meted out, 'the first and only subject to the particular punishment is the criminal himself'.[52]

Political offences

In Sierra Leone, the crime of treason as a political offence was punished with a death sentence.[53] The Akan of Ghana and Cote d'Ivoire punished treason with a death sentence. Treason included breaches of the oath of allegiance to a ruler or the cowardice of a war leader in battle.[54] The same applied to the Ba-Mbala people of the Democratic Republic of Congo, the Banyarwanda and the Barundi. In the kingdoms of Rwanda and Burundi, the Mwami tried treason himself. The supreme council sitting at the Mwami's bench (*Abacamanza*) tried other serious offences such as murder.[55] In Rwanda, persons convicted of political crimes were hurled on the rock of *Nkuli* (at the time of Mwami Rwabugiri) or abandoned to wild beasts in the valley of *rwabayanga* (*Urwobo rwa Bayanga*).[56] In Southern Africa, military offences were generally punished with a death penalty in the harshest way, while an assault on the king's wives called for a summary execution.[57]

The Bamoum of Cameroon had a very long list of *lèse majesté* offences: the use of goods belonging to the king like goats or wine, eating buffalo meats, the illegal use of the kingdom's insignia, any kind of behaviour from which lack of allegiance to the king could be inferred, friendships with the king's enemy, a long stay in the village, gifts to foreigners, commercial activities outside the kingdom

52 Chukwuemeka (n 8) 90.

53 Ayittey (n 4) 80.

54 ibid 82.

55 Augustin Buzora, *La peine de mort en droit Rwandais* (Mémoire de licence, Faculté de Droit, Université Nationale du Rwanda, Butare 1990) 8; Jan Vansina, *Les tribus Ba-Kuba et les peuplades apparentées* (International African Institute, London 1954) 28; René Bourgeois, *Banyarwanda et Barundi: La coutume* (Institut Royal Colonial Belge, Brussels 1954) 397.

56 Bourgeois, ibid 398.

57 *Makwanyane and Another* (n 33) para 381B per Justice Sachs.

without the king's authorisation, defaming the king, adultery with the king's wives or lustful contemplation of the king's wives. All these offences incurred a death sentence.[58]

A representative of the king or of the king's wives would publicly accuse the offender before the *Mitngu*. Cases of murder and adultery were never punished by compensation. Death was the appropriate sentence. Rebels were sentenced to death, their village was destroyed and their people dispersed.[59]

The death penalty was a means of protecting the king's exclusive rights, his property and his wives, and a weapon for combating any assumed or real opposition against his ruling.[60] Until the last king, Njoya (early twentieth century), half of those occupying the position of *Titamfom*, the highest functionary in the palace, and deputy to the king, had been executed for political reasons.[61]

Among the Zulu, any petty offence against the king was considered a capital crime. Entering *Isigodlo* (the king's wives apartments) or coughing, spitting or sneezing while the king was taking his lunch meant a death sentence.[62] A case was reported in which King Shaka surprised his soldiers while they engaged in sexual intercourse with the women of the *Isigodlo*. The sentence was immediate. Nearly 175 men and women were sentenced to death and executed.[63]

It was also an offence to criticise rulers. In addition to their political position, kings held religious positions. Their authority derived from God. The Dagaaba (Ghana and Burkina Faso), as other Africans, held that law could not be separated from morality, ethics, religion and social norms. There was thought to be no way of invoking law and ignoring its moral or utilitarian qualities. For this reason the system was seen to belong to the living, individually and collectively, the dead and supernatural forces. This collective ownership guaranteed that the legal system conformed to moral and religious norms.[64] Therefore, any disobedience or conspiracy against the ruler was a crime against society and constituted blasphemy. 'The position of the rulers and authorities is similar throughout Africa … In the past, execution was the punishment for recalcitrance against the rulers … The kings were fathers, judges, counsellors and priests.'[65]

Despotism was also a capital crime. The chief ruled for life as long as he showed no tendency towards dictatorship and tyranny. Otherwise, various punishments including the death penalty were applied. Despotism, dictatorship or tyranny were

58 Claude Tardits, *Le royaume Bamoum* (Armand Colin, Paris 1980) 825.

59 ibid.

60 ibid 826.

61 ibid 935.

62 Krige (n 37) 229.

63 ibid 223.

64 Yeplaala Kojo, 'Circular Arguments and Self-Fulfilling Definition: "Statelessness" and the Dagaaba' (1983) 10 *History in Africa* 349, 349–385.

65 SA Adewale, 'Crimes and African Traditional Religions' at www.afrikaworld.net/afrel/atr-crime.htm (accessed 16 May 2008).

expressed through the chief's life-style, decisions and treatment of his people: dispossessing people of their cattle, unjustified killing, waging war, seizing young girls of the tribe and so on. 'In such cases, when it became evident that the ethnic group was discontent and not likely to tolerate such oppression much longer, the fathers (or advisers) … would denounce the chief for his wrongdoings … A chief so deposed would be murdered ….'[66]

Supernatural crimes

Witchcraft and sorcery were themselves formal offences. Witches and sorceress were punished even if the result of their act did not qualify as an offence. This is a highly relevant aspect of indigenous criminal laws. It further demonstrates that Africans distinguished formal offences from material offences. The latter exist when the result of the act is an offence. A witch was prosecuted and perhaps executed even if the victim did not die. *A contrario*, a person could not be prosecuted for murder if the injured party did not die or if death resulted from other causes such as neglecting to use available and appropriate medicines for the victim's wounds. By way of legal logic and argumentation, Africans differentiated between murder and culpable homicide and theories of causation.[67]

Witchcraft is different from sorcery, although they resemble each other and are often confused. The distinction lies in the fact that sorcery involves practising a magic that is illicit and immoral, while witchcraft is 'a manifestation that is inherent in persons having a supposed psychic emanation from witchcraft-substance, a harmful material, thought to be present in the bodies of certain persons, that may be diagnosed by oracles in the living and discovered by autopsy in the dead'.[68] Scientifically and objectively, the process of witchcraft does not exist, although it is always dramatically described. But sorcery, in which people use evil magic to harm others, does exists. However, false accusations of it are doubtlessly often made.[69]

Although the killing of crocodiles was not prohibited among the Banyarwanda, it remained a serious offence to be caught cutting a crocodile's skin or pieces of one. The offender was immediately convicted of sorcery against the king. It is even said that the poison that the *Abiru* – functionaries tasked with keeping royal secrets, and nominating and enthroning the monarch – gave to the king when his

---

66 Ayittey (n 4) 171.

67 Nkambo PJ Mugerwa, 'Status, Responsibility, and Liability: A Comparative Study of Two Types of Society in Uganda' in Max Gluckman et al. (eds), *Ideas and Procedures in African Customary Law* (Oxford University Press, London 1969) 284. See also *Makwanyane and Another* (n 33) para 376A–B per Justice Sachs.

68 Simon Ottenberg and Phoebe Ottenberg, *Cultures and Societies of Africa* (Random House, New York 1960) 63.

69 ibid.

first grey hair appeared was made from crocodile bile or gall. This product was highly toxic and resulted in immediate death.[70]

Witchcraft and sorcery were and still are used in so-called hired killings, which occur on a very large scale in Africa. Many aggrieved persons frequently seek spells or potions from witch doctors with the intention of causing sickness or death. Relatives of the deceased will also pay frequent visits to diviners to discover who is bewitching them. The belief that someone is behind the death provides a motive for further killing.[71]

The Nandi sentenced a repeat-offender of witchcraft to death. If the witch was a woman the death would sometimes be preceded by torture. Women who were suspected of witchcraft were warned, however. 'An incorrigible witch … might … be executed.'[72] This was not a summary execution because 'executions were carried into effect on the orders of the *kokwet* (council of elders of the tribe) by the condemned's relatives'.[73] The same applies to Kapchchepsaos, Kapsamechei, Kamwagei, Kapchemuri, Kametere and Kapketui clans.[74] This practice was different from that of the Laibons. The Laibons community at large took part in the execution. Their condemned were executed by being clubbed to death.[75]

Witches known as *Mapamosavy* were much feared in Madagascar. It is believed that they were born witches and voluntarily harmed whomever they wanted. Bad spirits imposed this role on them. Although the community felt they were not primarily responsible for their fate, everything was done to execute them as soon as possible and in the most inhuman way.[76]

In the Democratic Republic of Congo, the Kuba had a very peculiar way of dealing with witchcraft. Most cases of murder were connected with witchcraft and were tried by the village court. A poison ordeal was the only legal instrument restricted to this offence. After the accusation was formally voiced, the accused had to drink a poison. The guilty party died and the innocent remained.[77] The Komo differentiated between involuntary and accidental homicides, which were punished by compensation except when connected with sorcery. When connected with sorcery, the offender was executed and the corpse thrown into a river or in a bush.[78]

---

70 Georges Sandrat, *Cours de droit coutumier*, Partie II (Groupe Scolaire Astrida, Butare 1951) 66.

71 Williams Clifford, *An Introduction to African Criminology* (Oxford University Press, Nairobi 1974) 121.

72 Geoffrey S Snell, *Nandi Customary Law* (East African Literature Bureau, Nairobi 1954) 77.

73 ibid.

74 ibid 76.

75 ibid.

76 Raymond Decay, *Mœurs et coutumes des Malgaches* (Payot, Paris 1951) 203.

77 Vansina (n 30) 113–114.

78 Hans Van Geluwe, *Les Bira et les peuplades limitrophes* (International African Institute, London 1957) 129.

In other areas, witches were summarily executed unless the chief or the public conscience opposed the execution. Olewale points out that 'African law permit[ed] the summary execution of the so called sorcerer or witch by the social group'.[79] Among the Nguni of South Africa, capital punishment was almost entirely limited to cases of suspected witchcraft. The sentence was spontaneously carried out after the diviner had established a case against the offender.[80]

Cursing was also considered a supernatural offence. As a Kikuyu tradition, a curse would cause panic when pronounced by elders. Very recently Kikuyu elders pronounced a curse against whoever might devastate the sacred hill of Karima, a hill traditionally believed to be used by God as a stepping-stone on his daily walk to Mountain Kenya.[81] For the Bali of the Democratic Republic of Congo, pronouncing a curse with bad side effects was a capital crime. The offender was tortured during the process of execution.[82]

Homicides

The political structure of the state determined the way that homicide cases were dealt with. In organised states, the death penalty was reserved for very limited offences and often imposed after a fair trial.

In the Democratic Republic of Congo, the death penalty was rare for murder but not absent among the Kongo.[83] For the Ba-Mbala and Kuba, the Supreme Council could impose the death sentence for murder. The court clearly differentiated between accidental homicide and voluntary homicide. The role of the king was to exercise his royal rights in granting mercy as only he could take a human life. He was not directly involved in the judicial process.[84]

If the judgment was upheld because the king had turned down the appeal of the *Mbeem* (headman of the culprit's village), who would beg the king to spare the life, the condemned would immediately be placed in an area reserved for the *Nkunkum* – enslaved criminals on death row who were sacrificed at the king's death. *Nkunkum* thus awaited an execution that was not eventual but real. The length of wait depended on the longevity of the king. Whenever the king fell sick or tribal war broke out the expectation of their execution increased, though it would never come if the *Nkunkum* died naturally before the king.[85]

If the offender was not *Nkunkum* and the death sentence was confirmed, special officers among the king's slaves accompanied the condemned to his home for

79 Olewale (n 2) 127.

80 *Makwanyane and Another* (n 33) para 377C per Justice Sachs.

81 Nick Wadhams, 'Kenyan Tribe Punishes Developers with Curse', *The Telegraph*, 27 October 2007.

82 Hans Van Geluwe, *Les Bali et les peuplades apparentées (Ndaka, Mbo, Beke, Lika, Budu, Nyari)* (International African Institute, London 1960) 90.

83 Marcel Soret, *Les Kongo nord occidentaux* (PUF, Paris 1959) 85.

84 Vansina (n 30). See also Vansina (n 55).

85 Vansina (n 30) 106 and 112.

a farewell. The royal decision and the death sentence were demonstrated to the headman of the village through symbolic objects and gestures. Afterwards, the condemned was urged to become intoxicated with palm wine and to hang himself in the forest. Execution of the condemned was an eventuality and not a widespread principle. In addition, those in the lineage of the culprit were required to hand over a slave in compensation.[86]

For the Banyoro of Uganda, the death penalty was the only recognised sentence for murder and was carried out regularly. Compensation was not an option in such cases. This practice differed from that of the Bonyoro's neighbours, the Baganda, for whom a death sentence was imposed when the deceased's relatives demanded it as a punishment for murder (itself rare).[87] However, the payment of blood-money was the general principle applied among the Baganda.[88] The Baganda knew that the death penalty was not a deterrent and found retribution unnecessary.

Among the Banyarwanda and Barundi, the *lex talionis* prevailed. Murderers were often sentenced to death by the Mwami's bench (*Abacamanza*), although the Mwami could exercise his right of mercy and overturn the Supreme Council's sentence, commuting it to compensation.[89] In cases where the offender had fled, the victim's clan had the right of vengeance and could kill someone from the murderer's family (*guhora*). The blood feud would continue until the Mwami decided to end the matter through compensation.[90]

In the Bamoum kingdom of Cameroon, the *Mitngu* was the only court that could impose the death penalty, should the king have no objection. The death sentence was in principle imposed for the crime of murder. The field where the crime was committed was confiscated.[91] However, a murder committed by a father against his son, between cousins, by the king's son or wife, except against her co-wives, and involuntary homicides were not deemed capital crimes.[92]

Sexual offences

Among the Bantu, compensation was generally the punishment for adultery. In the Democratic Republic of Congo, the Bira[93] and the Mangbetu imposed the death sentence on male adulterers.[94] Among the north-western Laadi, such men were buried alive at a market place. The offender's family carried out the execution.[95]

---

86 ibid.

87 For example, Mugerwa (n 67) makes no reference at all to intentional or voluntary homicides in Buganda.

88 Hone (n 20) 183–184.

89 Bourgeois (n 55).

90 ibid.

91 Tardits (n 58) 824.

92 ibid 825.

93 It should be remembered that they are not Bantu people. See footnote 182 below.

94 Geluwe (n 78).

95 Soret (n 83) 86.

For the Balese, the woman was executed whatever the circumstances, whereas the co-offender paid a fine of one goat. The Balese had always handed out death sentences to women convicted of adultery.[96] The harshest punishment for adultery existed among the Budu. There were two alternative punishments to the death sentence, namely castration and phallus ablation for male adulterers. Women convicted of adultery were sentenced to the burning of their genital parts.[97]

In Uganda, the Baganda inflicted the death sentence for adultery. The woman was compelled by torture to name her seducer by indicating notable marks on his body when the co-offender denied the fact. An adulterer or *mussi* (murderer) was sentenced to death when discovered.[98] Adulterers with upper-class women were often fully armed and killed those who caught them. Consequently, a principle was made that all adulterers were considered potential murderers and deserved a death sentence.[99] A slave who committed adultery with his master's wife was invariably put to death.[100] Compensation could be resorted to mainly when the offence involved non-slaves from the peasant class. The offender was also maimed; a limb was removed and an eye gouged out to show the public that he was convicted of such an offence. Among the Banyoro, a woman ran the risk of a death sentence if she committed adultery with a stranger. Adultery with one of her husband's relatives was praised as an act of hospitality.[101]

The Asante (or Ashanti) of Ghana punished adultery by what they called the dance of death (*atopere-goru*), which resembled sacrificial capital punishment.[102] In Cameroon, the laws regulating adultery were exceedingly severe. The death penalty was seen as the right punishment. A king's wife who committed adultery was sentenced to death by flogging.[103] In West Africa, adultery was simultaneously a religious and criminal offence. It was most commonly punished by death. The deceased was not mourned as capital punishment was a deserved punishment.[104] The Ife (Nigeria) sacred scriptures, which have influenced the Yoruba and most of the West African coast countries (Benin, Sierra Leone, and some parts of Ghana), warn against adultery:

> She destroys the members of the household of the husband,
> She destroys the members of the household of the concubine.

---

96 Hans Van Geluwe, *Mamvu-Mangutu et Balese-Mvuba* (International African Institute 1957) 150.

97 Geluwe (n 82).

98 Mugerwa (n 67) 283.

99 Hone (n 20) 184.

100 Mugerwa (n 67) 283.

101 Hone (n 20) 183.

102 Clifford (n 71) 437.

103 Mary H Kingsley, *Travel in West Africa (Congo Français, Corisco and Cameroons)* (Macmillan, London 1897) 255.

104 Olewale (n 2) 136.

Thereafter she destroys herself
And goes the far journey to heaven
So declares the adulterous oracle of the woman who is servant of death.[105]

In Southern Africa, King Gaika only abolished the death penalty for adultery in 1820. Prior to that, a woman caught in adultery was executed.[106]

In Rwanda, the law was particularly severe for girls. A girl's body and virginity were sacred. The law already provided that she was a diviner (*Umukobwa ni Nyampinga*). For this reason, when a mother gave birth to twins of different sex, the boy could be executed.[107] Furthermore, a girl who conceived a pre-marriage pregnancy (*ikinyendaro*), or girls whose breasts were not properly developed (*imhenebere*) or who did not menstruate at the age of puberty (*imha*) or who were far beyond the age of marriage and could not get a lover due to ugliness or misbehaviour (*igishubaziko*) were sentenced to death by drowning (*kwohera*).[108] Only the court could order this sentence. Royal officials had the task of carrying it out. The abomination would affect the entire country if the girl was not executed.[109]

Among the Nguni, Venda, Shangana-Tonga and Tswana of South Africa, incest, bestiality and other perverse sexual aberrations were considered ill-omened actions deserving of a death sentence.[110] The Baganda also applied the death penalty in cases of sexual offences against nature.[111] Although there is no clear indication of what the Baganda classified a sexual act against nature, they would have included homosexuality, obscenities and more than likely bestiality.[112]

Incest was not a great concern in some African societies. Joseph Ki-Zerbo states that the Egyptian Pharaohs freely practised incest.[113] Elsewhere, it was an immoral act combated by severe punishments and taboos. Two reasons are provided for this. First, family unity and the basis of society were threatened when a father and his son shared the wife, when a mother and her daughter shared the husband or a girl was shared between her father and brother. This created tension among individuals and within the community at large. Exogamous marriage strengthened the family, extended its interests and security and promoted economic development. The second reason, 'the remarkable absence of erotic feeling' between relatives, seems

105 Kojo (n 64). See also Tardits (n 58) 829.

106 Olewale (n 2) 138.

107 Alexis Kagame, *Les organisations socio-familiales de l'ancien Rwanda* (Académie Royale des Sciences Coloniales, Brussels 1954) 242.

108 ibid 299–301.

109 ibid.

110 Schapera (n 35) 212.

111 Hone (n 20) 182.

112 Clifford (n 71) 127.

113 Joseph Ki-Zerbo, *Histoire de l'Afrique noire* (Hatier, Paris 1972) 75.

doubtful. The erotic argument implies that all cases of incest amounted to rape, which is not always the case.[114]

Incest was a capital crime among the Bantu of Kavirondo in Tanzania[115] and the Baganda.[116] There is no justification for capital punishment for incest among these Bantu who punished murder through compensation, as shall be seen later.

Dangerous and habitual offenders

The death penalty was imposed for heinous and shocking crimes or on incorrigible criminals, even among indigenous people who resorted to compensation for murder.[117]

The Baganda had an aversion to theft. A man caught red-handed when stealing food was killed on the spot and the stolen food tied around his neck. His body was thrown into the road as a public message regarding the grounds of his execution. If he broke into a house, his relatives would disown him and were prevented from burying his body. Although a modern mind may see this as an extrajudicial execution, it was considered a punishment only so long as the public conscience was shocked and local leaders accepted the carrying out of the execution. It became an arbitrary killing when chiefs and the community did not support the execution.[118] The Banyarwanda and Barundi allowed the execution of a thief caught in the act without further consequences. Cattle and food thieves during famine were crucified or executed by impalement.[119]

There is no easily understandable justification for the death penalty for food theft when murder was punished by compensation in Buganda . Theft was not even an offence in many African indigenous laws. It was, however, the best example of a private wrong in Nigerian indigenous law.[120] The Odu-Ogbe Ale oracle made it, rather, a religious offence.[121] There is no indication that theft among the Baganda was more widespread than among other Ugandans so as to deserve summary execution. Rather, the Karamoja tribes (Karamojong) were considered the famous thieves in Uganda to the extent that soon after independence, Parliament and the Minister of Justice passed legislation and regulations specifically related to Karamoja thieves.[122]

---

114 Clifford (n 71) 125–126.

115 Olewale (n 2) 113.

116 Clifford (n 71) 124. See also Hone (n 20) 182.

117 Hone, ibid 181. See also *Rex v. Petero Mukasa and Katabazi Yamumbi* (1944) 11E.A.P.L.R. 115.

118 Mugerwa (n 67) 283. See also Hone (n 20) 184.

119 Bourgeois (n 55).

120 Chukwuemeka (n 8).

121 Adewale (n 65).

122 The Administration (Karamoja) Act 1963 as amended by The Administration (Karamoja) (Amendement) and The Administration of Justice (Karamoja) Act 1964, Karamoja (Maintenance of Public Order) Regulations, 1964 and The Restitution of Cattle

Apparently theft became a serious offence during the Kabaka dynasty.[123] In the African mind, theft is immoral and is perceived as a sign of laziness that every tribesman must combat. Stealing tarnishes the entire family's reputation and integrity. Africans strived to maintain a good name and a good image. Even a family without a very good reputation would try to avoid the disgrace of theft. A theft is always recalled when other family members or future generations are considered for positions or titles of honour or when demanding a girl in marriage from another family. A man who steals food instead of earning it by the work of his hand corrupts the youth and dishonours his clan. This is why male thieves and female thieves were treated differently among the Baganda. The female simply paid a fine.[124] We remain, however, unconvinced that the death penalty aimed to combat the laziness and immorality associated with theft.

As far as habitual offenders are concerned, the Bantu of Kavirondo would not execute a habitual offender directly. They put him in a situation in which he could be rehabilitated or killed by a stranger. The offender was placed outside the legal protection of the tribe. Anyone could kill him if they caught him committing his next offence.[125] The Nandi had no death penalty except for incorrigible habitual offenders. The offender's family was also required to give blood-money to the victim's clan.[126]

The Specificity of the Egyptian Case

The richness of the Egyptian civilisation goes back to antiquity, and Egypt remains a country with unprecedented cultural depth and unique features.[127] Even prior to the prosperous period of the pharaohs, the principal legal branches in Egypt had attained a higher level of perfection than in any other country.[128] Long before

---

and Payment of Blood-Money (Procedures) Regulations, 1965 respectively in Statutory Instruments no 265 of 1964 and 101 of 1965 as quoted by Mugerwa (n 67) 286–287.

123 Hone (n 20) 184.

124 Mugerwa (n 67) 283.

125 Gunther Wagner, 'The Political Organization of the Bantu of Kavirondo' in Meyer Fortes and Edward Evans-Pritchard (eds), *African Political Systems* (Oxford University Press, London 1970) 219.

126 Snell (n 72) 63.

127 Ivan Hrbek, 'Egypt, Nubia and the Eastern Desert' in Roland Oliver (ed), *The Cambridge History of Africa: From c.1050 to c.1600* (Cambridge University Press, London, New York and Melbourne 1975) 10–98 and Peter M Holt, 'Egypt, the Funj and Darfur' in Richard Gray (ed), *The Cambridge History of Africa: From c.1600 to c.1790* (Cambridge University Press, London, New York and Melbourne 1975) 14–58.

128 The first of their eight categories of law was related to crimes and police matters. King Bocchoris was eventually one of the great Egyptian legislators. See Arnold HL Heeren (tr), *Historical Researches into the Politics, Intercourse, and the Trade of the Carthaginians, Ethiopians and Egyptians*, vol 1 (D.A. Talboys, Oxford 1832) 165–166 and 341.

the Old Testament's Ten Commandments were recorded,[129] the 42 Egyptian commandments neatly divided human wrongs into three categories (transgressions against mankind, sins against god and personal wrongs).[130] There was no room for private justice.[131] Criminal cases were decided by the highest court of justice. Kings did not serve as judges[132] except for important cases where the pharaoh or a special commission that he appointed could try the case.[133]

Ancient Egypt was a relatively crime-free place and the death penalty was seldom applied. Neither the death penalty nor mutilation even existed before the eighth dynasty.[134] There was also a period of 150 years that passed without any execution taking place. Even when the court was obliged to impose it, 'there was some support of basic human rights'.[135] Respect for human rights can also be seen through the judicial process. 'There is no arbitrariness, judgments are equals for everyone, the rich and the poor, the noble and the meek ....'[136] Thus the harshness of ancient Egyptian punishments is sometimes associated with the influence of barbaric immigrants.[137]

However, there is no doubt that 'in extreme cases, capital punishment was inflicted by impalement on a stake, burning alive, drowning or decapitation'.[138] The death penalty was imposed on everyone who infringed Ma'at, or the universal law, by violating tombs, committing murder, treason or by spying on or by making an attempt on the life of the pharaoh who was seen as the guarantor of the law. All murders were punished equally regardless of the victim's or offender's social

129 Exodus 20:1–17, Deuteronomy 5:1–17.

130 'The Egyptian Forty-Two Commandments: Ma'at Right and Truth' at www.parankhgroup.com (accessed 16 October 2009).

131 S Allam, 'Un droit pénal existait-il 'stricto sensu' en Egypte Pharaonique?' (1978) 64 *Journal of Egyptian Archaeology* 65, 66.

132 Heeren (n 128) 342.

133 'Law and the Legal System in Ancient Egypt' at www.touregypt.net/featurestories/law/htm (accessed 16 October 2009). Violet MacDermot rejects the view that there existed a secular judicial system in ancient Egypt. She argues that judgments were 'the prerogative of gods rather than men'. See Violet MacDermot, *The Cult of the Seer in the Ancient Middle East: A Contribution to Current Research on Hallucinations Drawn from Coptic and Other Texts* (Welcome Institute of the History of Medicine, London 1971) 144.

134 Harco Willems, 'Crime, Cult and Capital Punishment (Mo'alla Inscription)' (1990) 75 *Journal of Egyptian Archaeology* 27, 33.

135 'Law and the Legal System in Ancient Egypt' at www.touregypt.net/featurestories/law/htm (accessed 16 October 2009) and MacDermot (n 133).

136 'The Death Penalty in Egyptian Ancient Law' at www.reshafin.org.il (accessed 16 October 2009).

137 Exodus 20:1–17, Deuteronomy 5:1–17.

138 'Law and the Legal System in Ancient Egypt' at www.touregypt.net/featurestories/law/htm (accessed 16 October 2009). Violet MacDermot (133).

status (freeman or slave).[139] Inscription no. 9 on the Hekaib sanctuary, the writings on the stela Cairo, the tombs III and IV at Assiut and the tomb of Chnumhotep II at Beni Hasan, and the graffiti in Lower Nibia indicate that the death penalty was indeed imposed and executed.[140] The Decree of King Demedjibtawi provided for the death sentence by burning of people who interfered with the Idy's cult installations in the Coptos temple. King Neferhotep I also decreed the death sentence for anyone who passed by the 'Holy land south of Abydos', which he declared to be a 'closed area' to the public. King Sesostris I once visited the temple of Tôd, finding it had fallen into ruin due to a group of hooligans, he ordered their arrest. They were sentenced to death by burning.[141]

Sometimes the punishment was extended to the offender's children. However, there is no evidence that leads to the conclusion that wives could be held liable for crimes perpetrated by their husbands. Children were condemned to prevent them from inheriting their fathers' ministries such as priesthoods, military services and so on. Wives could not inherit these. Death by burning turned the condemned into a sacrifice to the gods. Judgments took place in the temple and culprits were burnt on the temple's altar. The imposition of the death penalty was exceptional and imposed by the highest court of justice.[142] The practice of the death penalty in Egypt continued under the successive monotheist beliefs of Christianity and Islam.

The Exclusion of Unusual Punishments and Unclassifiable Cases

In criminal law, a punishment can be meted out only if it meets four criteria: legality, equality, individualisation and human dignity. The legality of a punishment is based on whether or not it is anticipatively provided for by the law. Furthermore, punishments must not vary according to social status or other subjective factors and they must be individual. This means that in cases of co-perpetrators, the sentence is individualised. The concept of human dignity is well known. This section considers whether summary executions, poison ordeals, vengeance and ritual executions as applied in the pre-colonial period met these criteria.

Unusual Punishments

These are punishments that, although they do not comply with the above criteria, existed in African indigenous laws. In applying the modern understanding of punishments, they may be excluded from the range of penal punishments.

---

139 Heeren (n 128) 342. See also 'The Death Penalty in Egyptian Ancient Law' at www.reshafin.org.il (accessed 16 October 2009).

140 Willems (n 134) 34–39.

141 ibid 39–41.

142 ibid 42–51.

Summary executions

In the *Makwanyane* case Justice Sachs stated that summary executions as applied in the pre-colonial period were not punishments. They were extra-judicial, spontaneous and irrational reactions of an angered crowd against unfortunate suspects of witchcraft.[143] Sorcery and witchcraft cannot be excluded from African indigenous laws. Studies on this phenomenon evoke even the existence of 'the law of sorcery' which in Guinea still allows certain parents to eat symbolically their relatives (symbolic anthropophagi) without reprisal unless rules are broken.[144]

Witchcraft and sorcery are thought to be generally levelled at established institutions and important pursuits. Therefore, witches and sorcerers were summarily executed to prevent any disturbance of the delicate fabric of social life. In the African great lakes kingdoms summary executions were allowed, provided the king had given permission to the lineage of the victim.[145] The practice is still alive. In 2003, 87 witchcraft suspects were executed in Congo Brazzaville. In 2005, old Burkinabé (Burkina Faso) women accused of eating the souls of children were compelled to drink a poison potion after which many died. In May 2008, a crowd of more than 100 people of the Nyakeo village in Kenya went door to door to the homes of suspected witches and burned 15 women alive.[146]

The Zulu, Venda and Nguni mainly resorted to diviners and ordeal to identify witches, not only because the crime was so serious but also because no number of witnesses could establish the innocence or guilt of a wizard due to the work of unseen forces. The judicial process could not work properly. After the diviner found the guilty person, the latter was put to death, often by torture.[147]

In indigenous African laws, summary executions were used as formal punishments when the execution was justified in people's minds or authorised by the king. Execution ceased to be a punishment and became an arbitrary and barbaric act in the absence of provocation or legitimate authorisation.[148] African laws allow summary executions mainly (but not exclusively) for supernatural crimes.[149]

Poison ordeal

Another confusing aspect of punishment is the poison ordeal. In the African mind, this acts as both a punishment and a method of investigation. Kuba courts felt

143 *Makwanyane and Another* (n 33) para 381B per Justice Sachs.

144 Maria Teixeira, 'Sorcellerie et contre sorcellerie: un réajustement permanent au monde, les Manjak de Guinée Bissau et du Sénégal' (2008) 189–190 *Cahiers d'etudes africaines* 59, 65.

145 Vansina (n 30) 112.

146 AFP, '15 Femmes accusées de sorcellerie brûlées vives dans l'ouest', Pascal Airault 'Forte croyance au Kindoki' and Charlotte Cans 'Chasse aux sorcières' at http://www.jeuneafrique.com/jeune_afrique/article_depeche.asp? (accessed 24 August 2010).

147 Krige (n 37) 225 and Schapera (n 35) 211.

148 Kinemo (n 31) 3 and Vansina (n 30) 105.

149 Olewale (n 2) 127.

comfortable when trying witchcraft. Instead of ordering a summary execution, the proper technique was to ask for a poison ordeal. 'The accused drinks poison; if he dies he is guilty; and if he survives he is innocent.'[150] In the Democratic Republic of Congo, the Bira considered death by poison ordeal to be the most severe punishment.[151]

The poison ordeal was familiar to various generations and in various areas. The second most common way to test defendants was the boiling water test. Suspects were compelled to plunge their hands into a container of boiling water and take out objects. Those who were not burnt were innocent. Husbands very often tested the fidelity of their wives in this way.[152]

Unclassifiable Cases

Other practices fall beyond any category of punishments. The death penalty was usually pronounced or authorised by a judicial body. In many areas, the principle was, however, that all blood belonged to the sovereign, who had the power of life and death. Sometimes, the sovereign abused his authority, allowed private justice, disregarded social anarchy and exacted death sentences on religious grounds.

The death penalty and the king's power of life and death

As an example, one could start with the Azande of the Democratic Republic of Congo and with a man who beat his wife every day. She could not take it any longer and took refuge at her friends' house. The husband brought the matter to King Azanga. He was famous for his severity and cruelty. The sentence came quickly. The fugitive wife was condemned to death with the prohibition of funeral and mourning. The same evening the king's council gathered and celebrated the sentence by eating meats and drinking beer.[153]

Unfortunately this was the fate of animals as well. The death sentence was applied to animals that killed other animals. 'A goat attacked by a dog hit the dog with its horns. Few hours later, the dog that belonged to an influential man died. The matter was discussed and much commented before being referred to the king. The king condemned the goat to death and ordered that its meat be shared among Mangbetu whereas the dog's meat was distributed to Medje.'[154]

In Rwanda, Mwami Rwabugiri is said to be famous for ordering the execution of people convicted of petty offences when he was drunk. When he sobered up, he would take care of the orphans probably to honour the principle '*Ingoma irahaka*

150 Vansina (n 30) 113.

151 Geluwe (n 78) 131.

152 Emmet V Mittlebeeler, *African Custom and Western Law: The Development of the Rhodesian Criminal Law for Africans* (Africana, New York and London 1976) 159.

153 Cyrille Van Overbergh, *Les Mangbetu (Congo Belge)* (Institut International de Bibliographie, Brussels 1909) 485.

154 ibid 486.

ntihora (the drum does not revenge, it forgives)'.[155] The family of the murdered person had no further appeal. The Mwami enjoyed immunity of jurisdiction according to the principle '*Ntihica Umwami, hica Rubanda* (it is never the King that kills but it is his people that kill)'.[156]

There were no safeguards against the king's abuse of his power of life and death. The death penalty was imposed and executed according to the sovereign's pleasure. The only exception was found among the Bamoum of Cameroon, where King Njoya decreed a law against abuses of power and persecution that were driving people to commit suicide.

> If someone hangs himself among the Nzi Pamom, a slave must be given to the King, three thousands couris to Taanggu and six hundreds to Mgbet Nyi [the deputy of Taanggu] and that is all. The King receives one slave because the master has ill-treated his slave who, due to anger, hanged himself. Do all people not belong to the King? The slave given as fine virtually replaces the dead.[157]

This decree shows the extent to which King Njoya subjected all his subjects to power without tyranny.

Vengeance or heroism in relation to the death penalty

In areas without capital punishment, the death penalty was a remedy for the failure to pay compensation. The Bukusu (Kenya) allowed the victim's clan to 'kill a member of the opposite sex of the murderer's clan' when the latter failed to pay the blood-fine.[158] The Lango (Uganda) found no way of compensating the wronged party and restoring the social balance in interfamily homicide. Cattle belonged to the entire family, the offender and the offended included. The death penalty for patricide and fratricide was therefore a reaction to the inefficacy of compensation in cases of interfamily homicide.[159]

The Teso and Karamajong (Uganda) historically settled homicides by killing the offender or taking revenge on a member of his family or clan, irrespective of whether the crime was intended or accidental.[160] However, the law developed to incorporate compensation for homicide when the offender was arrested. Members of the deceased's clan retained the right to kill a member of the offender's clan if

155 The drum symbolised the kingship in most African kingdoms. René Bourgeois, *Banyarwanda et Barundi: Ethnographie* (Académie Royale des Sciences Coloniales, Brussels 1957) 760.

156 Bourgeois (n 55) 65–66.

157 Tardits (n 58) 829.

158 Snell (n 72) 75.

159 Hone (n 20) 182.

160 Mugerwa (n 67) 282.

the criminal escaped.[161] This also applied to the Wakamba and Kikuyu of Kenya.[162] The Basoga (Uganda) killed the murderer to appease the deceased's ghost. For them, the death penalty was a divine sanction.[163]

Ritual murders: were victims sentenced or sacrificed?

Ritual killing was a common practice in many African kingdoms. It is argued that human sacrifice and the death penalty served the same purpose of deterring political opponents, punishing those who violated traditional norms and 'keeping the mass of the people in check'.[164] However, it is worth noting that the executed persons were not necessarily criminals.

Among the Kuba, the king's death was always accompanied by sacrifices. The *Nkunkum* or enslaved criminals on death row constituted the human stock for sacrifice.[165] A similar practice is found among the Swazi. The king had 'a house where he commanded bodies of men who died at the hands of the law to be hung up, and where thus hanging all the humidity of their bodies falls into vases placed underneath ….'[166] That 'humidity' was afterwards used by the king as an ointment oil that procured new strength.[167]

That is what occurred in cases where the death sentence was applied. The only issue was that among the Kuba the duration of the offender's stay on death row depended on the eventuality of the king's death.

Instances of ritual murder also form part of indigenous laws.[168] This refers to the killing of innocents or execution without judicial process for religious purposes. During the slave trade, West African kings enjoyed cheap lives. They organised annual carnivals to send messages of their filial loyalty and victory to their ancestors by killing slaves who could not be sold. Executions were carried out in public during periodic parties organised to commemorate ancestors and distribute war plunders. Sometimes, the abundance of unsold slaves transformed the festivities into scene of butchery. The royal palace reserved a door for the evacuation of slaves. The door was 'with a macabre humour baptized "passage of luggage to the other world"'.[169]

In Ghana, the rate of sacrifice of war prisoners, political opponents and returned slaves led the first British witnesses to believe that the victims were condemned to capital punishment. It was common that slaves, wives or relatives accompany

161 ibid.

162 'Some Notes on Native Laws and Customs' in East Africa Protectorate, *Laws Reports* (Stevens and Sons, London 1906), Appendix 1. See also Olewale (n 2) 139–140.

163 ibid.

164 Clifford (n 71) 438.

165 Vansina (n 30) 106.

166 Tor Irstam, *The King of Ganda* (Hakan Ohlsssons Boktryckeri, Stockholm 1944) 90.

167 ibid.

168 Olewale (n 2) 126.

169 Ki-Zerbo (n 113) 280.

dignitaries at their death. It is reported that early in the nineteenth century, 80 Fantis were decapitated for the king. A further 2,000 Fanti war prisoners were sacrificed at the funeral of the Asantehene's mother (the queen mother) of the Asante and in 1818–1819, 2000 Gyaman war prisoners were 'slaughtered over the royal death stool'.[170]

War prisoners were kept in a special village, Akyerekuro, as sacrificial stock. British authorities sought to address this by demanding an oath from the Asante who brought the unsold slaves to the Asante kingdom. The oath, to the effect that misfortune would strike the Asante kingdom if the slaves were mistreated, became a powerful deterrent against human sacrifices. With the abolition of the slave trade, British authorities felt compelled to be more vigilant in imposing fines or making a demonstration of force against chiefs who abused the abundance of slaves. It is said that the chiefs preferred breaking the oath they made with the British than violating their traditional practices. In 1844, however, coastal chiefs signed an agreement on the abolition of human sacrifice. The British continued to employ Christian preaching and education to deter the Asante over whom they had only a limited influence.[171]

Jukun kings (Nigeria and Cameroon), after seven years' reign, speared slaves as human sacrifices to maintain their longevity. Each slave's death symbolised the death of the king, who would afterwards go into the bush. On his return, he was newly clothed and seated on a white horse as a sign of rebirth.[172] For the Falli of the Congo, the ceremony was to symbolise the slaying of an enemy and the head would be paraded before the chief. During the three days between the Bushongo king's death and his funeral, people were hunted as sacrifices.[173] Baganda kings were famous for ritual murders (see Table 2.1).

---

170 Clifford (n 71) 438–440.

171 ibid.

172 Irstam (n 166) 89.

173 Emile Torday, *On the Trail of the Bushongo* (Seeley, Service and Co, London 1925) 177.

Table 2.1 Ritual murders in Baganda

Ritual sacrifice	Period	Number of people killed	Purpose
New skin for Kaula (royal drum)	Whenever	One man	Human blood had to run into the drum when beaten. The victim's life refreshed the king's life.
Coronation ceremonies	Whenever	Eight men	One man was shot by the king and another seven were killed at *Segaku* (the sacrificial site). The victim's bowels were hung around the neck of *Kawonawo* (another man chosen for the purpose). The killing increased the king's vigour and made *Kawonawo* strong and faithful.
Leopard hunt	Two to three months after coronation	One man	The captive was killed in the evening at the king's palace and the body hidden forever.
Confirmation	Two to three months after coronation	One man	The king slightly wounded the man who was killed for the invigoration.
Strengthening the king	Two to three years after coronation	One man	The man was speared outside the palace enclosure to give life-force to the king.
Great feasts for the kingdoms	According to the tradition of the kingdom	One man	All drums were beaten except one. The person who reminded the king that it was time for the great feast was killed and his blood put in that drum.
Sickness of the king	Whenever	Many people	*Mutebi*, the priest, would identify people who had peculiar marks and ask that they be killed for the life of the king.
King's death	Whenever	One man	After the king's death, the chief of the king's fire was strangled.

Source: Tor Irstam.[174]

174 Irstam (n 166) 25, 33–34 and 90.

Methods of Execution

Methods of execution varied. According to Olewale, '[in] criminal cases such as sorcery or witchcraft, wilful murder and alike, the penalty is death by shooting, spearing, hanging, drowning or impalement of the convicted person. These penalties also avail for treason and certain types of political offences.'[175] However, this general rule did not prevent the executioner from enjoying a large discretion that enabled him to determine the appropriate method of carrying out the death penalty.[176] As mentioned above, Egyptians preferred burning culprits on the temple's altar, whereas the Laadi of the Democratic Republic of Congo buried adulterers alive at a market place.

The most usual method of execution in Nandi customary law consisted of placing the noose of a rope made from a tree bark around the condemned's neck. A group of the offender's relatives would then pull the rope in opposite directions until the victim died. Beating and stoning also took place among the Nandi.[177]

Beside the drowning of girls, spearing, and impalement upon a sharp stick from the anus to the chest, the primary methods of execution among the Banyarwanda, and Barundi included beating, torture, mutilation, cutting the throat with bamboo, crucifixion as the condemned lied on his back on the ground and was impaled in the arms, legs and womb with sharp wooden sticks, strangling, abandoning the offender to wild beasts and hurling from a rock.[178]

In Rwanda, the immediate execution by means of spear, beating or cutting the throat was perceived as a favour for old persons, royal personnel and women. Strangling was applied to royal personnel or sycophants that the king intended to execute discretely. They were forced to starve for four days before the execution in order to make the executioner's task easier. Death by the amputation of hands and legs was reserved for robbers, who were abandoned to carnivores while still bleeding. Similar practices existed among the Toro of Uganda, where it was reported that this method was used to execute Ndahura, the king of the Abatshwezi. Persons convicted of political crimes were drowned in the abyss. This was the common method of executing the Abiru, who had the function of nominating and enthroning the king. They also swore an oath not to disclose royal secrets. Violation of the oath was a capital crime.[179]

There were, however, more atrocious methods of executing the death penalty. Although very rare, one method consisted of partially cutting human tissues on the offender's body after which the executioner would release dogs in order to finish the execution. It is said that this was the method kings used to exact revenge. Impalement was commonly used to execute incorrigible thieves of cattle or food

175 Olewale (n 2) 261.
176 Sandrat (n 70) 87.
177 Snell (n 72) 76.
178 Bourgeois (n 55) 398.
179 Sandrat (n 70) 85.

during periods of famines. This was seen as the most deterrent punishment. The corpse remained exposed to the public until predators and carnivores stripped the skeleton. As mentioned above, girls convicted of conceiving prior to marriage, of having underdeveloped breasts or of not getting married in good time were drowned in one of the lakes located at the border of the country.[180] Crucifixion was common among the Banyoro and Bahima of Uganda, and the Barundi who applied it to those caught stealing food during a time of famine. It was rare in Rwanda.[181]

Exclusion of the Death Penalty in Pre-colonial Africa: Selected Case Studies

Justice in some areas was built on principles of arbitration, mediation and restoration, even in very sensitive criminal matters. The death penalty was inconsistent with the purpose of justice among some Bantu and in the Horn of Africa.

The nonexistence of the death penalty in some Bantu law has created an imbroglio in some modern states. There is juxtaposition of tribes that applied the death penalty and those that were death penalty free. Given that the modern states are the result of arbitrary boundaries that amalgamated tribes regardless of their indigenous values, the application of the death penalty represents a step backward if modern law cannot recognise fundamental rights that indigenous laws acknowledged. Accordingly, since the modern state cannot apply the death penalty only on those tribes customarily attached to it without violating the right to equality and breaching principles of criminal law, countries where the death penalty was non-existent should simply abolish it.

In other countries, not all tribes resorted to capital punishment. That penalty was introduced through colonisation (Lesotho) or modernisation (Ethiopia). Lesotho has been studied with other Bantu customary laws. Detailed study of the exclusion of the death penalty among Ethiopians demonstrates that Ethiopian indigenous law speaks for itself as regards abolition.

Exclusion of the Death Penalty among the Bantu

The Bantu are an African people who in their languages commonly call a human a 'ntu' in the singular and use the prefix 'Ba' or 'A' for the plural. This is how '*Bantu*' or '*Antu*' is formed. The linguistic classification of Bantu has been preferred to the old classification that identified Bantu people with their economic *modus vivendi*, namely agriculture. The word 'Bantu' is still misused in many instances to refer invariably to all sub-Saharan Africans when in fact many do not meet the linguistic criterion.[182]

180 Kagame (n 107) 299–301.

181 Sandrat (n 70) 86–87.

182 For example, in South Africa and Botswana, Basotho, Bapedi and Batswana are Batho. In Swaziland, Swazi are Batchu. In Zambia, Lozi are Batu. In Namibia, Herero

Unfitness of the death penalty for sexual offences

The term 'sexual offence' can have a broad meaning, including sexual acts that are deemed unnatural like homosexuality and bestiality. Here, we are only concerned with classical sexual offences, namely adultery and rape. Similarly to modern law, indigenous laws define adultery as sexual intercourse between a married person and another person who is not his or her spouse.[183]

Marriage is a very valuable institution. Religious rituals are performed to ensure its stability. Ancestors and divinities are approached and consulted for their support and blessings. Family members and friends provide their advice to the new couple and are involved in every single part of the process.[184] Infidelity is therefore deemed an outrageous crime, striking out against the norm of society. When it results in conception, it inflicts a spurious offspring on the husband. Adultery is a crime not only against the husband but also against those corporate bodies related to him. It is a shameful act, the effects of which offend both the wife's and husband's families and the ancestors, gods and others supernatural beings because of the sanctity of marriage.[185] Hence adultery can be considered very serious. Among the Basoga of Uganda, adultery (*bwenzi*) could describe simply having control over a woman in such a manner that sexual relations were possible.[186] As mentioned above, adultery was a capital crime elsewhere.[187]

Some Bantu people reacted differently. Within the Shona (Mozambique and Zimbabwe), the guilty party would give a goat whose meat would be shared by both parties as a sign of public reconciliation.

> In cases like adultery, or others in which one party feels grievously insulted or his reputation seriously impaired, the court may, if it fears further trouble between parties, insist that they be publicly reconciled ... The guilty party is made to produce a goat or fowl which is killed at the court. The chief has a

are Ovanu. In Angola and the Democratic Republic of Congo, Bayazi and Bambunda are Bar, whereas Kwanyama and Luena-Lubale are Ovanu. In these countries still, Mongo are Banto, Basakata are Bare, Bant are Bat, Mbala are Hadu, Kwese are Hatu and Umbundu are Omanu. In the Eastern Democratic Republic of Congo, Bakonjo and Banande are Avandu, Banyanga are Beya, Babira are Bahuhu, Huku are Vumbi and Bahamba are Bakpa. In Congo Brazzaville, Ifumu are Baru and Tege are Bari. In Gabon, Bakele are Batyi, Mpongwe and Galuwa are Oma and Fang are Bur. In Cameroon, Fang are Bur, Basa and Ewondo are Bot and Bakwiri, Bankom and Isubu are Botu or Boto. See Alexis Kagame, *La philosophie Bantu comparée* (Présence Africaine, Paris 1976) 52–55.

183 Adewale (n 65).

184 ibid.

185 ibid. See also Max Gluckman, 'Limitations of the Case Method in the Study of Tribal Law' in Gordon R Woodman and Akintunde O Obilade (eds), *African Law and Legal Theory* (Dartmouth, Aldershot, Singapore and Sidney 1995) 104.

186 Lloyd A Fallers, *Law without Precedent: Legal Ideas in Action in the Courts of Colonial Busoga* (University of Chicago Press, Chicago 1969) 115–118.

187 Adewale (n 65).

> piece of meat prepared, which he divides between the parties making them eat together. Or they are required to take snuff together [as] one does not take food or snuff with one's enemy.[188]

The meat or snuff is shared also by members of the court and public as an expression of public support for the decision reached. The same sentence was applied *mutatis mutandis* to incest and unlawful sexual intercourse during a period of mourning.[189]

For the Pokot of Kenya, two brothers from the Dove clan were accused of committing adultery with wives of the Hawk, another clan. The sentence was compensation of a hut of goats and two calves.[190] The Iteso of Uganda imposed a sentence of from three goats to three heads of cattle for confessed adultery.[191] The Ndengese, Lulua, Tetela and Yansi of the Democratic Republic of Congo punished adultery using ritual purifications, as the gods had been insulted and the bodies of adulterers sullied. Adultery with the chief's wife was considered to be an attempt on the life of the chief and thus became a political and capital crime.[192] The practice of purification by a doctor also existed among the Tswana of Southern Africa. The woman is first washed with an irritant medicine to wash away any pollution that may prevent the fall of rain.[193] It is worth noting that the same rule of compensation for adultery has been found among non-Bantu people like the Ibo of Nigeria.[194] Despite the sanctity of marriage for the Bantu, they found no reason to impose harsh punishment. Compensation and ritual purifications were acceptable remedies.

Rape consists of non-consensual sexual intercourse. The definition of rape has always been 'a male having unlawful and intentional sexual intercourse with a female without her consent'.[195] Among the Shona (Zambia and Mozambique) and the Bemba (Zambia and the Democratic Republic of Congo), penetration was necessary.[196] Consent is assumed if the woman did not call for help or immediately report the case. Then it is adultery instead of rape.[197]

Cases of pregnancy without any evidence of coercion were likewise treated as adultery or unlawful sexual intercourse. For the Bemba tribe, alleging to have

---

188 Holleman (n 13) 14.

189 Jeater (n 7) 194.

190 Gluckman (n 185) 101.

191 Mugerwa (n 67) 281.

192 'Adultère chez les Ndengese, Lulua, Tetela et Yansi' at www.ceeba.at/so (accessed 20 May 2008).

193 Schapera (n 35) 211.

194 Otonti Nduka, 'The Traditional Concept of Justice Among the Ibo of South-Eastern Nigeria' in Gordon R Woodman and Akintunde O Obilade (eds), *African Law and Legal Theory* (Dartmouth, Aldershot, Singapore and Sidney 1995) 25.

195 Carel R Snyman, *Criminal Law* (4th edn, Butterworths, Durban 2002) 445.

196 Jeater (n 7) 183.

197 Max Gluckman et al. (eds), *Ideas and Procedures in African Customary Law* (Oxford University Press, London 1969) 67.

been raped without witnesses was considered an abomination.[198] In all instances, the victim had to lay down the relevant evidence, which was often irrational in terms of divination.[199]

In principle, the rapist had to pay dowry if the victim was a girl or compensation to the husband or father should the victim be a wife or a widow staying with her parents. Compensation amounted to a certain number of goats or amount of money.[200] There was no room for a death sentence even when the victim was a teenager.

Compensation for assault and homicides

Cases of assault were solved by compensation. Assault consists in unlawfully and intentionally applying force to the person of another either directly or indirectly.[201] The first illustrative case comes from the Mbeere of Kenya. Ireri injured his father Njiru with an arrow and smashed his gourd of beer. The two had been engaged in hurtful verbal exchange while drinking together. The father decided to kill his son either physically or socially. When the matter was put before the court, the elders found that both men were wrong and ordered a goat be paid in terms of compensation.[202] The court explained its findings:

> We have decided this because you beat an old man, although we know that Njiru made a mistake in throwing soil (issuing verbal insults). Even if you appeal anywhere else you will be told to provide a goat because you beat your father. Even if you go to London, you will be told to bring a goat. With the goat, Njiru will take an oath 'may this oath kill me if I throw soil and curse my son'.[203]

For the Kuba, the appropriate sentence for assault was a fine paid to the king and compensation in the form of a serf woman.[204]

Furthermore, before the middle of the nineteenth century, many Bantu laws did not differentiate between murder and involuntary homicide.[205] This was not a general rule, however. The offender had the same degree of culpability provided he was found guilty. For Kikuyu, Kamba and Pokot of Kenya,[206] and Arusha of Tanzania,[207] if the offender had inadvertently thrown a spear into his fellow hunter

198 ibid.

199 Woodman (n 3) 17.

200 Jeater (n 7) 182–183.

201 Snyman (n 195) 430.

202 Jack Glazier, *Land and the Use of Tradition among the Mbeere of Kenya* (University Press of America, Lanham 1985) 146.

203 ibid.

204 Vansina (n 30) 105.

205 Hone (n 20).

206 Gluckman (n 185) 100.

207 Philip H Gulliver, *Social Control in African Society: A Study of the Arusha: Agricultural Masai of Northern Tanganyika* (Routledge and Kegan Paul,

instead of striking a lion, he would be held responsible in the same way as if he took such an opportunity to defeat a challenging contemporary or enemy. Be it a case of intentional homicide or culpable homicide, the sentence remained compensation. This provided insurance for the dependants of the victim. Compensation was called a 'blood-debt'.

A case from the Pokot tribe elegantly illustrates this. A member of the Hawk clan fought and killed a member of the Doves clan. In the absence of immediate compensation, the Doves performed a military demonstration in the killer's village until the elders of both clans were obliged to settle the matter. Upon agreement, the near kin of the deceased was asked to claim reasonable compensation. He asked for a hut of goats and a calf, this being the 'blood-debt'.[208] An identical process is found within the Mbari, a clan of the Kikuyu tribe still in Kenya.[209] For the Baganda of Uganda, deliberate killing was not common but it was generally punished by compensation. Killing one's slave or wife was not an offence unless the perpetrator lacked acceptable grounds.[210]

For the Luo (Kenya), restitution for homicide involved a girl from the clan of the murderer bearing progeny in the deceased's name.[211] A similar practice existed among the Shona of Zimbabwe and Mozambique. The family of the victim found it inhumane to engage in bloody vengeance, feeling the loss a second life was unnecessary. Therefore, the family of the offender had to pay with a woman or, sometimes, two girls as a sign of acknowledging the offence, expressing remorse and redressing the loss of a family member. Such compensation is called *maropa*.[212] The same practice may have existed among the AmaXosa of South Africa as well.[213]

Furthermore, the death penalty did not exist for murder among the Tsonga and the Nguni of South Africa.[214] Montshiwa and Moshoeshoe, the kings of Barolong and Basotho respectively, expressively opposed the death penalty even when applied in other kingdoms. They believed that such punishment divided the community and that it was useless to take a second life.[215] Two wrongs do not make a right. In all cases of murder, property of people and females constituted a reserve for justice debts.[216]

London 1963) 127–129.

208 ibid 101.

209 Vincent G Simiyu, 'The Democratic Myth in the African Traditional Societies' in Walter O Oyugi and Afrifa K Gitonga (eds), *Democratic Theory and Practice in Africa* (Heinemann, Portsmouth 1988) 65.

210 Hone (n 20) 83.

211 Gulliver (n 207) 104.

212 Jeater (n 7) 186–187.

213 John Henderson Soga, *The Ama- Xosa: Life and Customs* (Lovedale Press, Lovedale 1932) 46.

214 Schapera (n 35) 209.

215 *Makwanyane and Another* (n 33) para 377C per Justice Sachs.

216 Jeater (n 7) 185–194.

Compensation was not exclusive to Bantu law. The practice of paying blood-debts for both intentional and accidental homicide existed elsewhere, such as in Kano (Nigeria).[217] Even though the above-mentioned Bantu tribes and kingdoms did not apply the physical death penalty, some of them resorted to social death, in terms of ostracism or banishment, as the only appropriate sentence for serious cases. Although today's society considers murder to be the worst crime, at that time witchcraft was considered the gravest offence.

Ostracism as the ultimate punishment for witchcraft

Ostracism involves treating an individual as non-human. He or she ceases to enjoy social status within the community, which withdraws its support. The individual becomes a pariah to all intents and purposes, cannot take part in social activities and ends up as a *persona non grata*.[218] This was considered the most feared punishment, because reciprocity plays a vital role in everyone's life.

Among the Bantu of Kavirondo dangerous witches were sentenced to ostracism. Driving the offender outside society was the paramount punishment, although at times there were extrajudicial killings of witches.[219] In Zimbabwe, ostracism was also the appropriate sanction for witchcraft. Witches were entirely exiled from the community. They were deprived of vital social support and denied their social identity. Despite that, their families remained liable for providing compensation to the victims.[220]

In the Democratic Republic of Congo, if it was proved that a death resulted from witchcraft, reparation was compulsory. Witchcraft and magic played a major role in traditional institutions and had a serious impact on individuals' behaviour. A chief of lineage found guilty of witchcraft was required to perform the *Nkwamur* rite to prevent vengeance. He often handed a goat or a dog to the deceased's family. If the animal was productive then the deceased had accepted the rite, otherwise he had refused it.[221]

Ostracism was the most feared punishment among the Luo. In one case, Ogalo engaged in a fight when he was away from home and both he and his adversary were seriously injured. Fearing a judicial process, he hid, but rumours started that he had been killed or was dying somewhere. His mother subsequently accused their neighbour, Augustino, of witchcraft and called on his wife to bear children in Ogalo's name, stating that Augustino's witchcraft was the cause of her son's involvement in the fight. 'Witches are so greatly feared, they are generally

217 Allan Christelow, 'Theft, Homicide and Oath in Early Twentieth Century Kano' in Kristin Mann and Richard Roberts (eds), *Law in Colonial Africa* (James Currey, London 1991) 217.

218 Chukwuemeka (n 8).

219 Wagner (n 125).

220 Jeater (n 7) 184 and Holleman (n 13) 16.

221 Tayaya Lumbombo and Tango Muyay, 'Sorcellerie et envoutement: les cauchemars de la société' at www.ceeba.at/soc/soc-psychologie (accessed 17 June 2008).

avoided and Augustino was at least threatened with ostracism if the accusation was believed.'[222]

Clearly no death penalty was applied to the aforementioned crimes in Bantu laws. Although this has been affirmed in respect of the states and tribes concerned, no general rule can be drawn.

The Ethiopian Model: The Pride of a Nation

Like anywhere in Africa, indigenous law formed the major part of the body of Ethiopian law. As regards capital punishment, it is stated in *The Itinerario of Jeronimo Lobo*, under a chapter headed 'Of the Customs, Religion and Civilization of the Abyssinians':

> many other customs, of the kind called civic, are in force and thoroughly accepted, and for us are very barbarous ... A man's life, death and property are often dispatched in half an hour, unless more time is needed to examine witnesses. ... If the offender does not wish to appeal, justice is done on the post. The culprit is arrested and handed over to the judge; and if he is to die, he is delivered to his opponents who kill him in any way they wish, joined by the relatives of the dead man, and all of them take part in striking the poor condemned man.[223]

There is no indication whether this statement applies to a particular tribe or not. This implies that all Abyssinians (Ethiopians) had the same custom under which the death penalty was a valid sentence.

Yet when referring to the Ethiopian antic kingdom of Meroë (probably in the eight century BCE), the Greek historian Diodorus, stated:

> [t]he laws of the Ethiopians differ in many respects from those of other nations, but in none so much as in the election of their kings; which is thus managed. The priests select the most distinguished of their own order ... The person thus selected immediately enjoys all the prerogatives, which are conceded to him by the laws, in respect to his mode of life; but he can neither reward or punish anyone, beyond what the usages of their forefathers and the laws allow. It is a custom among them to inflict upon no subject the sentence of death, even though he should be legally condemned to that punishment; but they send to the malefactor one of the servants of justice who bears the symbol of death. The Greek custom of escaping punishment by flight into a neighboring country is

222 Abel L Richard, 'Customary Laws of Wrongs in Kenya: An Essay in Research Method' (1969) 17 *American Journal of Comparative Law* 573, 573.

223 Donald M Lockhart (tr), *The Itinerario of Jeronimo Lobo* (The Hakluyt Society, London 1984) 174.

> not here permitted. When the criminal sees this he goes immediately to his own house and deprives himself of life ....[224]

However, Diodorus' additional comments have been misunderstood and sometimes misinterpreted. The statement that '[i]t is a custom among them to inflict upon no subject the sentence of death' is veiled. Dr Richard Lepsius affirms that Diodorus meant the opposite as regards a judicial verdict.

> Diodorus narrates exactly the same resignation to death in those who in Ethiopia were to die by judicial verdict; a person who had been condemned, and who had at first intended to save himself by flight, had nevertheless allowed himself to be strangled without resistance by his mother, who had obstructed him in his design.[225]

Ethiopian researchers corroborate Diodorus' statement on the exclusion of the death penalty under indigenous law. *Guma* (blood money) was the prescribed punishment for murder among Ethiopian tribes.[226] Recent researchers have inventoried 60 customary laws in Ethiopia and few of them have been studied by lawyers or anthropologists.[227] However, as shall be demonstrated by a sample of 10 of them, the death penalty was not a valid punishment for homicide under Ethiopian customary laws.

The Amhara had a gradual process of imposing more and more severe punishments starting with advice from relatives and neighbours, moving to reprimand by the *guagne* (the local assembly), a warning from the *abat* (the people's nominee), being required to feed more people than he or she has the capacity to feed, conspiracy by the whole village and finally ostracism (*eroge*). All matters were resolved by arbitrator and the death penalty was unknown. Their guiding principle was: 'even a swarm of bees would not leave their hive and go to a new one before they settle down to a nearby tree or fence'.[228] All offences were compoundable.[229]

The Tigray (Tigreans or Tigrawi) are located in today's Eritrea. Their customary law, considered one of the most developed laws, was written and kept in the church or by elders. Serious crimes were settled through agreements on blood money, the

---

224 Diodorus, I, p. 177, and so on, as quoted by Heeren (n 128) 412.

225 Richard Lepsius, *Letters from Egypt, Ethiopia and the Peninsula of Sinai* (Henry G. Bohn, London 1858) 202.

226 Jembere (n 1).

227 Dolores A Donavan and Getachew Assefa, 'Homicide in Ethiopia: Human Rights, Federalism and Legal Pluralism' (2003) 52 *American Journal of Comparative Law* 505, 507.

228 Jembere (n 1) 48–49.

229 Stanley Z Fisher, 'Traditional Criminal Procedure in Ethiopia' (1971) 19 *American Journal of Comparative Law* 709, 713.

amount of which was confirmed by elders and submitted to the High Court for final approval. The High Court tried the case if no agreement was reached.[230] It is argued that this court was entitled to impose a death sentence. Whether it did in fact impose such a sentence remains unproved.[231] Tigreans usually resolved cases of homicide with blood money and sometimes the victim's family required girls.[232] The giving of a girl aimed to prevent blood feuds between communities.

The Oromo were characterised by principles of fair justice and women played a major role in criminal cases. In olden days they practised the death penalty for homicide, but later the law developed to the extent that the death penalty was replaced by a payment of cattle when the victim was an Oromo. The *lubas* (representatives of the village) took charge of enforcing the judgment, taking the offender's cattle and feasting with it. If he had no cattle, he was flogged, warned and set free. Should the victim be a stranger, the offender would be anointed with perfumed butter and blood by his sister-in-law. Elders would bless him so that he would not become the victim of revenge. He was obliged to hide for three days at least.[233] Women were meanwhile sent to the victim's clan to beg for arbitration. Women played the role of messengers to avoid any revenge being taken, as the custom prohibited exacting vengeance against women. They were the peacemakers between clans. On their return, they informed the elders of the agreed date and place of meeting. At the meeting the amount of blood money was determined. On the due day, the culprit was required to say that he had accidently killed the deceased and that he agreed to pay this and that as *Guma*.[234]

The Kunama used a conciliatory body called the *sanga nenay*. Any person fearing revenge would go to stay at a *sanga nenay* house. If the crime had been perpetrated in an open place, such as a market, the offender was required to run and embrace any member of the *sanga nenay* household, even a little child. That was the end of revenge. The matter then had to be brought before the conciliatory body. During the event, a bull would be killed and eaten by all the members. Females from both sides would exchange utensils, males would exchange weapons and the offender's and the victim's families would exchange butter. Afterwards, the *sanga nenay* would announce the amount of blood money.[235]

The Somali tribe of Ethiopia treated homicides similarly to the Kunama and revenge was rare. It is worth noting that Somali customary law applies to all the Somalis in Ethiopia, Djibouti, Kenya and Somalia. They 'claim solidarity and unity under shared norms of culture and self-governance'.[236] The offender stayed

230 Jembere (n 1) 44.

231 ibid.

232 Franklin F Russell, 'Eritrean Customary Law' (1959) 3 *Journal of African Law* 100, 100–101.

233 Jembere (n 1) 45.

234 ibid.

235 ibid 56.

236 Donavan and Assefa (n 227) 516 and 527.

hidden and asked his relatives to beg for arbitration. If his cattle did not meet the requirements of blood money, the whole family would rescue him with additional cattle.[237] In some instances, the victim's family would demand a girl fitted out for marriage. The practice intended to bring the two families in conflict together. The decision was not spontaneous. It resulted from inter-clan contracts that have existed since time immemorial and which are upheld by the *Heer* (Somali customary law).[238]

The Gurage had a high court with jurisdiction over violent crimes such as murder, attempted murder, arson and so on. Homicides were punished by blood money. The offender and all the adult males in his lineage up to the third ascending generation were banned from the clan or tribe district until they had paid compensation. If they failed to pay, a blood feud would usually erupt and there would be no expectation of compensation should the criminal or one of his kinsmen be caught and executed. Only provocation was a valid defence. Vengeance after a court's decision was always severely punished. Vengeance was deemed to be an act of aggravated violence. The offender could suffer other punishments, the most severe being ostracism. Subsidiary punishments including not attending the offender's burial ceremonies, feast, refusal of fire from neighbours and keeping away his cattle could also be imposed.[239]

The Afar (or Danakil) had a penal code that determined criminal responsibility and matched offences with precise punishments. *Mada* determined 'the nature and type of crimes, the degree of responsibility together with the corresponding penalty'.[240] Furthermore,

> [a]cts that are considered to constitute crimes were categorized into five: *Eido* (killing), *aymissiya* (assault), *rado* (looting), *sammo* (adultery) and *oaffu* (insult). The corresponding types of punishment in descending order of their gravity are: *hane* (vengeance), *diat* (compensation for murder) and *deikha* (compensation for cases other than murder). *Maruso* (imposing fines) is also employed as a supplementary measure ....[241]

Whether vengeance was an institutionalised punishment is not clear. The use of the terms 'killing' and 'murder' is confusing. It is likely that murder corresponds to cases wherein the victim's family could not avenge the death and thus brought the matter to trial. *Hane* or vengeance, therefore, should not be listed among the punishments as it entails private justice. It has been argued that 'the highest penalty

237 Jembere (n 1) 65.

238 Donavan and Assefa (n 227) 526–527.

239 William A Shack, 'Guilt and Innocence: Problem and Method in the Gurage Judicial System' in Max Gluckman et al. (eds), *Ideas and Procedures in African Customary Law* (Oxford University Press, London 1969) 160–161 and Jembere (n 1) 57–59.

240 Jembere, ibid 60.

241 ibid.

that might be imposed by any court having the competence to try serious crimes was expulsion from tribal membership, [that is ostracism]'.[242]

The Wolaitta belonged to the independent kingdom of Wolaitta until their absorption in 1894. All important criminal cases were tried by the *Balmola* (legislative and judicial council) which played the role of the Supreme Court in criminal trials. Only princes were sentenced to ostracism. Other people found guilty of homicide were executed.[243]

Among the Kafecho (or Kafa), the *Tato* (the king) had among his functions the duty of presiding over the Supreme Court which was seated at the foot of *Bonga* hall. Although compensation was the most regular punishment, *Tato* had the power to pass death sentences.[244]

> Punishments consisted of chaining, flogging, and enslaving, and compensation was to be paid in cattle or money. The most common forms of punishments were mutilation, [that is] cutting off of one hand, finger or toe; execution by beheading, or in case of a woman, pegging down to the ground. Violent robbery was punished by hanging, while a thief received from 40 to 50 lashes.[245]

The Anuak dwell in western Ethiopia. There is no indication of violent crimes within this group. This is the result of communalism and collective responsibility. It has been argued that 'since they live together and work together, the chance of conflicting opinions is very much reduced'.[246]

We may conclude that only three tribes imposed the death penalty: the Tigray, the Wolaitta and the Kafecho. Its practice remains doubtful, however, in the case of the Tigray. The Wolaitta, who effectively practised the sentence, joined Ethiopia only at the end of the nineteenth century. The same is true of the Kafecho who were annexed to the kingdom of Abyssinia by Emperor Menelik II in 1894.[247] This implies that before the influence of Coptic law in 1434, Wolaitta and Kafecho were independent kingdoms whose laws fell outside the indigenous laws of Abyssinia. The logical conclusion is that no death penalty existed among the Ethiopian tribes studied.

The Kafecho were the only tribe to use mutilation and decapitation as punishments. It has not been established whether this resulted from any contact with a foreign legal system. Their geographical location (south-western Ethiopia)

242 Jamuluddin A Redo, *The Afar Customary Law* (unpublished Amharic manuscript), p. 2 as quoted by Jembere, ibid 62.

243 Jembere, ibid 66.

244 ibid 72.

245 ibid.

246 ibid 75.

247 ibid.

makes it likely that if any influence from canon law and *Shari'a* existed, it would have first affected coastal tribes.[248]

Conclusion

The above discussion aims to resolve the broad question of whether the death penalty existed in Africa before foreign legal influences arrived. As a punishment, it insinuates the presence of a rule of law and specifically of criminal law. Overgeneralisations have led to imply that criminal law exists only if serious crimes are harshly punished.

Accordingly, societies without the death penalty were thought to be still primitive. Such a conclusion deliberately ignores the fact that indigenous laws had already catalogued crimes and their punishments and distinguished between intentional homicide and accidental homicide. These brutal conclusions were likely influenced by a punitive mind and are blamed for their failure to consider the grounds on which the death penalty was either excluded or retained.

A lot of illegal conduct was simultaneously immoral and against religion. The death penalty was sometimes applied in the form of a divine punishment, or to prevent the abomination resulting from the crime affecting the entire community. The supernatural influenced both substantive and procedural law. In procedural law, because of their omniscience and superpowers, supernatural forces were resorted to when judging the probity and sincerity of a witness. In most African traditions, the witness's oath was made in the name of cosmic forces, ancestral spirits or God and witnesses swore to being struck by lightning or to being killed if they perjure themselves. Ordeal evidences were also common all over Africa.[249]

In most of the organised states, a competent court imposed the death sentence only after a formal trial with the right of appeal and the right to seek the king's mercy.[250] The death penalty was imposed for supernatural crimes such as witchcraft, poisoning, pronouncing a curse, political offences, homicides, malicious injuries and sexual offences. The conclusion is that the death penalty existed in Africa before foreign legal influences arrived. Many Bantu laws, thought to be the most humanitarian in Africa provided for the death penalty as well.

In other areas, harsh punishments including the death penalty were avoided on religious grounds. Restorative justice was itself lodged in religious beliefs. Sacred rituals and ceremonies were an integral part of the legal process. African gods and

248 The historical map of the ninth and ten centuries indicates that Kafecho or Kafa were (or are) located between the rivers Baro, Akobo and Omo. See Taddesse Tamrat, 'Ethiopia, the Red Sea and the Horn' in Roland Oliver (ed), *The Cambridge History of Africa: from c.1050 to c.1600*, vol 3 (Cambridge University Press, London 1977) 99.

249 Ayittey (n 4) 100–101.

250 ibid 85.

spirits were not focused on individual wrongdoing and punishment. They dealt with wellbeing and good relationships within communities as a whole.

The law was regarded as a compensatory device, which often prescribed the amount of compensation to be paid by the offender or his family.[251] It ceased to be punitive in the modern familiar sense. It was a tool of peace used to facilitate good relationships.[252] An offence against the law was simultaneously an offence against religion and inevitably involved the community.[253] Thus, the exclusion of the death penalty in some indigenous laws was justified by the idea that an appropriate punishment should not destroy the offender. Any punishment looked beyond the culprit and the crime in considering the society at large, the potential widow and orphans included. Compensation better served the aim of justice as a tool of restoration, retribution, deterrence and rehabilitation. There was no reason to lose a second life, given that two wrongs do not make a right. Foreign laws introduced the death penalty where it did not exist and dealt with its scope where it existed and introduced new methods of execution.

251 Chukwuemeka (n 8).

252 Ayittey (n 4) 80.

253 Chukwuemeka (n 8).

Chapter 3
The Death Penalty during the Period of Peaceful Legal Influences in Africa

Introduction

Pre-colonial foreign legal influences started in the seventh century CE when, from the Arabic peninsula, Muslims invaded North and East Africa. Later, Islamic law extended to Maghreb and West Africa. Before the scramble for Africa in 1885, Muslim law had become an unchallengeable legal system on the continent.[1] Ethiopia adopted Christianity around the fourth century as a result of its long history with Israel since the time of King Solomon. It would have introduced Judaic law from then.[2] However, the codification of this law only happened in the fourteenth century when Ethiopia adopted the Coptic law. There are also traces of Judaic law in North Africa (Morocco and Tunisia) and Hindu law in East Africa (Madagascar and Zanzibar). However, they left no substantive legacy in criminal matters. They were more concerned with family matters, personal status and commercial contracts.[3]

European legal systems were present in pre-colonial Africa too. In the seventeenth century, commercial interests led the Dutch government to create a station in the Cape (South Africa) and to import the Roman Dutch law there. At the beginning of the nineteenth century the anti-slavery movement in America incited the American government to create Liberia as a repository for free slaves so that they could exercise and enjoy full social, civil and political rights there. Liberia declared its independence a few decades before the scramble for Africa.

The period between the introduction of Islamic law and the scramble for Africa is commonly referred to as 'the period of imported laws' or the 'period of peaceful legal influences'.[4] This does not mean that Africans welcomed pre-colonial foreign laws with open arms. It rather implies that, contrary to colonial laws, pre-colonial foreign legal influences peacefully coexisted with indigenous laws although they later accommodated and unsuccessfully attempted to suppress them.

These influences eventually introduced the death penalty where it did not exist or extended it to apply to offences that had previously been punished in other ways. What is undisputed is the fact that these influences introduced new methods

1 Jacques Vanderlinden, *Les systèmes juridiques Africains* (PUF, Paris 1983) 27.
2 ibid 233–234.
3 ibid 39–41.
4 ibid 25.

of execution. This chapter studies the extent to which they introduced or extended the death penalty and new methods of execution in Africa.

European Peaceful Legal Influences in Africa

The Greeks, Romans, Portuguese and Spanish were among the first to interact with Africa through military invasions, trade, religious civilisation and exploration. They did not leave a lasting legal heritage upon their departure, however. This study is limited to Anglo-American law and Roman Dutch law, both of which peacefully and effectively influenced indigenous laws in Africa.

It is commonly accepted that ancient European punishments consisted of outlawing the recalcitrant offender and placing him beyond the social pale.[5] The law of homicide, for example, indicates that it was the duty of the family or of the tribe to avenge a victim by taking the life of his murderer.[6] Then the law developed and the practice of private justice and private reprisals was supplanted by decisions of an organised justice system.[7] Still, the law was characterised by punitive sanctions including death sentences.

In England as on the Continent, several crimes were punishable by death which was often ritually executed.[8] In 1820, there were over 200 capital crimes in England. These crimes were dispersed in at least 160 statutes and one provision could be interpreted as covering several capital crimes. It is said that 'the actual scope of the death penalty was often as much as three or four times as extensive as the number of capital provisions would seem to indicate'.[9] Capital crimes included witchcraft, treason and homicides. This was the result of the English law maturing under the influence of the Indo-European legal system. This process ironically upgraded English law to the status of state law and left the death penalty in the hands of the state.[10]

Thereafter, this same law crossed the Atlantic as North America was colonised. English law became the absolute master of the land. Although American law is also seen as a synthesis of English law, Native American customs and Spanish law, its main source is English law as contained in English legal practice, custom and

5 Henri S Maine, *Dissertations on Early Law and Custom: Chiefly Selected from Lectures Delivered at Oxford* (John Murray, London 1883) 36–45.

6 'Early Law and Custom' (1885) 2 *Cape Law Journal* 28, 28.

7 Maine (n 5) 31–45.

8 Bruce Lenman and Geoffrey Parker, 'The State, the Community and the Criminal Law in Early Modern Europe' in VAC Gatrell et al. (eds), *Crime and the Law: The Social History of Crime in Western Europe since 1500* (Europa Publications Limited, London 1980) 13.

9 Leon Radzinowicz, *A History of English Criminal Law and its Administration from 1750*, vol 1 (Stevens and Sons, London 1948) 4–5.

10 'Early Law and Custom' (1885) 2 *Cape Law Journal* 28, 28.

philosophy.[11] This law, dressed in an American suit, crossed back over the Atlantic to establish itself permanently in Liberia.

The Dutch had quite a different way of practising justice. While in England foreigners were the most likely to face the death penalty when involved in serious crimes, the Dutch referred to foreigners as *amicitia* (a friendly group) and exacted from them a peaceful living oath, in which they swore 'to live in love with [them]'.[12] In terms of the death penalty, until the eighteenth century most criminal cases were resolved through a *compositie* or a peaceful extrajudicial agreement.[13] Serious cases were punished by death until 1860.[14]

Dutch law remained a community law until the influence of Roman law in 1570. Establishing the date that Roman law penetrated the Netherlands has been and still is controversial; however, it is generally accepted that in 1570 Roman law became effective in Holland due to the enforcement of the criminal ordinance. This led to the *Gelderland* revolt which the Dutch Republic survived in 1795. The revolt aimed to restore the old community law, sourced from local customs that the citizens were used to.[15]

Thus, Roman Dutch law is Roman law grafted onto Dutch customs. From 1650, it enjoyed exclusive application at the Cape for almost 250 years until English law became a concurrent system in 1815.[16] Later efforts to maintain it were made by white Afrikaner nationalists who succeeded in introducing it in law schools and courts until 1980. Although the true picture of today's South African law is of a mixed legal system whose substance and form originate from Roman Dutch and English legal systems, Roman Dutch law remains the basis of South African criminal law.[17] Its influence on the South African criminal policy, including the death penalty, can only justify a debate as regards to its form and content as no execution was carried out in Holland after 1860[18] and the country abolished the death penalty for murder in 1870.[19]

---

11 Lawrence M Friedman, *American Law: An Introduction* (Norton and Company, New York 1984) 37.

12 Lenman and Parker (n 8) 14 and 25.

13 ibid 26.

14 William Tallack, 'The Penalty of Death' (1890) 7 *South African Law Journal* 82, 87.

15 CH Van Zyl, 'The Study of Law' (1893) 10 *South African Law Journal* 185, 203. See also Bruce Lenman and Geoffrey Parker (n 8) 33.

16 Francois du Bois, 'Introduction: History, System and Sources' in Cornie G Van Der Merwe and Jacques E Du Plessis (eds), *Introduction to the Law of South Africa* (Kluwer Law International, The Hague 2004) 1.

17 Jonathan Burchell, 'Criminal Law' in Cornie G Van Der Mwerwe and Jacques E Du Plessis (eds), *Introduction to the Law of South Africa* (Kluwer Law International, The Hague 2004) 447–448.

18 Tallack (n 14).

19 Roger Hood and Carolyn Hoyle, 'Abolishing the Death Penalty Worldwide: The Impact of a "New Dynamic"' (2009) 38 *Crime and Justice* 1, 5.

The Death Penalty in the Liberian Anglo-American Law

Liberia was initiated by the American Colonization Society created in 1817. Its purpose was to settle ex-slaves in West Africa.[20] Liberia and the United States of America have close ties. They share institutions and concepts of law. Article 6 of the 1820 Constitution provided for the application of the American common criminal law in Liberia.[21] The country eventually declared its independence in 1847 as a preventive measure against European colonial ambitions.[22] It never underwent European colonisation. Liberia applied a dual system that reflected the origin of its inhabitants until 1964 when the indirect rule policy was abolished.[23] American settlers were subject to the jurisdiction of modern law while African tribes were governed by their respective local customs. Liberian indigenous law was described as 'excellent and eminently adapted to the requirements of the country'.[24] Death by burning was the most severe punishment for witchcraft. A death sentence for murder was rare. Murder was generally redressed by the heaviest fine possible.[25]

From 1859, English law was gradually introduced and it became an authoritative legal component of Liberian law. In the 1900s Liberia initiated penal reform intending to substitute retributive punishments for reformative punishments. In 1914, Liberia codified its criminal law and government officials declared that the primary aim of criminal justice was rehabilitation.[26] The statutory death penalty was not applied until 1971.

The implied de facto *abolition of the death penalty*

The Liberian Declaration of Independence is somewhat a remake of the American Declaration of Independence. It contains the following paragraph:

> We were animated with the hope that here we should be at liberty to train up our children in the way they should go to inspire them with the love of an honourable

20 Harrison RJ Church, *West Africa: A Study of the Environment and of Man's Use of It* (Longman, London 1963) 330.

21 Gerald H Zarr, 'Liberia' in Alan Milner (ed), *African Penal Systems* (Routledge and Kegan Paul, London 1969) 196.

22 Declaration of Independence in Convention of the Commonwealth Republic of Liberia, 26 July 1847, page 5. Available at www.digital.library.cornell.edu (accessed 23 August 2009).

23 Monday B Akpan, 'Black Imperialism: Americo-Liberian Rule over the African Peoples of Liberia, 1841–1964' (1973) 7 *Canadian Journal of African Studies* 217, 217–236.

24 Wallis C Braithwaite, 'Tribal Laws of the Mendi' (1921) 3 *Journal of Comparative Legislation and International Law* 228, 233.

25 ibid.

26 Zarr (n 21) 210, footnote no 20.

> fame, to kindle with them, the flame of a lofty philanthropy and to form strong within them, the principles of humanity, virtue and religion.[27]

Accordingly, the first section of the Republican Constitution created an unrestricted right to life.[28] Limitations were set out in section 8 and provided that '[n]o person shall be deprived of life, liberty, property, or privilege, but by judgment of his peers or the law of the land'.[29] The death penalty as a limitation to the right to life could therefore be pronounced as a verdict of the jury or by a court of law.

The penal code further subjected the execution of the death penalty to the presentation of a signed and sealed death warrant from the Head of State.[30] It appears that Liberia did not resort to the death penalty until 1971. The only account of the death penalty being exercised was obtained from the personal letter of a teenager, Salomon S. Page, writing to his former father's master in April 1849. After narrating the war with local tribes in which he fought beside his father and uncle, he wrote:

> … time would fail me to give you a complete history therefore I stop here. 5 murderers were hung [and] one of our own citizens for shooting another at about 7 o'clock P.M., 4 natives of Africa for killing an American on an Island up the St. John river, commonly called the Factory Island.[31]

No other correspondence corroborates this story. If Salomon's letter is given credit, it would stand as the only recorded case before 1971. Liberia had become famous for not applying the barbaric punishments that were common in neighbouring British colonies.[32] The death penalty was also and still is regularly executed in the United States of America. The idea of liberty, so vital to former slaves, added to the concern of unifying the country where indigenous tribes remained hostile to the foreign invasion led to cautious decision making. Section 232 of the penal code, which provided for capital punishment by hanging in cases of murder, remained unapplied until 1971. President William Tubman simply refused to sign execution warrants. Death sentences were *de facto* commuted to life imprisonment.[33] From

27 Declaration of Independence in Convention of the Commonwealth Republic of Liberia, 26 July 1847, page 5. Available at www.digital.library.cornell.edu (accessed 23 August 2009).

28 Section 1 of the Liberian Constitution of the 26 July 1847, printed in *The Herald Office*, March 1847.

29 Section 8 of the Bill of Rights of the Liberian Constitution, printed in *The Herald Office*, March 1847.

30 Section 36 (1) of the Liberian Penal Code of 1973.

31 Mary F Goodwin, 'A Liberian Packet' (1951) 59 *Virginia Magazine of History and Biography* 77, 77.

32 Wilson J Moses, *Liberian Dreams: Back-to-Africa, Narratives from 1850s* (Pennsylvania State University Press, Pennsylvania 1998) 55.

33 Zarr (n 21) 207–208.

the time when the Declaration of Independence was signed in 1847 to 1971, Liberia *de facto* abolished the death penalty.

In 1965, President William Tubman formally opposed the death penalty by suggesting that the responsibility of signing and sealing a death warrant be given to the Chief Justice. The president was not compelled to perform that duty and there existed a constitutional provision supporting the suggestion. Liberians approved the idea and local newspapers found the recommendation logical. The Chief Justice was already required to follow the legal process of homicide cases. He would therefore be comfortable with the responsibility of signing or not signing a death warrant.[34] No further action was taken, however.

In 1969, a call for complete *de jure* abolition was launched to prevent future heads of state from introducing the practice of hanging.

> … [T]here now appears some likelihood that capital punishment may be utilized in the more immediate future. As a result of the widespread public concern over the pronounced increase of crimes of violence, some suggestion has been made in the newspapers and other media that capital punishment be used.[35]

It was not long before this prophesy of calamity was fulfilled. As soon as President Tubman died, his former vice president (now president) began signing death warrants.

The era of brutality

From the beginning (1971), President William Tolbert applied the Biblical saying 'An eye for an eye and a tooth for a tooth'. Tolbert was an ordained Baptist church pastor. He often declared that if you kill, you will be killed too. The first death warrant he signed was that of Justin Obi, a Nigerian lecturer convicted of having murdered an Episcopalian Bishop.[36] A few weeks later, he signed a death warrant authorising the hanging of three convicted criminals, one of whom was his cousin.[37] In 1974, he again ordered the hanging of four convicted criminals.[38]

The regime became more barbaric when Tolbert started punishing those who perpetrated ritual murders. In 1976, 12 people were arrested and accused of ritual murder. The case was known as 'the trial of the gang of 12'. Before the end of the trial, two of the accused were released and another two died. On 9 June 1978, a jury convicted Allen Yancy and others of the murder of a very famous singer and fisherman named Moses Tweh, sentencing them to death by hanging. On

34 *Liberian Star*, 9 June 1965 as quoted by Zarr, ibid 211, footnote no 42.

35 Zarr (n 21) 208.

36 Fred PM Van Der Kraaj, 'The Open Door Policy of Liberia: An Economic History of Modern Liberia' (Bremen 1983), found at www.liberiapastandpresent.org (accessed 26 August 2009).

37 ibid.

38 ibid.

appeal, the Supreme Court upheld the conviction and confirmed the lower court's death sentence.

The gang's last resort was to apply for a presidential pardon. Influential persons attempted to obtain a review of the court's decision but the president simply replied, 'I will never permit myself to be influenced in one way or another by sentiments. I will do my duty when it is time to do my duty in the fear of God in keeping with the oath of office of the President.'[39] Some family members tried to poison their convicted relatives to save their family from the public humiliation of a hanging. All these attempts failed and the president signed the death warrant.

The scene of the 1979 execution was one of macabre horror for the Liberians who gathered to watch. The pitiless heart of their president silenced a crowd of 15,000 persons for half an hour.[40] The close ties between Liberia and the United States of America have resulted in the international community turning a blind eye to the abuses of human rights in Liberia. In the 1977 Annual Human Rights Report that was presented by the United States' Department of State to Congress, no mention of the trial is made. Rather, Liberia is applauded as having one of 'the best human rights records in Africa'.[41] On 12 April 1980, Samuel K. Doe overthrew and assassinated William Tolbert. In 1986, article 11 of the new Constitution reconfirmed the provision on the death penalty imposed through a judicial process.[42]

The legacy of the death penalty in Liberia

In short, the fact that Liberian indigenous tribes only imposed a fine for murder demonstrates the absence of a retaliation policy in that society. The amount of the fine was set as a deterrent, with the purpose being to ruin the offender.[43]

Thus it was Anglo American law that introduced the death penalty for murder in Liberia. Its practice is evidence, however, of the extent to which the death penalty served different politicians. Death penalty provisions remained dormant within the Constitution and the penal code when society was in need of peace and national unity. The executive found ways of excluding executions for more than a century. The resurgence of executions in the 1970s was simply the consequence of not having *de jure* abolition and further evidence of the fragility of *de facto* abolition. Executions started one year after the death of the abolitionist president,

39 'Yancy and Others to be Noosed', *The New Liberian*, 1979 and 'Gang of Seven Executed: Thousands Thronged the Cemetery', *Express Special*, 1979 as quoted by Van Der Kraaj (n 36).

40 ibid.

41 See Annual Human Rights Issues submitted to the Congress by the US Department of State, 65 (1976–1977), Liberia, at www.heinonline.org/HOL/ViewImageLocal? (accessed 1 September 2009).

42 The Constitution of the Republic of Liberia of 6 January 1986, ICL Doc status, 6 January 1986.

43 Braithwaite (n 24) 234.

William Tubman. The new regime, whose slogan was the *lex talionis* principle, hanged 16 people between 1971 and 1978.[44] Liberia's last execution occurred in 2000 and the death penalty was legally repealed in 2005. We shall return to this in the final chapter.

The Death Penalty under Roman Dutch Law in South Africa

Roman Dutch law in South Africa has never been a death penalty free law. It inherited concepts and theories of Roman law that according to the Law of XII Tables prescribed the death penalty for a range of crimes including treason (*perduellio*), murder, theft, defamation and perjury. It also contained influences of local Germanic customs, which, in addition, imposed the death penalty for rape, sodomy, bigamy and heresy.[45] English law influences on South African law, moreover, had little to do with abolition, favouring the death penalty as well. Its effects were limited to shortening the list of capital crimes, introducing the discretionary death penalty for treason and the mandatory death penalty for murder. The efforts of the British coloniser were not immune to Afrikaner nationalism and its apartheid racial ideology.

The death penalty prior to the influence of English law

When Dutch settlers landed at the Cape of Good Hope in 1650, one of the laws at their disposal was the 1540 Edict of Emperor Charles which made bankruptcy a capital crime. Van der Linden, a prominent and learned early Roman Dutch lawyer, argued that the Edict never found favour with South African settlers due to its absurdity. Temporary imprisonment became a reasonable alternative.[46] However, the exclusion of the death penalty for its unreasonableness remains doubtful. It is instead thought that Van der Linden was expressing a more modern view. The old Roman Dutch legislation (*Placaat*) of commercial honesty imposed the death penalty for a breach of faith among businessmen[47] and 'those at the Cape considered themselves governed by the Roman-Dutch law'.[48] There is, however, no indication in the Cape archives of the death sentence being passed for insolvency.

These archives indicate that until formally prohibited by the Netherlands, notorious cases deserving of the death sentence were often returned in Europe.[49]

44 Van Der Kraaj (n 36).

45 Exton M Burchell and Peter MA Hunt, *South African Criminal Law and Procedure* (Juta, Cape Town 1970) chapter 1, at 2–11.

46 'Capital Punishment' (1897) 14 *South African Law Journal* 122, 122–123.

47 ibid.

48 Burchell and Hunt (n 45) 17.

49 'Extract from the Despatch of Seventeen to India, 2 July 1703', as quoted in Hendrik CV Leibbrandt, *Precis of the Archives of the Cape of Good Hope: Letters Received 1695–1696 by Governor S Van Der Stel* (Cape Times, Cape Town and London 1900) 332.

This means that the Roman Dutch penal law was not yet extended to Africans. In reaction to the Cape Governor's letter of 19 February 1701 requesting that in accordance with the judgment of the Court of Justice, sailor Jan de Vos be transferred to Holland to be executed there, on 2 July 1703 Dutch authorities replied that '… such desperate people are no longer to be sent over to us – no criminals whatever – for trials …'.[50]

This made it clear that there were to be no more transfers of convicted or suspected criminals to the Netherlands. The prohibition also contained firm instructions on the timeframe of execution, the place of execution and the automatic refusal of pardon in such cases. The aforementioned letter stated:

> It is somewhat incongruous that those of Ternate sent all the papers connected with the case of the skipper, condemned to death for murder, to Batavia, as the case was so clear and all punishments, of this nature especially, should be promptly inflicted, without leaving the delinquents so long in uncertainty regarding their fate. Moreover, it is advisable that such sentences should be executed on the spot where the crimes have been committed, in order to impress and deter others, and not in another place. The reasons adduced … are, moreover, not so favourable and weighty as to justify the postponement of the execution so long, or a request for pardon. Accordingly such verdicts shall henceforth be carried out without delay where the crime has been committed.[51]

These firm instructions opposed the Cape authorities' practice of avoiding the death sentence as best they could. There were different ways of avoiding an offender's execution. The first was commutation of the death sentence to that of banishment. On 30 November 1697, the death sentence by shooting of J.C. Overvran, a former soldier convicted of murder, was commuted to banishment to Robben Island. The Governor said he found no reason to execute him.[52] This only happened once. Commutation was then restricted or even forbidden in application of the1650 law regulating the death penalty. On 23 July 1701, Dutch authorities felt obliged to reiterate that,

> [t]he Governor-General had no power to assume unto himself such a right, which not only does not belong to him, but which he is strictly forbidden to assume, as will be seen from our instructions to you of the year 1650, in which pardon from death (or the remission of capital punishment) has been strictly forbidden to all and everybody, and the Governor-General in particular is forbidden to do so on his own authority … This law has always steadily been kept in view as far as we know ….[53]

50 ibid.
51 ibid.
52 ibid 133.
53 ibid 276–277.

Judicial authorities reacted to the prohibition by reducing death sentences. Convicted persons had to be given the impression that they were being executed without killing them. On 27 August 1696, one Frans Coentsen drew his sword against a sergeant on guard. He was 'sentenced to be blindfolded on the place of execution, a bullet to be fired over his head and after that to be put in irons and serve as convict for three years'.[54] On 23 December 1696, Jerla was convicted of human trafficking for having bought a child with the purpose of selling it afterwards. The court condemned Jerla to 'be brought to the place of execution, there to be bound to a pole and rigorously scourged and branded ....'[55]

On 13 October 1699, soldier Jan Abrahams was convicted of stabbing his mother in the loin with a knife. The sentence reads: 'The knife to be tied above his head, and after having been severely whipped and branded on the back, he was to be banished for 10 years as a convict.'[56] On 14 October 1699, soldier Jan Stekelman was convicted of a crime that is not mentioned and sentenced 'to stand with the rope around his neck under the gallows; to be severely whipped, branded and sen[t] in chains for 10 years to Robben Island'.[57]

The third way to avoid the death sentence was to resort to legal technicalities. On 1 September 1699, two Chinese were convicted of sodomy, a capital crime. However, the court was unable to secure a confession from the accused. They were sentenced to banishment.[58] On 27 November 1699, Oeydsoeko was also convicted of sodomy. Although tortured, he refused to confess. The court stated 'that the mildness of our laws requires that no one shall be executed or condemned unless he personally confesses to the crime of which he is accused ... [T]he prisoner although tortured, would not confess ... [T]herefore he should be banished for life ....'[59] On 12 December 1699, Binko was convicted of murder and sentenced to be banished for life after first serving six years in irons.[60] Confession was a precondition for the imposition of the death sentence according to Philip II's criminal procedure ordinance of 1570.[61]

Nevertheless, the Dutch authorities were sometimes inconsistent in their criminal policy. The Netherlands refused, for example, to uphold an execution when doing so would undermine their position in the colony. In 1703, the colony faced probably what was its first challenging death penalty case. Ninety men planned an expedition into the interior to steal cattle. They spent almost two months moving from village to village, attacking and killing Hottentots and taking

54 ibid 210.
55 ibid 72.
56 ibid 216.
57 ibid.
58 ibid 214.
59 ibid 233.
60 ibid 234.
61 Burchell and Hunt (n 45) 19.

possession of their cattle. More than 2,000 cattle were stolen during a war in which many Hottentots lost their lives.

Applying the Resolution and *Placaat* of 11 July 1702 and likely bearing in mind the aforementioned 2 July 1703 letter, the judicial council of the Company[62] started by explaining why the court painfully excluded the death sentence in previous similar cases. First of all, half of the population (550 people at the time) was involved in this kind of dirty business. Second, widows and orphans, already far from their fatherland, would be exposed to extreme misery if their breadwinner was executed. Third was their fear of inciting general chaos. If some convicted criminals escaped execution, they could flee into the uncontrollable mountains creating a climate of insecurity for the Hottentots and for their fellow Europeans.[63] However, based on the circumstances of the case, judges found that only the death sentence was appropriate and made the following ruling:

> ... In order to preserve the peace of the Government and to free the natives for the future from similar violence committed on them so unjustly by fully half the number of inhabitants by the abuse and violation of the free barter, we have unanimously decided ..., on pain, that offenders will, according to circumstances be punished corporally or capitally ....[64]

Despite the determination of Cape authorities to execute the sentence, they wisely submitted the matter for approval to their hierarchy in the Netherlands. On 24 July 1704, a reply stated:

> ... in reply to your [letter] of 1st April 1703, ... regarding the violence committed by some freemen on the Hottentots, whom they had visited in order to barter cattle, from whom they took, and whom they robbed of their cattle, likewise murdering some of them, as fully set forth in your letter; ... We now say that although those violent men have deserved a rigorous punishment commensurate with such a horrible deed, we share your hesitation because of the great number of people who, according to your evidence, are guilty of this crime ....[65]

62 General Netherlands Chartered East India Company.

63 Hendrik CV Leibbrandt, *Precis of the Archives of the Cape of Good Hope: The Defence of Willem Adriaan Van Der Stel* (W.A. Richards & Son, Cape Town 1897) 136.

64 ibid 135.

65 Hendrik CV Leibbrandt (n 49) 347. Accordingly, the Cape Government passed *Placaat* against trifling barter with natives three times (8 December 1739, 26 April 1770 and 16 June 1774) and recidivism led it to take a resolution on the 19 July 1786, authorising the Landdrost to make the so-called trade of cattle with Kafirs, a trade that often turned into a raid in the Hottentots territories, at most twice a year for bringing good cows for the benefit of the entire company. See Hendrik CV Leibbrandt, *Precis of the Archives of the Cape of Good Hope, Requesten (Memorials) 1715–1806*, vol 2 (Cape Times, Cape Town and London 1905) 493.

Until 1862, most of the prevalent offences under Roman Dutch law were capital crimes. It appears, however, that courts seldom pronounced it. Sometimes, the prosecutor's references to the Imperial statutes lying in the criminal code and to Biblical *lex talionis* verses were unsuccessful.[66] Capital crimes were treason, murder, assault with intent to murder, rape, sodomy, bestiality, incest between people in a consanguineous relationship, arson, robbery, theft aggravated from former conviction, housebreaking, theft and killing of cattle, coining, falsity and forgery. For the crime of sodomy, a 1730 *Placaat* added that the offender should be hanged in public, his body burnt or thrown in the sea or left to wild animals.[67]

Nevertheless, interest in executions gradually lessened. In 1731, one person was convicted and sentenced to death for sodomy. In 1831, four people were executed, two for sodomy, one for assault with intent to murder and one for rape and robbery. In 1832, three persons were executed, one for assault, housebreaking, theft and killing cattle, the second for theft, shop-breaking and assault with intent to murder and the third for aggravated theft. In 1835, only two people were executed respectively for arson, incest and rape. In 1836, again two persons were executed, one for arson and the other for housebreaking with intent to steal, theft and assault with intent to murder. The death penalty fell out of vogue until 1844 when one person was executed for rape. In 1862, soldier William Nicholas was convicted of rape and executed as well. In 1891, McKeone and Cooper were executed for highway robbery and assault on a policeman.[68]

Cape sentences were described as being as barbaric as those formerly in vogue in Europe during the same period. They included breaking on the wheel, hanging, impaling, strangling, burning, drowning, smothering and torture accompanied by a *coup de grace*.[69]

After the execution of William Nicholas, it was commonly thought that the death penalty would be abandoned for all crimes except murder. The government seemed to have substituted it with banishment. The convicted were banished and sent to Robben Island for custody or hard labour.[70] Surprisingly, three decades later the Transvaal High Court imposed a death sentence for highway robbery and theft.[71] The sentence provoked intense legal controversy. In fact, the court was

66 Leibbrandt (n 49) 341–342.

67 'Capital Punishment' (1897) 14 *South African Law Journal* 122, 123. For bestiality and coining see also Clarkson H Tredgold, *Handbook of Colonial Criminal Law* (Juta, Cape Town 1904) 74 and 101.

68 'Capital Punishment under the Common Law' (1891) 8 *South African Law Journal* 232, 232.

69 'Capital Punishment' (1897) 14 *South African Law Journal* 122, 122–123. See also Burchell and Hunt (n 45) 18–19.

70 Leibbrandt, *Precis of the Archive of the Cape of Good Hope, Requesten (Memorials) 1715–1806*, vol 2 (n 65) 234, 374, 616 and 632.

71 'Capital Punishment under the Common Law' (1891) 8 *South African Law Journal* 232, 232.

blamed for not following legal developments in England where the death penalty was restricted to treason and murder.

In 1891, one of the writers exclaimed:

> The common law in this country seems to have followed in its growth the legislative development of the English criminal law, and one would have thought that the criminal law of Transvaal would have advanced in a similar way, but …, the world has been astonished to find that this was not the case.[72]

In reaction, Transvaal Chief Justice Kotzé admitted that the sentence was outdated but stated that he had a feeling it conformed to Roman Dutch law.[73]

The influence of English law on the law of treason

Roman Dutch law regarded treason to be a very serious crime. The offender and his or her descendants were put to death as a warning to potential criminals. Alternatively, they were subjected to extreme persecution, misery and poverty to the extent that death became a relief.[74]

In Roman Dutch law, high treason is referred to as *perduellio* which always implies hostile intent against the ruler.[75] No cases of treason appeared before the courts before the British war.[76] The early Roman Dutch law of treason had three sources: the *Grondwet* (as modified and completed by amendments and additions), statutes and resolutions and the works of Van der Linden, Van Leeuwen and Grotius. The latter were applied in cases where the two previous sources were silent.[77] Section 31 of the Transvaal *Thirty-three Articles*, which was a complement to the *Grondwet*, stated that cooperating with foreign states or their officials or

72 ibid.

73 Ellison Kahn, 'Crime and Punishment 1910–1960: Reflections on Changes since Union in the Law of Criminal Punishment and its Application' (1960) 191 *Acta Juridica* 191, 199.

74 Frederick G Gardiner, 'Notes on the Law of Treason' (1901) 18 *South African Law Journal* 142, 151–152.

75 Treason (*perduellio*) was different from *seditio* that involved a riot. Riot would become treason under certain circumstances, namely when the assembling endangered the state. There was no treason if the hostile intent resulted from personal hatred or revenge although these motives were often ignored when the killing had endangered the state. See Gardiner, ibid 147–148.

76 ibid. See also 'The Crime of Treason, etc., in the Transvaal' (1896) 13 *South African Law Journal* 182. The first British occupation in South Africa dated 1795 but left no legal legacy. The second occupation started in 1815 and lasted until the Union of South Africa in 1910. See Eduard Fagan, 'Roman Dutch Law in its South African Historical Context' in Reinhard Zimmermann and Daniel Visser (eds), *Southern Cross: Civil and Common Law in South Africa* (Oxford University Press, London 1996) 46.

77 'The Crime of Treason, etc., in the Transvaal' (1896) 13 *South African Law Journal* 182, 182.

servants with hostile intent was treason and any attempt to do so was attempted treason, all punishable by a fine of Rix Dollars 500 and banishment from the country.[78] In Natal, the 1868 legislation aimed 'to assimilate the [existing] law to the law of United Kingdom in relation to treason offences'.[79] There is no record of any execution for treason under Roman Dutch law.

In 1816, five Boers were executed for high treason. They had rebelled against the British rule. These were likely the first executions in the colony for this crime. The executions created a long lasting bitterness that became one of the contributing factors to the Great Trek. On the ground, people considered those executed to be political martyrs.[80] Apparently in reaction to the consequences of the 1816 executions, the death penalty became rare for treason. From 1832, English authorities decided to introduce legal reforms. The charter creating the Supreme Court empowered that court to reshape Roman Dutch law along English law lines. Judges were granted full authority and jurisdiction to incorporate into the existing legal arsenal new principles as developed by the Cape government.[81] In 1833, eventually as a result of the reform, chiefs Mampuru and Niebel were sentenced to death for public violence and rebellion among other things. Although veiled, the charge amounted to treason. Mampuru was executed the same year and Niebel's death sentence was commuted to life imprisonment.[82]

Roman Dutch lawyers, however, continued resisting the reintroduction of the death penalty for treason. In the *Lionel Phillips and Sixty-three Others* case,[83] the so-called 'Reform committee' case, the defence argued that capital punishment was repealed for treason under Roman Dutch law in reference to Holland law, Transvaal law and Van der Linden, who limited punishments for treason to corporal punishment, imprisonment and banishment.[84] Van der Linden warned that a more severe sentence would make the offender an 'unfortunate victim of political dissentions'.[85]

---

78 See the *Law of the Thirty-Three Articles* as interpreted in *The State v Lionel Phillips and Sixty-Three Others*, 1896, reprinted (1900) 17 *South African Law Journal* 21 and 28. See also 'The Crime of Treason, etc., in the Transvaal' (1896) 13 *South African Law Journal* 182, 183.

79 Law no 3 of 1868 (N) as quoted by Burchell and Hunt (n 45) 29.

80 Ellison Kahn, 'How Did We Get our Lopsided Law on the Imposition of the Death Penalty for Common Law Crimes? And What Should We Do about It?' (1989) 2 *South African Journal of Criminal Justice* 137, 141.

81 Stephen D Girvin, 'The Architects of the Mixed Legal System' in Reinhard Zimmermann and Daniel Visser (eds), *Southern Cross: Civil and Common Law in South Africa* (Oxford University Press, London 1996) 96.

82 Kahn (n 80).

83 *State v. Lionel Phillips and Sixty-three Others*, 1896, reprinted (1900) 17 *South African Law Journal* 15.

84 ibid 21.

85 Johannes Van der Linden, *The Institutes of the Law of Holland* (Amsterdam 1806), 319 as quoted in *State v. Lionel Phillips and Sixty-Three Others*, 1896, reprinted (1900) 17

Some judges were reminded that, although disused, the death penalty still existed for treason.[86] They would still not revive it, however. Many were even reluctant to impose the death penalty for treason under occupied South Africa. Only Reinhold Gregorwski J imposed a death sentence on four men convicted of high treason in the *Reform Committee* case. The judge said that the existing legal anarchy did not help in sentencing. One had '... to select one or other of the laws under which the punishment should be met out'.[87] But he immediately added, '[t]he laws ran upon parallel lines with each other and the one had nothing to do with the other'.[88] A death sentence was imposed in the belief that it was legal. His judgment became controversial and was strongly criticised to the extent that the government took the step of commuting the four death sentences to imprisonment.[89] The record shows that only Jopie Fourie was executed for high treason in 1914.[90] Eventually a number of treason convicts were summarily executed. It is submitted that early after the Anglo-Boer war 'over fifty [Boers] were executed for treason' in the Cape Province.[91] Records of these cases are still missing and some of their graves did not contain their bodies.[92]

Judges concluded that in leaving to courts the power of imposing a discretionary death sentence, the legislator had excluded vindictive sentences.[93] Even in England, no person had suffered a death sentence for treason since 1861.[94] Murder had become the only capital crime. The *de facto* abolition of the death penalty for treason had therefore met the aspiration of Roman Dutch lawyers beginning with Van der Linden who had 'an incipient reprobation of it [the death penalty]'.[95]

The influence of English law on the law of murder

Roman-Dutch law defines murder (*moord* or *doodslag* – archaically used as *doodslach*) as the intentional killing of a human being by another sane human being; cases of gross negligence (*lata culpa*) were excluded as they lead to a charge of culpable homicide.[96] Legal development of Roman Dutch law did not

South African Law Journal 25.

86 'Cape Treason Trials' (1901) 18 *South African Law Journal* 164, 168.

87 *State v Lionel Phillips and Sixty-Three Others*, 1896, reprinted (1900) 17 *South African Law Journal* 29.

88 ibid.

89 Girvin (n 81) 116.

90 Barend Van Niekerk, 'Hanged by the Neck until You Are Dead' (1969) 86 *South African Law Journal* 457, 459.

91 David Harrison, *The White Tribe of Africa: South Africa in Perspective* (Ariel Books, London 1985) 4.

92 ibid 45.

93 'Cape Treason Trials' (1901) 18 *South African Law Journal* 164, 165.

94 Van Niekerk (n 90) 461–462.

95 ibid 461.

96 Manfred Nathan, 'The Roman Dutch Law of Homicide' (1902) 19 *South African Law Journal* 115, 117–118.

aim to abandon the death penalty. 'Once a court has decided that an act amounts to murder, there is irrespective of persons, mode, time or place, but one penalty to inflict [that is the death penalty].'[97] Manfred Nathan calls this a 'simplification of crime and of its punishment'. There was no longer any need for the ornate embellishments of torture and degradation for the court to be satisfied with the definitional elements of murder.[98] Mercy was an alien concept even in cases where the murderer was intoxicated.[99]

South African law inherited the broad definition of murder, the mandatory death penalty and the secret process of mercy from English law as a consequence of British colonisation of the Cape.[100] Section 135 of the Native Territories Penal Code Act of 1886 introduced a new definition and confused murder with culpable homicide under the heading of homicide. It read:

> homicide is culpable when it consists in the killing of any person either by an unlawful act or by a culpable omission to perform or observe any legal duty, or by both combined, or by causing a person by threats or fear of violence or by deception, to do an act which causes that person's death, or by wilfully frightening a child or sick person.[101]

It is submitted that English law differentiated between categories of homicide by determining whether the act was perpetrated in secret, in a calm and coldblooded manner (murder) or because of anger, provocation or insult (manslaughter).[102] This categorisation did not much impress Roman Dutch lawyers.[103] In homicide cases, courts seldom resorted to English terminology for murder and manslaughter, both being part of intentional homicide under Roman Dutch law.[104] Courts instead referred to deliberate murder and determined murder, both of which were punishable by death.

The mandatory death penalty for murder did not enjoy unanimity either. In the *Bodenstein* case, the judge regretted the absence of judicial discretion in cases of murder before recommending mercy. He stated that 'the charge of murder against the prisoner has been fully proved, and … he should be convicted. We have no

---

97 ibid 139.

98 ibid 23.

99 ibid 124.

100 Robert Turrell, *White Mercy: A Study of the Death Penalty in South Africa* (Praeger, London 2004) 4.

101 Section 135 of the Native Territories Penal Code Act 24 of 1886. For details see Nathan (n 96) 116 and Tredgold (n 67) 119–120.

102 William Wilson, 'Murder and the Structure of Homicide' in Andrew Ashworth and Barry Mitchell (eds), *Rethinking English Homicide Law* (Oxford University Press, New York 2000) 20–23 and Burchell and Hunt (n 45) 25.

103 Turrell (n 100) 1 and 27, footnote 11.

104 Nathan (n 96) 117–131.

alternative but to inflict the sentence of death. If any mercy has to be extended ..., such mercy lies in higher hands than ours.'[105]

In Natal and at Rustenburg, judges were more courageous and substituted the mandatory death penalty for temporary imprisonment.[106] As the Eastern District Judge President, Kotzé opposed this initiative on the grounds that under Roman Dutch law discretionary sentences should be limited to junior offenders.[107] It is submitted that the learned judge was referring to the Tryn Jansz case, where a Leiden court had found it inappropriate to strangle and break the body on the wheel of an 11-year-old girl who had used rat poison to murder her master's family. Tryn Jansz was sentenced to 70 years imprisonment and general forfeiture as a 'humane punishment' at the time.[108]

Judge President of Griqualand Laurence stated that the precedent was outdated in terms of meeting the needs of justice. The judge maintained that the court had the power to withhold the death sentence 'in very special circumstances, on very exceptional occasions and for very cogent reasons'.[109] One such special circumstance that justified discretion and the imposition of an alternative sentence was infanticide.[110] The debate indicates the extent to which the confusing legal situation led judges to forge their own paths, which were sometimes totally new to both Roman Dutch law and English law.

The pre-apartheid distaste for the death penalty in South Africa

The absence of legislative guidance on precise punishments for precise crimes created uncertainty. The courts were obliged to dig into old authorities that stemmed from two opposite legal systems. Transvaal was the only exception as it had enacted the Criminal Procedure Code 1 of 1903 which created a statutory death penalty.[111] Although Van der Linden appeared to be alone in his desire for abolition,[112] capital punishment did not have much support among the founders of Roman Dutch law. This led to increasing doubt regarding its mandatory nature for murder. It was remarked that 'though these old laws are still on our statute book, the extreme penalty has ceased to be exacted. In practice, death sentences are now passed only in cases of murder. Whether even in those cases, it is a compulsory sentence, is open to question.'[113]

105 *Rex v. Bodenstein* (30 September, 2 October 1901), reprinted (1901) 18 *South African Law Journal* 425–426.

106 Burchell and Hunt (n 45) 123 and Kahn (n 73) 199.

107 Kahn, ibid.

108 Nathan (n 96) 121–122.

109 Kahn (n 73) 199.

110 ibid.

111 Chapter 18 of the Criminal Procedure Code (Transvaal) Ordinance 1 of 1903.

112 Van Niekerk (n 90) 461.

113 'Capital Punishment' (1897) 14 *South African Law Journal* 122, 123.

There is no record indicating that Roman Dutch law founders consistently recommended the death penalty. The few pre-union cases of hanging are attributed to foreign influences, mainly the development of Dutch customs in the Netherlands and the English law of murder.[114] The nineteenth-century discretional death penalty was restricted to treason and rape and the mandatory death sentence was only for murder as in England. Property crimes no longer incurred the death penalty.

Furthermore, executions were to be humanely carried out in conformity with the English requirement of 'swift execution of the condemned and atomization by surgeons'.[115] All of the terrors previously attached to the punishment such as breaking the body on the wheel, decapitation, torture accompanied by *a coup de grace*, and so on became outlawed. Hanging became the only acceptable method of execution.

In South Africa, the death penalty became more problematic from 1910 with the unification of the four provinces. In the same year, there were 57 executions. The figure increased to 268 during the first decade of the union.[116] During the first half of the twentieth century, Louis Botha's government (1910–1919) executed more people than all the other governments that succeeded him.[117] It is certain that the reasons that provoked the increase in death sentences are alien to Roman Dutch law. As we shall see below, the discriminatory policies that the British coloniser left to Afrikaner nationalists, added to the bitterness of the Anglo-Boer war, framed the policy behind the resort to capital punishment after the Union of South Africa.

Asian Legal Influences in Africa

Two major Asian legal systems influenced Africa prior to colonisation, Islamic law in East, North-East, North and West Africa and Coptic law in Ethiopia.

African Islamic countries came under the influence of Islamic law (*Shari'a*) with the Muslim invasion. Chapter 2, verse 178 of the Quran clearly proclaims that there is life for you in retaliation.[118] The Islamic death penalty law did not impress African tribes, however, as they were used to the blood money system.[119] The

114 Kahn (n 73) 198.

115 Greg T Smith, 'Violent Crime and the Public Weal in England, 1700–1900' in Richard McMahon (ed), *Crime, Law and Popular Culture in Europe* (Willan Publishing, Devon 2008) 193.

116 Van Niekerk (n 90) 458.

117 Turrell (n 100) 260.

118 Medina Sura II: The Cow 178, in Abdullah Yusuf Ali, *The Glorious Koran* (JM Dent & Sons 1909) 356. Sura V: The Table 32 and Sura XVII: The Night Journey 33 also provide for retaliation.

119 Sayed Hassan Amin, *Islamic Law in the Contemporary World* (Royston, Glasgow 1985) 24–28.

friction between Islamic law and customary laws sometimes resulted in clashes, with Africans preferring their customs to the imposed religious norms.[120]

Ethiopia received the Coptic law from the Coptic church of Alexandria. Ethiopia (former Empire of Abyssinia with Aksum as its capital) became a theocratic empire with close ties to Israel at the time of King Solomon and during and after the era of Jesus Christ.[121] Biblical modes of punishment, including the *lex talionis*, were introduced with the codification of the *Fetha Negest* in 1434.[122]

The Death Penalty in Ethiopian Law

Like Liberia, Ethiopia never underwent Western colonisation. Although Ethiopians claim to apply the civil law system,[123] the marvellous picture of their law stems from a well-balanced symbiosis of traditional customs, canon and Islamic laws and Western laws (common law and Romano-Germanic law) received in modern times.[124]

Ethiopian legal history is usually divided into three periods: the traditional period that ended with the reign of Emperor Zär'a Ya eqob (1434), the period from Emperor Zär'a Ya eqob (1434–1468) up to the end of the monarchy and the beginning of the Ethiopian revolution (1974) and the post-revolution period (from 1974 to the present).[125] Without prejudice to this subdivision, the study of the death penalty under Ethiopian law requires consideration not of the country's important political events but solely of the criminal law in force at a given time even if the studied period of time bridges different political periods.

The previous chapter established that the death penalty did not exist in Ethiopia before the arrival of Coptic law. The period of customary law ended in 1434 when Emperor Zär'a Ya' eqob instructed scholars of the Ethiopian Orthodox Church to compile legal norms, later known as *Fewuse Menfessawi* or spiritual remedies. Also during his reign, the emperor ordered a copy of the law in force in Alexandria and required its translation into Ge'ez, the Semitic language formerly praised as the Latin of Ethiopia. The Code is known as *Fetha Negest* or the Law of the King, partly based on Roman Byzantine law. This second period ended in 1930 with the first codification of the Ethiopian penal code. The 1930 penal legislation, which

120 Sayyid Muhammad Abu Rannat 'The Relationship Between Islamic and Customary Law in Sudan' (1960) 4 *Journal of African Law* 9, 13.

121 1 Kings 10:1–13, Mathew 12:42, Acts of Apostles 8:26–39.

122 Genesis 9:5–6, Exodus 21:14.

123 Dolores A Donavan and Getachew Assefa, 'Homicide in Ethiopia: Human Rights, Federalism and Legal Pluralism' (2003) 52 *American Journal of Comparative Law* 505, 511.

124 Aberra Jembere, 'Legal History of Ethiopia 1434–1974: Some Aspects of Substantive and Procedural Laws' (PhD Thesis, Erasmus Universiteit, Rotterdam 1997) 9–15.

125 ibid 3.

had retained aspects of the *Fetha Negest*, was repealed by the 1957 penal code, which was inspired by the French Indochina penal code.[126]

The death penalty under the monarchic law

Although indigenous laws remained a valid component of Ethiopian law until 1930, the codification of *Fetha Negest* limited their scope. The *Fetha Negest* codified a law already in force in Egypt. It was partially based on the Coptic principles of the Orthodox Church of Alexandria, the canon law of the Roman Byzantine Catholic Church, doctrines from the Old and New Testaments, *Shari'a*, glosses from Nicaea and Antioch, and Roman law.[127] It introduced new criminal sanctions including the death penalty and principles of criminal responsibility. The law that developed from it was called the *Atse ser'at* or the deeds of the sovereign originating from *afe-negus* (the King's mouth). Justice was carried out in the King's name. The term *Atse ser'at* refers to the procedural law, substantive law and case law initially formed by local justice bodies and then confirmed by the Supreme Court.

The *Fetha Negest* introduced capital punishment without instituting the prosecutor. It did not indicate the executioner either. Accordingly, individuals personally initiated and prosecuted the case. They were even required to execute the sentence except when the offence involved the state (blasphemy, perjury, banditry and treason). State organs, mainly the emperor and priests, prosecuted these public offences. Emperor Tewodros is said to have been pitiless as regards treason. He regularly resorted to capital punishment by crucifixion, burning, beheading, famine or hurling against rocks for real or supposed political dissidents. He personally supervised most of the executions. The death penalty could be preceded by accessory punishment of amputation of hands and legs. His rule had no mercy for women, whether pregnant or not, and children. Beside formal trials, he resorted to summary executions as he pleased.[128] It is doubtful whether the emperor was applying the *Fetha Negest*. Treason might have been a capital crime even under customary law.

However, homicide had always been treated as an interpersonal issue. What Coptic law altered was the punishment by replacing compensation with capital punishment. Nevertheless, the absence of a precise criminal procedure in homicide cases gave a green light to revenge, and it was sufficient to prove an intentional homicide for the revenge to take place.[129] The law only forbade revenge on culprits

126 ibid 3 and 10.

127 Steven Lowenstein, 'Ethiopia' in Alan Milner (ed), *African Penal Systems* (Routledge and Kegan Paul, London 1969) 35. See also Comité de Législation Etrangère et de Droit International, *Le code pénal de l'Empire d'Ethiopie (du 23 juillet 1957)* (Centre Français de Droit Comparé, Paris 1959) 6–7.

128 Weld H Blundell, 'History of King Theodore' (1906) 21 *Journal of the Royal African Society* 12, 12–42.

129 Stanley Z Fisher, 'Traditional Criminal Procedure in Ethiopia' (1971) 19 *American Journal of Comparative Law* 709, 742.

of involuntary homicide. The *Fetha Negest* had instituted a sanctuary similar to the *sanga nenay* institution of the Kunama. The Coptic Church, highly respected by citizens and the government, played the role of sanctuary to offenders involved in involuntary homicides.

The offender entered the churchyard and rung the bell as a sign that he had placed himself under the protection of the church.[130] The violation of a legitimate sanctuary on the grounds of revenge was a serious crime punishable by exile for life. However, boastful offenders who did not hide until the end of the mourning exposed themselves to revenge without further consequences.[131]

This anarchy meant that the victim's family had the latitude of determining the method of execution. Private prosecution of criminal cases and execution of penal sanctions undermined the policy of reconciliation. Indeed, the new law had not formally repealed compensation as a means of reconciliation. Over the years, the government felt concerned by this private justice and took measures.

First of all, the emperor became the sole person to decide on capital cases. A decree was issued also prohibiting blood revenge without judicial mediation.[132] It is also argued that principles of individual criminal responsibility, personal punishment, grounds of justifications and mitigating circumstances were observed.[133] The second important resolution regarded control of the methods of execution. Initially, the monarch determined the place and method of execution under government supervision. Still, the victim's family retained the executioner's duty.[134] In 1925, Haile Sellasie, then Regent and later Emperor of Ethiopia (1916–1974), introduced a method of swift execution. He established a device in a village near to Addis Ababa where the executioner (from the victim's family) had only to pull a lever which caused a rifle to fire at the condemned person's heart from a fixed position.[135]

All these measures indicate the uneasiness that the death penalty imposed on the rulers and the citizen. Later the government strongly encouraged a return to the customary law remedy of blood money.

The survival of compensation under the Fetha Negest

The death penalty was not mandatory for personal injuries or homicide cases. It could be converted into compensation for the sake of reconciliation. The *Fetha Negest* established the amount of blood money for all kinds of offences including homicide. In some areas, judges overlooked the statutory provisions and applied customary methods. This means that even in homicide cases, the *Fetha Negest* never had full control of the country. It is indeed established that it

130 ibid 725.
131 ibid 726.
132 ibid 742.
133 Comité de Législation Etrangère et de Droit International (n 127) 10.
134 Fisher (n 129) 743.
135 ibid 743.

operated more as an esoteric document that was hardly and likely rarely applied outside imperial courts. Imperial judges, who were generally from the Ahmara tribe, preferred resorting to their customary law that was indeed death penalty free and encouraged reconciliation.[136] The consequence of having introduced the *Fetha Negest*, however, was that the victim's family would refute reconciliation and become intransigent on capital punishment. In such circumstance, the death penalty was upheld and executed.[137]

Certainly, the most interesting part of Ethiopian law was the fact that almost the entire country invested in the process of reconciliation. It was the function of elders, church officials and judges to negotiate with the winning party of the case that he or she accepts blood money from the adversary.[138] In capital cases, the emperor personally pleaded with the victim's family to accept compensation.

During the reign of Menilik II (1889–1913), a man fell off a branch of a tree that he was busy cutting and killed the unfortunate person who was sleeping under the tree. There is no record on whether judges convicted the offender of murder rather than involuntary homicide. However, the deceased's family refused blood money and demanded the death sentence. They appealed to the emperor for the sentence. The emperor agreed with the victim's family in terms of the legal principle and said that 'to satisfy the requirement exactly, death must be inflicted on the criminal in the same way as that in which he had disposed of his victim'. In other words, one of the members of the victim's family was required to go up the tree and fall on the offender. No one dared to do it and they accepted the blood money.[139]

The judicial process was so transparent that judges did not hesitate to point out the emperor's responsibility in some cases. Emperor Tewodros (1855–1868) was once held liable for the death of a soldier who had been killed by his colleague due to the emperor's contradictory instructions. When the matter was brought before the court for adjudication, the court courageously stated that 'had the Emperor not been the eyes of the nation, the consequence of giving contradictory instructions might have reverted to him'.[140] The emperor concurred with this wisdom and accepted responsibility, paying 500 birr as blood money.[141]

The legacy of the death penalty in Ethiopia

The introduction of the death penalty in Ethiopia was an important change in the country's legal system, as the paying of blood money had always been the most severe punishment for homicides and similar cases. Only the emperor's wisdom

136 ibid 712.
137 ibid.
138 ibid.
139 Jembere (n 124) 89.
140 ibid 84.
141 ibid.

could temper the severity of the *Fetha Negest*, which provided that 'whoever kills a person, should, likewise, be killed'.[142]

However, this *lex talionis* principle clashed with a strong custom of blood money that could not be easily overridden. The death penalty was perceived and mostly practised as a mechanism for revenge rather than as a punishment, with the far-reaching consequence of indefinite blood feuds that tore apart the community. There is no doubt that the death penalty was rarely applied. So far, all attempts to replace compensation for homicide have been unsuccessful.

Even when imprisonment was imposed in recent years, Ethiopians felt that the cases were not yet settled. In consequence, victims' families have sworn revenge on culprits that the state has released as long as blood money has not been paid. This is evidence that Ethiopians have opposed and are still resisting retributive and supposedly deterrent punishments and that 'traditional proceedings [are] far more successful than states proceedings in restoring peace to the community as a whole'.[143]

The Shari'a Death Penalty Law in Pre-colonial Africa

A state's criminal policy cannot be dissociated from its political, religious and socio-economic regime. Thus, the study of the death penalty in Islamised Africa cannot be separated from the death penalty in the Muslim world. This justifies a general overview before considering its implementation in Africa, which was dominated by the school of Malek ben Anas.

An outline of the death penalty in Shari'a

The law stemming from the Quran, the sacred book, and from Sunna, which refers to the prophet's practices, is known as *Shari'a*.[144] When sentencing on the basis of *Shari'a*, a Muslim judge can draw on three kinds of punishments depending on the nature of the offence: *hudud* or fixed penalties, *qisas* or retribution and *ta'zir* or discretional punishments.[145]

Hudud is imposed for seven crimes: adultery, false accusations of fornication, drinking alcohol, highway robbery, apostasy, theft from a secure or private place and insurrection against Islamic leaders.[146] Of these, only apostasy, insurrection, sexual offences and theft committed in prison by a convicted criminal serving a life sentence are punishable by death.[147]

---

142 ibid 89.

143 Donavan and Assefa (n 123) 522.

144 William A Schabas, 'Islam and the Death Penalty' (2000) 9 *William and Mary Bill of Rights Journal* 223, 231.

145 Amin (n 119) 23.

146 ibid. See also Schabas (n 144).

147 Amin (n 119) 24. See also M Cherif Bassiouni, 'Death as a Penalty in the Shari'a' in Peter Hodgkinson and William A Schabas (eds), *Capital Punishment: Strategies*

There has been some controversy over whether the death sentence was a prescribed punishment for adultery and sodomy. The Quran provides for 100 lashes in cases of adultery involving a married person[148] while there is a *hadith* showing that the prophet was reluctant to stone a woman who came four times to confess her adultery to him.[149] The Quran does not set out a clear punishment for sodomy; only Chapter 4, verse 20 refers to such acts. However, it is submitted that 'the prescribed punishment for adultery, as well as for homosexual intercourse by a married person is death'.[150] This is apparently a new policy that falls outside a strict interpretation of the Quran. Cases of insurrection and criminal gang activities followed by murders cannot be punished by death either if the offender has repented.[151]

Qisas are retributive punishments prescribed by the Quran. Verse 2:178–179 provides: 'O believers! Retaliation for blood shedding is prescribed to you: the free man for the free, and the slave for the slave, and the woman for the woman ….'[152] Retaliation, or the right to revenge in the sense of the Biblical *lex talionis*,[153] is therefore applicable to five crimes: 'premeditated murder, seemingly premeditated murder, erroneous murder, intended offences other than homicide and unintended offences other than homicides'.[154] It is unfortunate that the principle of proportionality lying behind the word *qisas* has been misunderstood and interpreted meaning retribution[155] due to its literal translation of 'equivalence'.[156]

The victim has a choice between taking revenge, exacting blood money or forgiving. If there is an agreement on blood money or *diyya*,[157] or if the offender is forgiven, the death sentence is excluded.[158] Verse 2:178–179 states *in fine*: '… but he to whom his brother shall make any remission, is to be dealt with equitably; and to him should he pay a fine with liberality'.[159] Forgiveness is much favoured by the Quran over the two other alternatives,[160] even though local customs have led to a misleading interpretation restricting punishments to the

for Abolition (Cambridge University Press, Cambridge 2004) 189.

148 Quran 24:2.

149 Bassiouni (n 147) 181.

150 After the 1979 Iranian revolution, two laws were passed imposing the death sentence for homosexual intercourse and adultery. See Amin (n 119) 24–25.

151 Wafaa H Wahba al-Mawardi (tr), *The Ordinances of Government* (Garnet Publishing, London 1996) 68–70.

152 Medina Sura II: The Cow 178, in Yusuf Ali (n 118) 356. Sura V: The Table 32 and Sura XVII: The Night Journey 33 also provide for retaliation. See Schabas (n 144).

153 Bassiouni (n 147) 182.

154 Amin (n 119) 29.

155 Schabas (n 144) 232.

156 Bassiouni (n 147) 182, footnote 51.

157 Sometimes written as *diya* or *diyah*. See Amin (n 119) 28–29 and 103.

158 Wahba al-Mawardi (n 151) 251.

159 Medina Sura II: The Cow 178, in Ali (n 118) 356.

160 Medina Sura II: The Cow 178, in Ali, ibid.

death penalty and compensation only. This misinterpretation has also had far-reaching consequences in that at the time of codification, some states excluded the *diyya* and forgiveness and prescribed only the death penalty for intentional homicides. Furthermore, under the penal code these crimes are prosecuted by the state and the victim no longer has the right to express consent as to the punishment imposed by the court.[161]

Ta'zir (correction) is an optional punishment decided by the judge for offences without prescribed penalties. It is different from *hudud*, *qisas* and *diyya*.[162] Professor Cherif Bassiouni opposes this view in stating that 'their penalties, according to several of the jurisprudential schools of *Sunni* and *Shi'a* traditions, can be the same penalty as provided for *hudud* and *qesas* crimes'.[163] The difference is that the death penalty may be discretionarily imposed since it is not expressively prescribed by the Quran.[164] Although Sayed Hassan Amin excludes the discretional death penalty and ranges *ta'zir* from admonishing the offender to a disapproving look,[165] it is established that the Prophet used crucifixion as a disciplinary chastisement.[166] Sometimes, crucifixion is combined with stoning.[167] This confirms the conclusion that the death penalty is the most severe *ta'zir* punishment, though discretionarily imposed.

In short, Islamic law grants the application of the death penalty for certain crimes. It is only mandatory for murder. It can even be made optional or excluded if the victim's family exacts blood money (*diyya*) and forgives the offender or if the offender repents. Indeed, 'the Quran specifically provides that an offender who has committed a crime may repent and, if the repentance is genuine, that person should not be punished'.[168] The trial will only inquire to as the sincerity of repentance. It follows that resorting to the death penalty in Muslim states is more a matter of policy choice than it is a strict adherence to *Shari'a*. *Hudud*, *qisas* and *ta'zir* offer other possibilities and alternative punishments remain consistent with the *Shari'a*.

Addressing the question of why states did not, at least, keep the spirit of the scriptures and the noble characteristics of Islam, Professor Cherif Bassiouni answered '[it] can only be explained by reasons extraneous to Islam'.[169] Indeed, although Islamic law keeps claiming its absolute validity, it accommodated local customs and enactments of political rulers from its origin. The failure of these

161 Bassiouni (n 147) 183.

162 Amin (n 119) 29.

163 Bassiouni (n 147) 183.

164 ibid 183–184 and Schabas (n 144) 232.

165 Amin (n 119) 29.

166 Wahba al-Mawardi (n 151) 259.

167 Rudolph Peters, 'Islamic and Secular Criminal Law in Nineteenth Century Egypt: The Role and Function of the Qadi' (1997) 4 *Islamic Law and Society* 70, 86.

168 Bassiouni (n 147) 184.

169 ibid 185.

norms to reach a real symbiosis has created an uneasy coexistence that gives room to arbitrary interventions from political leaders.[170] It follows that today, the law and its practice in the Islamic World is fundamentally inconsistent.

The death penalty in the Malek ben Anas school in Africa

Abou Abd El-Salâm ben Saaïd Et-Tenoukhy, who was known as Sehhnoun, a famous Syrian scholar, introduced the Maliki rite in Africa immediately after his appointment as the *Qâdhy* of Egypt. To spread its ideology he nominated disciples of the Maliki school for key political and judicial positions.[171] Though Sehhnoun did not succeed in expanding the Maliki rite beyond Egypt until the Muslims gained control of Spain, he did, at least, manage to plant it in the hearts of the Egyptians.[172] Northern Africa inherited the glorious and famous Spanish Maliki rite from a devoted Spanish graduate, Abd Allah ben Yacin, who crossed the Mediterranean to catechise the Islamic religion.[173]

Reluctant people were forced by sword to adopt and convert to the Maliki rite. Abd Allah ben Yacin first converted the Djedala people and then used them to compel the Lemtouna, who had rejected him. The Lemtouna tribe later became a powerful resource for his mission. He then used his people to convert other neighbouring tribes at the point of a sword. By the beginning of the nineteenth century, inhabitants of northern and north-east Africa had embraced the Maliki rite.[174]

According to the principles of this rite, intentional homicide means a murder resulting from hatred or anger. This is different from an assassination committed in the course of robbery or a clandestine assassination. Intentional homicide is punishable by death unless the victim's family accepts the *diyya*.[175] There is no pardon for the two forms of assassination. It is even submitted that for one victim, many members of the offender's family can be executed.[176] Attempted assassination is subject to optional sentences determined by the Imam. Punishments include simple death, death on the gallows, amputation, imprisonment and ostracism. The crime is forgiven if the offender repents immediately.[177]

In both intentional and involuntary homicides, victims can forgive the offender. Forgiveness from one member of the family suffices. This then excludes the death sentence and opens the door to alternative punishments. Females cannot forgive

---

170 Joseph Schacht, 'Islamic Law in Contemporary States' (1959) 8 *American Journal of Comparative Law* 133, 133.

171 MB Vincent, *Etudes sur la loi musulmane (Rit de Malek): Législation criminelle* (Joubert, Paris 1842) 25.

172 Ivan Hrbek, 'Egypt, Nubia and the Eastern Desert' in Roland Oliver (ed), *The Cambridge History of Africa: From c.1050 to c.1600* (Cambridge University Press, London, New York and Melbourne 1975) 15.

173 Vincent (n 171) 29.

174 ibid.

175 ibid 64–65.

176 ibid 92.

177 ibid.

if there are males in the family. When a family cannot provide a male who was close to the victim, forgiveness must be granted by a male from the wider family. His consent plus one female's consent validate the forgiveness.[178] A father who voluntarily kills his child is due to pay *diyya*. There is no death sentence. The law does not attempt to establish whether the father intended the killing.[179] An unanswered question relates to the person to whom the *diyya* is paid in such circumstances, as the father wears two hats: he is the criminal and the victim. The rule remains that 'retaliation is excluded if the guilty party comes to inherit any part of the right of blood against himself ....'[180]

A death sentence is also imposed in cases of intentional assault that can result in death or which causes severe suffering (for example castration or a wound that reaches the bone). Involuntary assault is punished by *diyya*.[181]

A *mohhcin*, a married person who commits an act of fornication, is put to death by stoning. If he or she was not married and thus was not a *mohhcin*, he or she is flogged and exiled to another country. Sexual intercourse with a slave or a servant (the *hhadd* of fornication) incurs correctional punishments.[182] The death penalty is also imposed for rape if the offender is an unbeliever.[183] In cases of homosexuality, the law does not take marital status into account. The two consenting males are put to death by stoning. Anal intercourse with a woman amounts to fornication or *hhadd*, depending on the marital status of the man and woman involved. Bestiality incurs correctional punishments. A confession or a deposition of four witnesses is a prerequisite for punishment.[184]

Theft is punished by imprisonment rather than death, even when the thief is a repeat offender.[185] In cases where the offender has committed many offences, some punishable by death and others by lesser punishments, the death sentence absorbs the other sentences.[186] It is worth noting that imprisonment for theft is not prescribed by the original 'traditions' of the Prophet. The Maliki rite opposed the Hanbali rite and joined the Hanifi and Shafi'i in finding that the prescribed sentence of a fine was unacceptable. Joseph Schacht submits that 'there were, it is true, attempts made in the formative period of Islamic law to introduce fines for theft by making the thief responsible for twice the value of the object stolen,

178 ibid 74.

179 ibid 75, footnote a.

180 James ND Anderson, 'Homicide in Islamic Law' (1951) 13 *Bulletin of Oriental and African Studies* 811, 814.

181 Vincent (n 171) 82.

182 ibid 95–96.

183 ibid 99.

184 ibid 100–101 and 107.

185 ibid 107–109.

186 ibid 105.

attempts which found expression in several "traditions" attributed to the Prophet'.[187] The disagreement is further evidence of inconsistencies in *Shari'a.*

Broadly speaking *Shari'a* and the Maliki rite share the structure of punishments (prescribed, retributive and discretionary punishments). However, the Maliki rite punishments are differently dispatched. In the Maliki rite, intentional homicide comprises three categories. The first is murder, which strictly speaking means a sudden attack resulting from anger or hatred without premeditation. It justifies a death sentence only if no agreement on blood money is reached. The second category entails premeditation, an ambush or follows or precedes the commission of another crime such as robbery. For this crime, the death sentence is mandatory and there is no alternative to it. The third category is an attempt to commit assassination. The sentence is optional and is imposed by the *Imam* although a death sentence is one of the options.

Furthermore, the Maliki rite differentiates between degrees of assault based on the mental element. In a voluntary assault, simple harm is different from harm that has created long-term suffering for the victim. The latter are the only crimes considered to be capital crimes. The death penalty is selectively imposed for sexual offences. Homosexuality is a capital crime regardless of the marital status of the offender and his accomplice.

The Maliki rite is unique in that it does not consider theft, even habitual theft, to be a capital crime. Instead the punishment can be amputation or imprisonment while in *Shari'a* the death penalty is an option for an incorrigible thief.

The death penalty in pre-colonial Islamised Africa

Before European colonisation, Islam had established itself as the most important religion in a major part of the upper Sahara and had supplanted African and Christian religions in different areas.[188] However, the interaction between *Shari'a* and the existing law, whether indigenous or Christianised indigenous law, varied in each country.

The following considers in detail the practice of the death penalty in Egypt, the Sudan, Morocco and Nigeria. Each received Muslim law in a different way and their geographical location, political and cultural backgrounds are important criteria for drawing a balanced and objective conclusion.

The death penalty in Egypt

The death penalty existed in Egypt prior to foreign legal influences. Its practice continued under the successive monotheist beliefs of Christianity and Islam. Christianity was probably introduced into Alexandria around 61 CE by St Mark

187 Schacht (n 170) 140.

188 Safiya Safwat, 'Islamic Law in the Sudan' in Aziz Al-Azmeh (ed), *Islamic Law: Social and Historical Context* (Routledge, London 1988) 231.

himself.[189] It became stronger with the introduction of the Coptic Church's doctrine in 284 CE.[190] The Coptic doctrine based on the Bible expanded the *lex talionis* law.[191]

Islam was introduced in Egypt after the country was conquered in 639 CE by an Arab army led by Amr ibn al-As.[192] The Sunni legal school was introduced by the Maliki rite under the *Qadi* Abu Tahir al-Dhuhli and lasted until 969 CE, when Jawhar's army invaded and took control of Egypt and installed the Fatimid dynasty which gradually introduced the Fatimid law, a branch of the *Ismaili Shi'a* legal school.[193] The Fatimid law, though not favoured by the majority of the population,[194] was tolerant towards Christians and Jews. It took an extremely severe attitude towards disciples of the Sunni school, despite their being quite similar.[195]

There are doubts regarding the use of the death penalty during the reign of the first Fatimid dynasties. For example historians disagree over whether a death sentence was handed down to al'Adid. Some state that he was sentenced to death by the jurists of Saladin and others affirm that he either committed suicide or died naturally.[196] It was only under *Khalif* Al Hakim (996–1021) that harsh punishments including torture and beheading were instituted for those who had, without necessarily infringing Islamic law, violated numerous prohibitions established by the *Khalif*.[197] The Ottoman administration that took over after the reign of the Fatimid dynasty exclusively applied the principles of the Hanafi legal school until the nineteenth century. Homicide cases were heard by the *Qadi* and were punished by death.[198]

Gradually the Islamic law was confined to evidence matters, with the penal code (of French inspiration) dealing with the substantive law of homicide. In 1860 a Nubian who had murdered a school girl was discharged by the *Qadi* court because the two witnesses were minors. The trying judge did not take into account the *post mortem* evidence that incriminated the offender. The plea of the deceased's mother for the death penalty in compliance with the penal code was refused even before the court of appeal that imposed three years of forced labour.[199] This is not a

189 C Wilfred Griggs, *Early Egyptian Christianity: From its Origin to 451 CE* (E.J. Brill, Leiden 1991) 13–14.

190 John Iliffe, *Africans: The History of a Continent* (Cambridge University Press, New York 1995) 37–38.

191 Exodus 21:12–26.

192 Iliffe (n 190) 43. For a discussion of legal schools in Islamised Egypt, see generally Yaacov Lev, *Saladin in Egypt* (E.J. Brill, Leiden 1999).

193 Hrbek (n 172) 10. For the doctrine of this school, see Michael Brett, 'The Mīm, the 'Ayn, and the Making of Ismā'īlism' (1994) 57 *Bulletin of the School of Oriental and African Studies* 10, 25–39.

194 Hrbek (n 172) 12.

195 Lev (n 192) 117–118.

196 ibid 82 83.

197 Hrbek (n 172) 12–13.

198 Peters (n 167) 78.

199 ibid 79.

Shari'a punishment. It is, however, an indication of the extent to which the system had become dual in nature.

Indeed only a few capital cases were left to the *Qadi*. These were limited to *maqatil* or causing death by exceeding the fixed numbers of lashes imposed for corporal punishment, infanticide, rebellion or resisting an official when resistance has provoked death.[200] In cases of intentional homicide, the *Qadi*'s court had the duty of inquiring whether victims preferred the death penalty or compensation.

The *Qadi*'s court referred the matter to the Council for trial code in three circumstances according to the penal legislation: satisfactory agreement on compensation, pardon granted by the victim and acquittal resulting from the lack of evidence. The penal code provided for a sentence of hard labour in addition to compensation. However, the death penalty (as *qisas* retribution) could not be executed unless confirmed by *al Jam'iyya al-Haqqaniya* or the Viceroy. Since the seventeenth century, the *Qadi* court had not been authorised to impose mutilation or death sentences by stoning or stoning combined with crucifixion (as *hudud* or *ta'zir* penalties).[201]

The dual system weakened the *Qadi*'s court. However, this court also appeared to be inclined towards reconciliation rather than punitive measures for homicide and assault. The aim of justice was not retribution. The victim-offender agreement regarding financial compensation determined the victim's intention to reconcile, though the matter could still be heard by the Council.[202]

The death penalty in the Sudan

In the fourth century CE, Sudan was divided into three Christian kingdoms: Nobatia, Makuria and Alwa with, respectively, Faras, Dongola and Soba (today's Khartoum) as their capitals.[203] In about the sixteenth century the Funj put an end to the kingdoms of Alwa and Makuria by unifying them at Sennar.[204] Although the Funj kingdom opened its doors to Egyptian Islamic scholars or Islamic scholars residing in Egypt, they were not much concerned with law and justice. There was no pure Islamic law, as their *Shari'a* encompassed other beliefs.[205] The effective application of *Shari'a* started with the Ottoman invasion in 1837 and gained significance under the Mahdiya regime. The Turkish administration in the Sudan is remembered for the cruelty of its justice.[206]

The Turks were pitiless and characterised by corruption and injustice. Their 'cruelty was also common in the execution of sentences. Sentences included

200 ibid 80.
201 ibid 86.
202 ibid 89.
203 Iliffe (n 190) 41.
204 Safwat (n 188).
205 ibid 232 and 235.
206 ibid 233.

mutilation, lashings, death and imprisonment for long periods.'[207] In being so harsh, Ottoman authorities departed from the basic rules of Islam. This gave weight to their opponents' argument that oppression, injustice and excessive taxation were not exclusively signs of bad governance but surely were indications of a bad religion.[208] A religious revolution to return to the ascetic roots of Islam became the battle cry in the Mahdiya Revolution led by Mohammad Ahmad al-Mahdi.[209]

From 1885, the Mahdiya imposed the observation of *Shari'a* in all areas. Murder, apostasy and adultery were capital crimes. However, the desire to build a purely Islamic state drove the Mahdiya to act outside the law. For example, the illegal cohabitation of two consenting adults became a capital crime.[210] Obviously, under *Shari'a* a case of illegal cohabitation between unmarried people amounts to fornication. The problem became that *Shari'a* gave no legal status to the customary marriage that was so common among peasants. The marriage was legal under customary law and a capital crime under *Shari'a*. The clash between customary law and *Shari'a* was not only limited to sexual offences. It also arose in homicide cases where indigenous people applied blood money while *Shari'a* imposed a death sentence.[211] The Mahdiya were aware of these discrepancies but they retained capital punishment for political reasons.

The death penalty was justified on the grounds of peace. Safiya Safwat points out that 'the severity of this legislation should not be dismissed as mere blind conservatism'.[212] The country's social order was strongly shaken after the revolution and the war against Egypt. Within the immense and ever-changing tribal forces upon which the new order depended, it was necessary to maintain discipline. People in need of peace believed the Mahdi's repressive regime was in line with *Shari'a*. 'Although the penalties for the infringements of his rules may sound mercilessly harsh ..., they were understood and accepted as the correct application of *Shari'a* by his own people.'[213]

Mahdi's first goal was to modify local customs as most of them were repugnant to Islamic law. Upon his death in 1885, the Khalifa Abdullahi continued to use the Quran and Sunna as the primary sources of law and organised a centralised kingdom within which severe punishments were in common use.[214]

This Islamic regime did not, however, survive the Anglo-Egyptian invasion of 1889. After the seizure of Khartoum, the British and the Egyptians agreed on a common administration of the Sudan under the Condominium rule. Sudan

207 ibid.

208 ibid 234.

209 Carolyn Fluehr-Lobban 'Islamization in Sudan: A Critical Assessment' (1990) 4 *Middle East Journal* 614, 614.

210 Safwat (n 188) 235.

211 Rannat (n 120).

212 Safwat (n 188) 235.

213 ibid.

214 ibid.

was neither an Egyptian nor a British colony. It was officially agreed that neither English law or any modification of it, nor Egyptian law would apply to Sudan. However, the British Governor-General exploited this gap using article 4 of the Condominium rule which gave him supreme legislative power in Sudan. Article 4 conceded that 'laws, as also orders and regulations with the full force of law … may from time to time be made, altered, or abrogated by proclamation of the Governor General ….'[215]

However, 'although the laws provided by them were not purely English, they were either an adoption or an adaptation of the English law'.[216] It is worth recalling that at the end of the nineteenth century, the death penalty was mandatory in English law.

The death penalty in Morocco

The application of Islamic law in Morocco[217] presents some peculiarities that make it a *sui generis* case. The way crimes punishable by *hudud*, *qisas* and *ta'zir* penalties were redressed was far different to the Quran scriptures and recommendations of the Islamic schools. Homicide cases were firstly redressed by vengeance. A relative of the deceased must take the offender's life. If he succeeds, justice is deemed to be done. If he fails, then the offender must be exiled from the area for a period of seven years. Upon his return, he may choose to pay blood money or co-organise a feast with his relatives, to which he invites the victim's family. The feast aims to reconcile families and to stop interfamily blood feuds.[218]

This collective nature of conflict resolution is attributed to Islamic law.[219] There is confusion over what was and what was not Islamic, as Islamic law is not built on the idea of collective criminal responsibility.[220] The first attempt to apply a pure Islamic law dates back to 1512. At that time Yahyà b. Ta'fuft made two decrees outlawing tribal customs and enforcing a firm Islamic law. It is submitted that

> … given mistakes of tribal ancestors, Yahyà b. Ta'fuft decided to apply the Islamic precept of *qisas* to whoever kills a Muslim brother: 'soul for soul, eye for eye, nose for nose, ear for ear, tooth for tooth'. Then, he prescribed the *diyya* for various offences: ten *uqiyya* [almost ten dinars] for theft, one *uqiyya* for

215 Michael W Daly, 'The Development of the Governor-Generalship of the Sudan, 1899–1934' (1983) 24 *Journal of African History* 77, 77.

216 Safwat (n 188) 237.

217 For a concise history of Christianity and Islam in Morocco, see Jean-Louis Miège, *Le Maroc* (PUF, Paris 1994).

218 Fernando Rodriguez Mediano, 'Les pratiques de la justice aux 16e-19e siècles: justice, crime et châtiment au Maroc au 16e siècle' (1996) 3 *Annales, histoire des sciences sociales* 613, 613.

219 ibid.

220 Anderson (n 180).

> assault with stone or stick, five *uqiyya* for an attempt to rape a woman, a half *uqiyya* for a woman who insults a man.[221]

In compliance with this *lex talionis* rule in Fez and Marrakech, convicted criminals were obliged to walk up and down the streets of the town towards the place of execution naked screaming the grounds of their conviction. Only wealthy criminals were exempted from this. They were executed before the procession, and while carrying their bodies to the place of execution, the executioner loudly read the reasoning behind the sentence. Methods of execution consisted of crucifixion, cutting the throat, emptying the stomach with a sword and strangling. The death penalty applied to murder and high treason.[222] Mutilation did not apply to robbery and theft at Fez and Marrakech. The punishment was flogging, in addition to the offender proclaiming the reason for his conviction in the town's streets.[223]

It is submitted that this was an initial application of *qisas* and *diyya*.[224] It is unquestionable that these reforms of customary law introduced another legal system which departed from both customary law and Islamic law. The Berber tribes of the Rif region or the Rifians resorted to vengeance in a way that lasted for centuries. Compensation was a foreign concept. For Berbers of the central Moroccan Atlas, the Arab Bedouins, the Semede, the Ait Dawud and the Banu, compensation was the most common punishment and ostracism the heaviest.[225] Therefore, bearing in mind that retaliation and compensation are not innovations of Islamic law, it makes sense that three elements exclude these punishments from the Maliki rite (in force in Morocco and in others parts of North Africa):[226] the offenders' public humiliations, proclamation of the reasons for their conviction and the public degradation or dehumanisation of the dead body. These practices were alien to both Islamic law and customary law.

Yahyà b. Ta'fuft's efforts at correcting ancestral mistakes led to a mixed system encompassing elements from Islamic law, customary law, canon law and personal initiatives. Christianity was indeed present on the Moroccan coast between the heights of the Roman Empire and 1578.[227] Islamic law matured with the beginning of the seventeenth century (1606). Death by decapitation was the appropriate sentence for murder, rebellion, robbery, theft and adultery.[228] Again this went far

221 Mediano (n 218).

222 ibid 614–615.

223 ibid.

224 ibid.

225 David M Hart, 'Murder in the Market: Penal Aspects of Berber Customary Law in the Pre-colonial Moroccan Rif' (1996) 3 *Islamic Law and Society* 343, 345. See also Mediano (n 218).

226 Robert Brunschvig, 'Justice religieuse et justice laïque dans la Tunisie des Deys et des Beys: jusqu'au milieu du XIXème siècle' (1965) 23 *Studia Islamica* 27, 28.

227 Miège (n 217) 17–18.

228 Mediano (n 218) 616.

beyond the Maliki school within which the death penalty is an option for homicide cases and non-existent for property crimes. The embellishments with which the sentence was carried out were introduced by Yahyà b. Ta'fuft, likely as a warning to potential criminals.

The death penalty in Nigeria

There is no consensus on the exact date Islam was introduced into Nigeria. Some point to the ninth century,[229] others to the eleventh century or fifteenth century.[230] It is undisputed, however, that, from the fifteenth century, *Shari'a* flourished in northern Nigeria and that the jihad war extended its legal principles and institutions into the nineteenth century.[231] Before British colonisation, the northern emirates were fully under *Shari'a*. Ubah points out:

> [T]here is at present no comprehensive study of the legal system of the emirates for the period preceding British occupation. But undoubtedly in its several aspects-organizational structure, substantive law, punishments for offences, and judicial procedure that system was basically Islamic, with variation from place to place according to the degree of Islamization.[232]

During the jihad, *Shari'a* courts were spread throughout the main urban areas. They were headed by a sultan, 'Amirul Mu'mineen', whose primary duty was to reduce injustice, retrain aggressors and ensure that *Shari'a* was applied as a mechanism of justice.[233] The courts were required to apply the Quran, Sunna and other relevant sources without restrictions. The absence of restrictions had two major consequences: the application of a dual system and an increase in local Muslim schools.

Criminal law remained under *Shari'a*, although it was confined to a very limited number of crimes, namely those acknowledged the most serious. These were homicides, assault, theft and economic crimes.[234] It became the only law under which the death penalty could be imposed. The creation of different legal schools also resulted in the systematisation and sophistication of the law. Despite local efforts, the Maliki rite remained dominant until the imposition of English law.[235]

229 Yadudu H Auwalu, 'Colonialism and the Transformation of Islamic Law in the Northern States of Nigeria' (1992) 32 *Journal of Legal Pluralism* 103, 111.

230 Abdulmumini A Oba, 'Lawyers, Legal Education and *Shari'a* Courts in Nigeria' (2004) 49 *Journal of Legal Pluralism and Unofficial Law* 113, 113–116.

231 ibid.

232 Chinedu N Ubah, 'Islamic Legal System and the Westernization Process in the Nigerian Emirates' (1982) 20 *Journal of Legal Pluralism and Unofficial Law* 69, 70.

233 Auwalu (n 229).

234 ibid 113.

235 Oba (n 230) 116.

Under the Maliki rite, the *Qadi* or *Alkali* for the *Haussa* area over which a political authority of the Emir presided held the legal administration. The Emir held the function of court of appeal and experts in Islamic law assisted him. The Emir was required to apply the Maliki provisions in all cases including homicides. 'The hearing of cases and passing of verdicts, as well as the punishments inflicted for various offences, were consistent with the prescriptions of the Maliki schools to which all Nigerian Muslims belonged.'[236]

Accordingly, the *diyya* was acceptable in cases of involuntary homicide. Murder was punishable by death. The execution was carried out by beheading the convict with a sword. This practice, that complied with the Maliki law, persisted as an alternative to hanging.[237]

It is worth noting that the application of *Shari'a* in this region was very inconsistent. The *Haussa* of Sierra Leone, still under *Shari'a*, had substituted 100 lashes for the death penalty by stoning in cases of adultery (*zina*).[238] The imposition of lashes indicates the distance between the Sierra Leonean *Shari'a* and the Nigerian *Shari'a*, which applied death by stoning for adultery.[239] Crimes were so punished if committed by or against a freeman. There was unequal treatment of slaves and freemen and crimes perpetrated against slaves were not seriously punished.[240]

Disparate practices in Islamised African countries

The implementation of *Shari'a* depends much on each country's social realities and this has been the case since its introduction in Africa. The Maliki legal school was the most important component of Islamic law in Africa. Nevertheless, under the Maliki, the Fatimid and the Ottoman, the death penalty was not received with much enthusiasm in Egypt. The Ottoman Empire even decided that any sentence of death should be re-examined before its execution or simply replaced by imprisonment or a fine.[241]

The situation was quite different in Sudan where Islamic authorities struggled with their subjects to impose the *Shari'a*. They tried to use it as a tool to crush any local resistance to their power. The clash between local customs and Islamic law also existed in Morocco, where the argument for 'a pure Islamic law' served as an alibi for the ruler who invented a law which was neither Islamic nor customary, but was probably a mixed law under which, from the sixteenth century, Fez and Marrakech inhabitants suffered an horrific era of brutality. Sentences alien to the

236 Ubah (n 232).

237 Alan Milner, 'Sentencing Patterns in Nigeria' in Alan Milner (ed), *African Penal Systems* (Routledge and Kegan Paul, London 1969) 264.

238 HM Joko Smart, 'Place of Islamic Law within the Framework of the Sierra Leone Legal System' (1980) 18 *African Law Studies* 87, 94.

239 Ubah (n 232).

240 ibid 71.

241 Centre Des Etudes de Sécurité (Arabie Saoudite), 'Légalité et commodité de la peine de mort en droit Musulman' (1987) 58 *Revue international de droit pénal* 431, 431–432.

Maliki rite such as the death penalty for theft and adultery, public humiliation of the convicted and degradation of the dead body were introduced. Nigeria departed from that school in terms of imposing the death penalty for adultery.

Though all these countries applied *hudud*, *qisas* and *ta'zir* punishments and some even went beyond this, the imposition of the death penalty was excluded when deemed inappropriate. Likely the best example is that of the Egyptian *Qadi* who, instead of imposing the death for homicide as a retributive punishment (*qisas*), imposed imprisonment and a fine as appropriate alternatives. It is deplorable that other Islamised African countries did not resort to that option.

Conclusion

There is a strong relationship between a society's criminal justice policy and its political, social, economic and religious values. Some of those values are enforced by legal norms such as penal laws. The ancient and the modern penal laws are characterised by punishments that indicate that they are built on force.[242] It seems to be true for all mankind that the remaining question concerns the nature of the punishment and the body entitled to impose it. Thus, while the foreign nature of the death penalty has justified repeals in recent years,[243] other heirs of the same punishment are vehemently pointing out that it is so enshrined in their history, culture and religion that its abolition would be tantamount to the abolition of their identity.[244] The two arguments are not necessarily diametrically opposed as the facts demonstrate that the death penalty was not enthusiastically embraced by one or the other.

Under Anglo-American law in Liberia, the death penalty was more a political instrument than a penal sanction. Liberians excluded its application at a time where executions were common worldwide. A whole century passed without executions, in the interests of peace and unity. Capital crimes did not increase during that period, but rather the threat of executing criminals and their effective execution corresponded with an increase of criminality. As customary law only reserved the death penalty for witchcraft, in Liberia the death penalty was the result of foreign influence.

The same applies to South Africa with regards to tribes that did not resort to the death penalty. However, compared to those in the Netherlands, Dutch settlers at the Cape displayed distaste for the death penalty. Despite the Dutch authorities' insistence that the death penalty be mercilessly carried out, the Dutch settlers did not cede to the pressure. Death sentences in the Cape were rare. Fortunately English

242 'Early Law and Custom' (1885) 2 *Cape Law Journal* 28, 28.

243 *S v. Makwanyane and Another* 1995 (3) SA 391 (CC), at para 377D–E per Justice Sachs.

244 See, among others, the position of Morocco, Egypt, Libya, Mauritania and Sudan as regards the death penalty as studied by Schabas (n 144) 226–236.

law became influential only after it had matured enough to limit death sentences to treason and murder. Even there, liberal Roman Dutch judges took profit of the legal anarchy and made it discretionary. From the nineteenth century onwards, no death sentence would pass without legal controversy. By that time, South Africa was already on the point of abolishing the death penalty. It had practically abolished it before the twentieth century. However, the twentieth century saw that situation reversed. The English view is that 'violence [is an] acceptable means of maintaining discipline in both public and private spheres'.[245] Those backward steps can be attributed to this view. Roman Dutch lawyers blamed English common law and equity for its 'mass of anomalies and antiquated rules often leading to positive injustice'.[246] English law practically introduced the foundation of the apartheid policy. We shall return to this.

Religious laws have played a major role in the imposition of the death penalty in countries where it did not exist previously or was rarely imposed. The modernisation of Ethiopian law in 1434 corresponded with the adoption of biblical retributive principles. A country that redressed homicide cases by using the principle of extracting blood money (*guma*) adopted the death penalty model. This punishment was completely alien to Ethiopians so the emperors painfully imposed it. Unfortunately, any amendment of the penal code would retain the death penalty.

Ethiopians knew that the death penalty was not an inspired punishment just as the Muslims knew that its sacred nature, as attributed in *Shari'a*, remains a 'popular impression'. 'Muslim penal law is characterized by a strong undercurrent of clemency and sympathy for the oppressed. Punishment is ordered to be free of any spirit of vengeance or torture.'[247] Differences among Islamised African countries concerning how *Shari'a* is received and practised show that there is no consistency across the board regarding punishments, including those prescribed by the Quran. *Shari'a* was generally superimposed on a customary law base without or with very exceptional death penalty instances.

Kenneth Roberts-Wray was correct when he concluded, '... it is clear that in many parts of Africa, indigenous customary law has been influenced and changed by the adoption of certain basic Islamic principles, and that what is claimed to be Islamic law has been modified by customary practice'.[248] Based on the discrepancies between *Shari'a* as applied by the Ottoman *Qadi* in Egypt and by Yahyà b. Ta'fuft in Morocco and the difference between the punishments for adultery in accordance with Nigerian *Shari'a* and with that of Sierra Leone, one

245 Smith (n 115) 191.

246 'Roman Dutch Law in the Transvaal and Orange River Colony' (1901) 18 *South African Law Journal* 398, 398.

247 Schabas (n 144) 230.

248 Kenneth Roberts-Wray, *Commonwealth and Colonial Law* (Stevens and Sons, London 1966) 537.

can conclude that harmony in Islamised Africa will be achieved by nothing less than abolition.

None of the laws that influenced Africa before colonisation was death penalty free. Some of those laws have been upgraded to become the sole legal system of the country (Liberia) or to constitute the basis of a country's modern law (South Africa, Ethiopia and most African Muslim countries), or they have been juxtaposed to the colonial law to form the current law (Nigeria). Although pre-colonial legal practices were characterised by a varied enthusiasm towards the death penalty, the history of capital punishment in some of these countries has been one of the most atrocious on the continent. This resulted from the fact that colonisation worsened a practice which was already heavily outrageous.

Chapter 4
The Death Penalty as a Colonial Policy in Africa

Introduction

Foreign influences changed indigenous laws in both their substance and their form. Already, limited pre-colonial influences had affected local perceptions of the death penalty in Liberia, South Africa, Ethiopia and West and North Africa. Countries that were death penalty free started justifying the retention of the death penalty on the grounds of its deterrent value or divine nature.[1] The policy continued during colonisation.

Nearly all colonisers resorted to the death penalty to enforce their system of order. There were seven colonial powers in Africa: Belgium, France, Germany, Italy, Portugal, Spain and the United Kingdom. However, the German era in Africa (Namibia, Tanganyika, Ruanda-Urundi, Cameroon and Togo) was short lived and left almost no legal legacy, although Africans – mainly Namibians – still remember it with bitterness.[2]

The Spanish legal system in Africa was limited to Equatorial Guinea, a small portion of Eastern Morocco and the coast of Western Sahara and had no widespread implications.[3] Legal historians qualify Western Sahara as stillborn and Equatorial Guinea as the poor parents' child to indicate that Spain left no substantial legal heritage in these countries.[4] Italy failed to implement the death penalty law in Somalia and there is no record of whether or not it succeeded in Libya. A few decades before colonisation (1867), Portugal had abolished the death penalty. In 1870, it adopted a decree extending the abolition of the death penalty to Portuguese territories in Africa, Asia and Oceania.[5] Article 55 of the Portuguese

---

1 William A Schabas, 'African Perspectives on Abolition of the Death Penalty' in William A Schabas (ed), *The International Sourcebook on Capital Punishment* (Northeastern University Press, Boston 1997) 31.

2 Dan Stone, 'White Men with Low Moral Standards? German Anthropology and the Herero Genocide' (2010) 35(2) *Patterns of Prejudice* 33–54. See also Allan D Cooper, 'Reparations for the Herero Genocide: Defining the Limits of International Litigation' (2006) 106 *African Affairs* 113–126.

3 Tony Hodges, *Sahara occidental: origines et enjeux d'une guerre du desert* (L'Harmattan, Paris 1987) 61–78.

4 Jacques Vanderlinden, *Les systèmes juridiques Africains* (PUF, Paris 1983) 50–51.

5 Fernando O Gouveia Da Veiga, 'Portuguese Africa' in Alan Milner (ed), *African Penal Systems* (Routledge and Kegan Paul, London 1969) 217.

penal code provided for a maximum punishment of 24 years' imprisonment, a policy that remains ahead of its time.[6] Portuguese territories in Africa thus enjoyed *de jure* abolitionist status during colonial times.[7] They introduced the death penalty when they became independent.[8]

Despite there being only slight differences between French law and Belgian law; only Belgium was a *de facto* abolitionist state during colonial times. This chapter focuses on the nature and scope of the death penalty in law and practice in territories under British, French and Belgian rule.

The Death Penalty in English Colonial Law in Africa

In principle, common law is more flexible than civil law as it evolves and adjusts to local environments. However, common law practice in Africa departed from this theory. The need for control that gave way to injustices superseded flexibility.[9]

Various colonies applied English law as it had been imported from England, except where political and local circumstances dictated a few adjustments.[10] Legal provisions conferring jurisdiction over offences had never been considered to be outside the competence of the British legislature. Crimes remained under the jurisdiction of British law even if they occurred elsewhere.[11] This calls for an analysis of the common characteristics of English death penalty law in different colonies to occur prior to any discussion of its actual application in Africa.

Common Features of the English Colonial Death Penalty Law in Africa

During colonisation, indigenous law as Islamic law continued to be applied where appropriate in private law, except in situations that were deemed repugnant to English law. The criminal law remained the Queen's *chasse gardée* for serious offences or in special circumstances. Africans, who were subjects rather than

6 Le Code Pénal Portugais de 1867, in Marc Ancel and Yvonne Marx, *Les codes pénaux Européens*, vol III (Centre Français de Droit Comparé, Paris 1957) 1529.

7 Clarence H Patrick, 'The Status of Capital Punishment: A Worldwide Perspective' (1965) 56 *Journal of Criminal Law, Criminology and Police Science* 397, 408.

8 Amnesty International, *Mozambique: Human Rights and the Police*, April 1998, AI Index: AFR41/01/98, Reuters, 'South Africa Keeps Hangman Occupied', *The Montreal Gazette*, 4 July 1969, 37, Agencia Angola Press, *Angola Constitution Bans Death Penalty*, 19 May 2010.

9 Sandra Fullerton Joireman, 'Inherited Legal Systems and Effective Rule of Law: Africa and the Colonial Legacy' (2001) 4 *Journal of Modern African Studies* 571, 571 and 578.

10 *R v. Joykissen Mookerjee* (1862) 1 Moo PC (N.S.) 172 at 190–191.

11 The Admiralty Offences (colonial) Act, 1860 (23 and 24 V. c. 123).

citizens, could not claim the jurisdiction of customary criminal law or *Shari'a*. Pre-colonial laws were to be eliminated.[12]

Specific legislation was enacted to ensure that British courts had the last word in criminal matters. Murder or manslaughter perpetrated either in a foreign country or on the high seas came under the jurisdiction of British courts.[13] In 1871, citizens of Sierra Leone, Gold Coast (Ghana), Gambia and Lagos were brought under the umbrella of English law. These people were still free despite a slight occupation of the coast. Articles 1 and 2 of the West African Offences Act proclaimed the extension of English law to them only when they committed an offence within 20 miles of the boundary of their territory against a subject of Her Majesty.[14] Probably the best description of those provisions is found in the Bond Agreement of 1844 between Britain and Gold Coast chiefs. Its sections 2 and 3 read as follow:

> 2. Human sacrifices and other barbarous customs, such as panyarring, are an abomination and contrary to law.
>
> 3. Murders, robberies, and other crimes and offences, will be tried and inquired of before the Queen's judicial officers and the chiefs of the district, moulding the customs of the country to the general principles of British law.[15]

Section 1 of the Sierra Leone Offences Act appeared to adopt the same style:

> The laws which are now or which shall hereafter be in force in the Colony of Sierra Leone for the punishment of crimes therein committed shall be and the same are hereby extended and declared applicable to all her Majesty's subjects within any Territory adjacent to the said colony, and being with the Limits as aforesaid; and every crime or offence committed ... shall be cognizable in any such courts, and shall be inquired of, tried and prosecuted, and on conviction punished, in such and the same Manner as if the same had been committed within the said Colony.[16]

---

12 Kenneth Roberts-Wray, *Commonwealth and Colonial Law* (Stevens and Sons, London 1966) 535.

13 Section 1 of the Murders Abroad Act, 1817 (57 Geo. 8, c. 58).

14 West Africa Offence Act, 1871 (34 and 35 V. c. 8).

15 Sections 2 and 3 of the Agreement of 6 March 1844 between Great Britain and Gold Coast as reproduced by NM Ollenu, 'The Influence of English Law on West Africa' (1961) 5 *Journal of African Law* 21, 23.

16 Section 1 of the Sierra Leone Offences Act, 1861 (24 and 25 V. c. 31). A similar phrasing appears also in the South African colonial legislation. See South African Offences Act, 1863 (26 and 27 V. c. 35) and sections 20 and 21 of the Fugitive Offenders Act, 1881 (44 and 45 V. c. 69).

In terms of capital punishment, violence, ritual execution and discriminatory and unfair process characterised the British colonial policy. The deterrent and didactic nature of the death penalty as professed by the colonial courts was combined with a dose of dehumanisation and discrimination. Both the prosecutor and the defence council, each serving personal interest but all resorting to the same prejudicial procedure, presented to the judge many stereotypes. The process of creating another identity started with the trial and ended with the sentence. According to the prosecutor, Africans were a dangerous race, with uncivilised values and violent behaviours. They were less than human, with a 'primitive mentality' and 'impulsive savagery'. The defence counsel reiterated that the court was dealing with irresponsible and mentally retarded people.[17]

Compared to the average Englishman, primitive people could not differentiate between good and evil or identify boundaries between right and wrong.[18] Where a young Englishman took for granted the triumph of forces of right, they strongly believed in evil spirits and were more responsive to them, as well as to forces of nature.[19] The death penalty cemented this belief. Public displays of judicial power through firing squad and hanging were just a transplantation of the method of execution in vogue in England until the nineteenth century. The motto 'deterrence, authority and efficiency' aimed to crush any resistance or subversion and change the savage into an obedient citizen.[20] Indians and mostly Africans were subjected to the death penalty when the victim was a European.

After witnessing the execution of his chief for subversion, a Nigerian elder realised that society had changed, 'it was giving place to something new, to new laws, different standards of conduct and to a foreign people'.[21] Prior to the period of emergency laws, the discomfort resulting from public executions for the colonial officers, the condemned and African society led London to instruct that executions be carried out *in camera*.[22]

The process of imposing the death penalty was unfair. The British coloniser arbitrarily controlled and limited rights of appeal, restricted rights to mercy and sped up executions. There were doubts about the power of the Judicial Committee of the Privy Council (the Queen in Council or the Committee) to grant a *dernier ressort* appeal in capital cases as it could no longer sit as a court in criminal matters.[23] Speaking on behalf of the Committee in 1941, Lord Simon LC provided a list of

---

17 Stacy Hynd, 'Killing the Condemned: The Practice and Process of Capital Punishment in British Africa, 1900–1950s' (2008) 49 *Journal of African History* 403, 405.

18 Frank Furedi, *Colonial Wars and the Politics of the Third World Nationalism* (I.B. Tauris, London 1994) 135–136.

19 ibid.

20 ibid; Hynd (n 17) 404; Michael Crowder, *Colonial West Africa* (Frank Cass, London 1978) 9.

21 Hynd (n 17) 407.

22 ibid 408–409.

23 Roberts-Wray (n 12) 433–463.

areas where the Committee could interfere. It appeared that 'the Committee does not concern itself with ... the award of particular punishments'[24] or 'the length of sentences'.[25]

The Committee expressed no compassion for the condemned even when the accused had successfully challenged the ruling of the court. A nineteenth-century precedent had compared appeals in capital cases from British colonies with stalling tactics intending to delay the carrying out of the sentence. According to the Lord Chancellor, with a successful application 'it would be easy for any person in any distant colony to stay execution and, which would be a very serious and grave misfortune, to interpret a long delay between the vindication of justice by a verdict and execution of the sentence ...'.[26]

The rule remained unaltered even when the offender alleged grievous miscarriage of justice. Based on illegal evidence, the Supreme Court of Nairobi convicted *Karuma* of unlawful possession of ammunition and sentenced him to death. The Committee looked at the merits and demerits of the case in depth and found no applicable precedent in English law. Only in the *Olmstead* case had the American Supreme Court stated that 'the common law did not reject relevant evidence on the grounds that it had been obtained by illegal means'.[27]

Unfortunately, that case did not indicate on which common law authority it was based. Scottish and South African cases, which could be relied on, mainly dealt with different circumstances.[28] The Committee was embarrassed but still did not advise mercy. It looked for 'an intermediate position between the American and Scottish views ...',[29] without managing to hide that 'there were matters of fact in the case which caused [their Lordships] some uneasiness'.[30] They advised that the condemned person's application be dismissed. The aforementioned uneasiness led them to open a salutary door by directing that the execution be conditional on the decision of the Secretary of the State.

The case highlights contradictions that existed between legal reasoning and the radical and oppressive position of the colonial policy. The Committee found that grounds for granting the application for mercy existed, but they still could not grant it. One wonders why they delegated their powers to the executive. Surely, a precedent undermining British colonial interests was not welcome.[31] It was important to terrorise the people, already reduced to subjects, with harsher or

24 ibid.

25 *Hardtmann v. R* (1963) A.C. 746 at 758; *Mondihar Sigh v. R.I.* (1950) A.C. 345.

26 *Ex parte Deeming* (1892) A.C. 422 at 426. See also *Hardtmann v. R* (1963) A.C. 746 at 758.

27 *Olmstead v. United States* (1928) 277 U.S. 438.

28 *Kuruma v. R.* (1955) A.C. 197 at 200.

29 ibid.

30 ibid 205.

31 *Rex v. Mohamed Shah s/o Lal Shah* (1939) 5 E.A.P.L.R. 103 at 104.

excessive punishment so that they fear the ruler. The purpose was to combine the domination of men and territories and to rely on legal violence.[32]

In dealing with death row or what it called 'delays in capital cases', the British coloniser issued new instructions. Indeed, applications for appeal or commutation of sentences delayed the execution of capital sentences. The Committee was not aware of the facts or even of the decision and no measures could be taken meanwhile. In London, as well as in various colonies, instructions were given that intended to speed up the execution of the death penalty.[33] After the reception of the petition in London, a speedy hearing was immediately organised. When a leave to appeal was granted, the Judicial Committee was also instructed to deliberate promptly on the matter.

The orders for reducing delays in execution of the death penalty are summarised below:

a. If the condemned intended to apply for a special leave for appeal or commutation of the sentence, the date of execution was postponed for three weeks. The application contained instructions, documents including the affidavit of means and the certificate of council justifying the rationale of the application and funds to a solicitor in London and to a specified government officer.
b. Upon reception of the file by the Solicitor in London, the Secretary of State could postpone the execution for a further three weeks.
c. No further delay could be accepted if the deadline was not respected.

Dismissals justified new applications, which were expected to go through the same process and take the same amount of time.[34] Though the Committee felt concerned and disapproved of this abuse of the procedure, it took no initiative to stop its dilatory use. In 1947, the Executive appeared increasingly concerned over delays of execution. It sought the authorisation of Parliament to delegate the Committee's power to the Governor. In lieu of the judiciary, if the Governor concluded that 'any proceedings taken by the accused persons either in the Colony or by way of petition in England were without real substance, he would not allow those proceedings to cause the postponement of the sentence'.[35]

The British coloniser was not concerned with protecting the process of justice. Speedy executions became common. Stacy Hynd recalls that 'early colonial hangings were often improvised affairs, the gallows being created from a nearby tree, or even a door-frame suspended over a river bed …'.[36] Following the new

32 Hynd (n 17) 403.

33 Roberts-Wray (n 12) 446.

34 ibid.

35 House of Commons, Debates, vol 441 (written answers), cols 230–233 as quoted by Roberts-Wray, ibid 447.

36 Hynd (n 17) 407.

instructions, executions fell under the Governors' discretion. The lodging of a special leave to appeal did not 'necessarily affect [the Governor's] position'.[37] This excessive politicisation of the judicial process prevailed in all British colonies.[38]

The Death Penalty in British East Africa and Somalia

In 1877, the Sultan of Zanzibar authorised the British East Africa Company to operate in the sphere formerly offered to Portugal. Later the area from the island of Zanzibar to the Eastern coasts of Somalia, Kenya and Tanganyika became a place of contention between Great Britain and Germany. Treaties with local chiefs, demonstrations of force against coastal Arabs, concessions, sale and leasing contracts among Europeans or between them and local chiefs allowed Europeans to control the area.[39] The agreement was that Germany would occupy Tanganyika and Great Britain would settle in Kenya and South Somalia, while Zanzibar would remain independent under a British protectorate. Uganda joined the team under a protectorate treaty in 1892. Later, Tanganyika was brought under British trusteeship in application of the Versailles Treaty of 28 June 1919.[40]

There were five Somalias: Italian Somalia, British Somaliland, French Somalia, the Ogaden Province of Ethiopia and the Northern District of Kenya. As regards punishments, compensation (*diyya*) characterised Somali customary criminal law of homicide. Even under the influence of *Shari'a*, Somalia like Zanzibar did not introduce the death penalty. Capital punishment was very rare under the *Ismaili Shi* School in Zanzibar and on the coast. Even murders that involved mutilation were punished by *diyya* provided the victim consented to receiving it.[41]

With colonisation, the British and the Italians introduced the Indian penal code and the Italian penal code respectively, both of which punished murder by hanging. These laws collided with a very strong custom of *diyya*, the repeal of which would result in political chaos for the fragile colonial administration. *Herr* (contracts or treaties), which determined the amount of *diyya* depending on the offence and its gravity, bound Somali clans for centuries. Under *Herr*, 100 camels was the

37 House of Commons, Debates, vol 441 (written answers), cols 230–233 as quoted by Roberts-Wray (n 12) 447.

38 Anthony I Asiwaju, 'Law in African Borderlands: The Lived Experience of the Yoruba Astride the Nigeria-Dahomey Border' in Kristin Mann and Richard Roberts (eds), *Law in Colonial Africa* (Heinmann, Portsmouth 1991) 232.

39 Roberts-Wray (n 12) 756–758.

40 Alan Sharp, *The Versailles Settlement: Peacekeeping after the First World War, 1919–1923* (Palgrave Macmillan, New York 2008) 173–174.

41 James S Read, 'Kenya, Tanzania and Uganda' in Alan Milner (ed), *African Penal Systems* (Routledge and Kegan Paul, London 1969) 105–106.

punishment for killing a man and 50 camels for killing a woman.[42] The punishment was doubled for intentional homicide, mainly when it resulted from hatred.[43]

Colonial laws interpreted *diyya* in terms of their own concepts and in comparison with principles familiar to them. They failed, however, to push it out. In British Somaliland, courts upheld the payment of full or partial *diyya* although they were applying the penal code.[44] Under Italian penal code, courts understood *diyya* to be the parallel of a civil remedy for torts resulting from the offence and the collective payment as the correspondent of the Italian principle of *responsabilità solidale.* This oversimplification resulted in the imposition of two punishments, namely imprisonment and *diyya.*[45] Tribesmen perceived the imposition of two sentences as double jeopardy.[46] However, hanging remained uncommon among the Somali in all cases.

Kenya, Uganda and Tanganyika joined to form a formal cooperation in 1926 through the Governors' conference.[47] Even prior to this, each country's practices influenced the others' without replacing them.[48] Petty offences, which constituted the majority of criminal cases, were left to indigenous courts that applied indigenous criminal law or what remained of it. The British coloniser had repetitively modified indigenous law and procedure in East Africa to make it more modern. The commission in charge of cataloguing customary crimes stated that 'some crimes ... were converted into civil wrongs and vice versa, some district representatives agreed to modify elements in certain offences, ... some offences were eliminated altogether where it was found that they were already covered under some written law'.[49]

The Westernisation of indigenous law through 'administrative pressures or directions, training courses conducted by courts advisers, handbooks of persuasive and binding authority and ruling by magistrates and high courts'[50] led indigenous judges to deliver justice in ways that flattered their masters.[51] The Native Tribunals Rules of 1911 provided that any sentence imposed by the Council of Elders was to be subjected to the approval of the District Commissioner. In Kenya, indigenous

42 Paolo Contini, 'The Evolution of Blood-Money for Homicide in Somalia' (1971) 15 *Journal of African Law* 78, 78–80.

43 Georges BN Ayittey, *Indigenous African Institutions* (Transnational Publisher, New York 2006) 80.

44 Contini (n 42).

45 ibid 81.

46 ibid 82.

47 Roberts-Wray (n 12) 447.

48 *Rex v. Tromoi and Another* (1919) 8–9 K.L.R. 6.

49 'Notes and News, Customary Criminal Law in Kenya' (1963) 7 *Journal of African Law* 1, 2.

50 James S Read, 'Criminal Law in the Africa of Today and Tomorrow' (1963) *Journal of African Law* 5, 16.

51 *Rex v. Weer S/O Muga* (1911) 5 E.A.P.L.R. 62 at 62–63.

courts specialised in applying statutory criminal provisions and usually imposed punishments that had never existed under their traditional law.[52]

Punishments were selected from the range of penalties with which the coloniser was more familiar.[53] The purpose of this policy was to break down the traditional penalty of compensation and emphasise the death penalty as a deterrent. Compensation became considered inadequate and repugnant.[54] The phrase 'repugnant to natural justice, equity and good conscience' was present in all colonial statutes and essentially referred to anything foreign to English law.[55] The death penalty was thus traditionalised.

However, the regularity with which the death penalty became imposed by traditional courts attracted the coloniser's attention. The Council of Elders ordered a group of eight men to execute a death sentence against one Kachau. During a trial for murder, the accused claimed immunity on the grounds that they were executing the order of a court of law. The East African Court of Appeal was asked whether, in terms of colonial law, the Council of Elders constituted a court of justice to pass a death sentence. Despite concluding the opposite,[56] traditional courts continued flattering the District Commissioner. In application of a supposedly traditional punishment, in 1908, a statutory Kikuyu Council (the *Kiama*) tried a suspected witch and imposed a sentence of death by stoning.[57] In 1913, the same Council imposed a death penalty by burning on two men convicted of witchcraft.[58] In a similar murder case from the Kamba, a tribal meeting imposed a death sentence on the culprit and ordered his hanging in the village.[59]

Discrepancies between methods of execution are per se an indication that the death penalty did not fit the so-called 'survival of indigenous punishments'.[60] In the *Karoga wa Kithengi and 53 others* case, the court established that in applying the death penalty by burning, stoning or hanging, native courts 'were no longer exercising their old customary jurisdiction, but only such jurisdiction as the Governor's rules allowed them to exercise ...'.[61] The appropriate sentence for witchcraft under traditional Kikuyu law was ostracism.[62] The death penalty was not

52 'Notes and News, Customary Criminal Law in Kenya' (1963) 7 *Journal of African Law* 1, 2.

53 Read (n 41) 95.

54 Section 2 of the Colonial Laws Validity Act, 1865 (28 and 29 V. c. 63).

55 Roberts-Wray (n 12) 396–399, 575–579; JN Matson, 'The Common Law Abroad: English and Indigenous Laws in the British Commonwealth' (1993) 42 *International and Comparative Law Quarterly* 753, 761.

56 *Kasan wa Muiga and others v. Rex* (1912) 4 E.A.P.L.R 103 at 103–105.

57 *Rex v. Kichingeri and others* (1908) 3 E.A.P.L.R. 1 at 2–4.

58 *Rex v. Karoga wa Kithengi and 53 others* (1913) 5 E.A.P.L.R. 50 at 53.

59 *R v. Komen Arap Chelal and 43 others* (1938) 5 E.A.C.A. 150.

60 *Rex v. Kichingeri and others* (1908) 3 E.A.P.L.R. 1 at 5 and Read (n 41) 96.

61 *Rex v. Karoga wa Kithengi and 53 others* (1913) 5 E.A.P.L.R. 50 at 53.

62 Lewis Tupper, 'Customary Law and Other Law in the East Africa Protectorate' (1907) 8 *Journal of Comparative Legislation* 172, 175–176 and Read (n 41) 105.

a valid punishment for Kikuyu, Kamba, Luo or Pokot of Kenya.[63] Its application was an indication of the foreign laws' influence on African indigenous laws.

Before pure English law, East Africa, particularly Zanzibar and the adjacent mainland areas, was for decades under the influence of the Indian criminal law.[64] With the Order in Council of 1884, the death penalty, already valid in the Indian penal code of 1860, became applicable in Zanzibar and its adjacent territories as part of the district of Bombay. The Indian penal code remained in force until the Colonial Office Model Code replaced it in 1930.

According to section 53 of the Indian penal code, the death penalty was its most severe punishment.[65] It was mandatory for political crimes and murder perpetrated by a prisoner serving a life sentence[66] and discretionary for other forms of voluntary homicide.[67] Section 194 *in fine* also punished perjury with death when it resulted in the judicial execution of an innocent person.[68]

There was distaste towards the death penalty in India. Drafters of the Indian penal code joined 'those who condemn the English statute book as sanguinary …'.[69] They sent a brief but strong message to the judiciary to prevent it from making use of the discretionary death penalty for gang robbery, cruel mutilation and rape and outlawed the death penalty for petty offences such as theft, cheating or mischief.[70] The scope of the death penalty was actually very limited even in practice:[71]

a. Only two crimes were punished by death and commissioners had called the judiciary not to abuse the use of the death penalty.
b. The personal jurisdiction of the penal code was restricted to non-natives. Indigenous people referred to their respective customary laws in criminal matters.
c. The death penalty, which was not new to the Europeans, Indians, Arabs and Muslim population of Zanzibar and the coast, at least for treason and murder, had to be executed without ritual torture. It was especially recommended that the convicted person not be broken on the wheel or burnt alive.

---

63 Philip H Gulliver, *Social Control in African Society: A Study of the Arusha: Agricultural Masai of Northern Tanganyika* (Routledge and Kegan Paul, London 1963) 127–129.

64 Matson (n 55).

65 This was section 40 in the draft presented to the Governor in 1838. See alternatively Walter Morgan and Arthur G Macpherson, *The Indian Penal Code Act XLV of 1860 with Notes* (G.C. Hay and Co, London 1861) 32 and 'Notes on the Chapter of Punishments' in Thomas Macaulay, *Indian Penal Code* (Lawbook Exchange, New Jersey 2002) 5.

66 Sections 121, 132 and 303 of the Indian Penal Code Act XLV of 1860.

67 Sections 302, 303, 305 and 396 of the Indian Penal Code Act XLV of 1860.

68 Morgan and Macpherson (n 65) 33 and163.

69 'Notes on the Chapter of Punishments' in Macaulay (n 65) 70.

70 ibid 69.

71 ibid and Matson (n 55) 760–761.

The new penal code for East Africa[72] departed from Indian law on the grounds that Indian and African living conditions were not the same.[73] It was inspired by the Northern Nigerian criminal code of 1904, which in turn was based on the Queensland criminal code Act of 1899. The later derived from the work of R.S. Wright, who, in 1877, drafted a criminal code for Jamaica, a colony settled by Sir James Stephen. The draft never became law in Jamaica.[74] The initial text, mistakenly attributed to James Stephen,[75] was deemed obsolete for its reference to the unfamiliar terms of intention and cause. It contained, however, basic principles of English law.[76] It became a reliable reference for different colonies. The Queensland code covered 717 provisions. Undoubtedly, the more detailed a code is, the more inflexible it will be. Its sections 8 and 664 together provided for death sentences to be carried out by hanging by the neck within the walls or enclosed area of the prison unless the sheriff decided otherwise. Capital offences were offences against public order, sedition, piracy and homicides.[77] A reading of the code causes one to think that it simultaneously applied to both Queensland and England.

The rationale behind the change in East Africa was the desire to see pure English law applied. The British Secretary of State disclosed that he was advised not to rely on the reasons behind the importation of the Indian code and to apply a code whose language and principles were familiar in England. In *Mawji and Another v. R.*[78] the clash between Indian law and English legal principles in courtrooms set those in London on edge. Lower judges rejected the English law of conspiracy because it did not exist in the law before them, namely the Indian code. Practical problems such as new terminology, the absence of textbooks and the unavailability of English case law also led local lawyers to boycott the brutal legal change. The State Secretary insisted that the basic problem was that Indian law needed to be replaced.[79] The East African Court of Appeal reiterated that codification was the only difference between East African law and English law.[80]

---

72 Model Penal Code for the East African Dependencies Act, 1929 in *The Gazette of the Colony and Protectorate of Kenya*, no 40, 1 August 1929.

73 C Clifton Roberts, 'African Natives under the English System of Penal Law' (1933) 15 *Journal of Comparative Legislation* 169, 169.

74 HL Stephen, 'A Model Criminal Code for the Colonies' (1899) 1 *Journal of Comparative Legislation* 439, 439.

75 Read (n 50) 14.

76 Stephen (n 74).

77 See sections 37 to 43 for treason, 44 to 53 for sedition, 79 to 82 for piracy, 305 for homicides in the Queensland Criminal Code Act, 1899 (68 Vic no 9, 1899).

78 *Mawji and another v. R* (1957) J.C. 126 at 130 and 133.

79 Read (n 50) 7. See also sections 2 and 4 of the Model Penal Code for the East African Dependencies Act, 1929 in *The Gazette of the Colony and Protectorate of Kenya*, no 40, 1 August 1929.

80 *Rex v. Kinanda Bin Mwaisumo* (1939) 6 E.A.C.A. 105 at 108.

Accordingly, English principles and methods of interpretation were incorporated into domestic law.[81] Local legislation provided, for example, that English law would serve as a reference to define treason and piracy.[82] Henceforth, the definition of crimes would depend on changes that took place in Britain. This drove some to conclude that 'no doubt this Penal Code is excellent where one has to deal with Europeans, but it hardly seems to fit the case when we picture a court scene with native prisoners in the dock'.[83]

The reform represented a step backwards. The death penalty became mandatory for treason, piracy and murder. Retribution was the motive behind most punishments. Magistrates started imposing excessive punishments on a regular basis.[84] In 1932, almost an entire village received a death sentence. This was considered the only appropriate punishment for the murder that the 60 offenders had perpetrated.[85] Courts vehemently rejected any complaint as to the severity of punishments. The court of appeal insisted that judges not read into the law punishments other than those written there.

In the *Kichanjele* case, the court of appeal quashed a sentence of five years' imprisonment and imposed a death sentence for treason because the judge erred in considering that the death penalty was the maximum sentence. The court pointed out that, unlike in rape cases where life imprisonment was a possible sentence, there was no alternative punishment to death for murder and treason.[86] Before this case, the practice of the death penalty in Kenya was such that rape or mere assault with intent to rape of European females justified a mandatory death penalty[87] while the rape of an African female could easily be reduced to adultery or defilement.[88] The sentence for rape of African females whether teenaged or adult was imprisonment.[89]

The coloniser's brutality and racism made the death penalty an instrument of oppression. Racial bias in the handling of capital cases increased as demands for independence increased and with the emergence of the *Mau Mau* movement. Murders perpetrated by Africans against Europeans and Asians became

81 *Mawji and another v. R* (1957) J.C. 126 at 133 and *Kimno Arap Kipturji v. Rex* (1934) 1 E.A.C.A. 190.

82 Section 40 of the Kenya Penal Code, cap. 24, section 53 of the Uganda penal code, cap. 22, in Uganda Protectorate, *The Penal Code, 1950 and the Criminal Procedure Code, 1950* (Government Printer 1950) 17.

83 Roberts (n 73) 170.

84 *Rex v. Kumwaka wa Mulumbi* (1932) 14 K.L.R. 137.

85 ibid.

86 *Rex v. Kichanjele s/o Ndamungu* (1941) 8 E.A.C.A. 65.

87 Uganda and Tanganyika resisted introducing the death penalty for rape. See Read (n 41) 105–106.

88 *Rex v. Odar Odeyu* (1918) 7 E.A.P.L.R. 108 at 109 and *Rex v. Farasisiko Sheshaho* (1938) 5 E.A.C.A. 110.

89 *Rex v. Opiri* (1927) K.L.R. 90 and *Rex v Hassan wa Saleh and Another* (1908) 3 K.L.R. 105.

systematically punished by death, regardless of procedural irregularities, while those against fellow Africans were regularly reduced to manslaughter. In the *Kamau* case, the accused was charged of murdering an Indian. Based on a medical report the court found that the accused was probably suffering from epileptic insanity both before and during the action. The court imposed a death sentence despite the doubt shed by medical report.[90]

The court adopted a different attitude when the victim was an African. Kibiegon Arap Bargutwa violently murdered his father on the allegation that his father attempted to have unlawful connexion with him, an accusation that his father denied before dying. The medical report concluded that the attack was so violent that it suggested that the accused was not in his right mind. The court found that 'although such incomprehensible facts are not in themselves sufficient to establish insanity in law, it seems to us that … there is good reason to think that he may at least have been labouring under an insane delusion to the effect that his father has made an indecent assault upon him'.[91] On the assumption that delusion existed, the court reduced the charge from murder to manslaughter.[92]

Despite their repeated unwillingness to impose the death penalty on juvenile offenders,[93] East African courts gained an interest in criminal cases and in particular the number of homicide cases steadily increased. Death sentences passed down in East Africa in the periods 1897–1930 and 1931–1950 are given in Figures 4.1 and 4.2 respectively.

Between 1897 and 1950, 76 per cent of those convicted and hanged for murder were Africans.[94] The fate of Africans became of major concern during the *Mau Mau* anti-colonial movement when Kenya had the largest recorded number of hangings. Most offences became capital crimes. Between 1950 and 1963, the rate of executions in Kenya (2,328 executions took place over this period) was almost seven times higher than that of Tanganyika (332 executions).[95] David Anderson states that it was a time of 'Courtroom dramas', where no rule of law or judicial process existed. There was only authority and hanging.[96]

The 1953 Lari massacre, where more than 200 Kikuyu people (mainly women and children) were murdered, resulted in a call for three priorities: bringing *Mau*

90 *Rex v. Kamau s/o Njeroge* (1939) 6 E.A.C.A. 133 at 133–135. See also *Rex v. Gerevazi s/o Lutabingwa* (1941) 9 K.L.R. 56 at 56–57.

91 *Rex v. Kibiegon Arap Bargutwa* (1939) 6 E.A.C.A. 142 at 143–144. See also *Rex v Mwandamere s/o Sefula* (1931) 8 K.L.R. 58 at 58–59.

92 ibid. Compare with *Rex v. Kamau s/o Njeroge* (1939) 6 E.A.C.A. 133 at 133–135; *Rex v. Gerevazi s/o Lutabingwa* (1941) 9 K.L.R. 56 at 56–57 and *Rex v. Mwandamere s/o Sefula* (1931) 8 K.L.R. 58 at 58–59.

93 *Rex v. Mvula s/o Irove* (1944) 11 E.A.C.A. 112 at 112–113 and *Rex v. Kulabirawo* (1947) 14 E.A.C.A. 116.

94 Hynd (n 17) 406; See also David Anderson, *Histories of the Hanged: Britain's Dirty War in Kenya and the End of Empire* (Weidenfeld and Nicolson, London 2005) 347–348.

95 Anderson, ibid 48 and 346–354 and Read (n 41) 126–127.

96 Anderson, ibid 151.

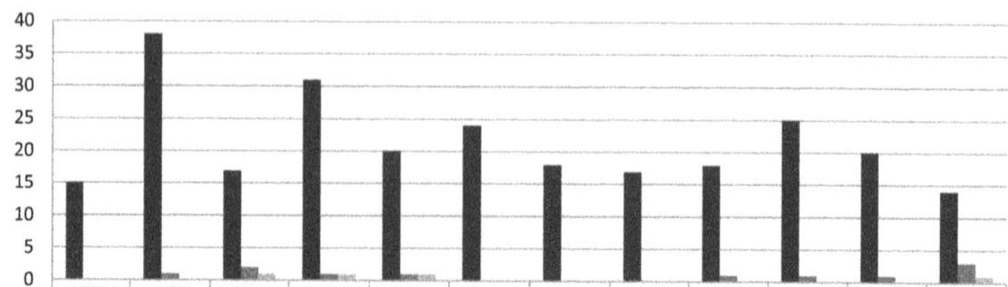

	1897-1905	1906-1908	1909-1910	1911-1912	1913-1914	1915-1916	1917-1918	1919-1921	1922-1923	1924-1926	1927-1928	1929-1930
■ Criminal cases	15	38	17	31	20	24	18	17	18	25	20	14
■ Capital cases	0	1	2	1	1	0	0	0	1	1	1	3
■ Death sentence	0	0	1	1	1	0	0	0	0	0	0	1

Figure 4.1 Death sentences in East Africa (1897–1930)
Source: East African Law Report (1897–1930).

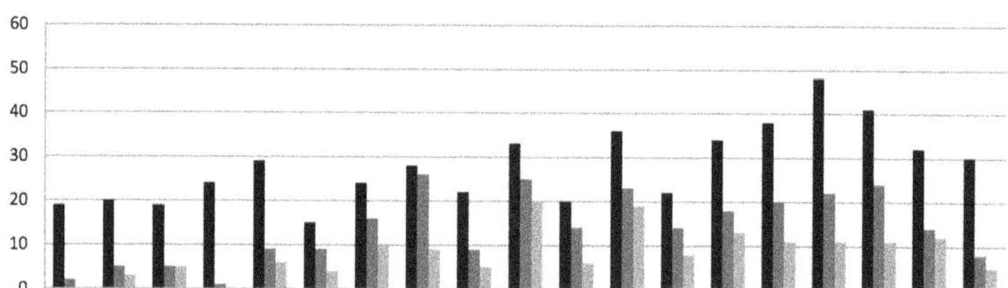

	1931	1932	1933-1934	1935	1936	1937	1938	1939	1940	1941	1942	1943	1944	1945	1946	1947	1948	1949	1950
■ Criminal cases	19	20	19	24	29	15	24	28	22	33	20	36	22	34	38	48	41	32	30
■ Capital cases	2	5	5	1	9	9	16	26	9	25	14	23	14	18	20	22	24	14	8
■ Death sentence	0	3	5	0	6	4	10	9	5	20	6	19	8	13	11	11	11	12	5

Figure 4.2 Death sentences in East Africa (1931–1950)
Source: East African Law Report (1931–1950).

Mau culprits speedily to justice, convicting them and executing them.[97] Capital offences were increased to meet this goal. Hate speeches and dehumanising conduct against Kikuyu led to the adoption of draconian measures. '*Mau Mau* adherents did not belong to the human race … they had to be eliminated.'[98] Five more offences were added to the list of capital crimes, such that anyone in connection with the movement had to be hanged. These offences were administering or taking the *Mau Mau* oath, being a member of the *Mau Mau*, carrying out acts prejudicing

97 ibid 151; John Lonsdale, 'Kenyatta's Trials: Breaking and Making an African Nationalist' in Peter Coss (ed), *The Moral World of the Law* (Cambridge University Press, London 2000) 196.

98 Caroline Elkins, *Imperial Reckoning: The Untold Story of Britain's Gulag in Kenya* (Henry Holt and Company, New York 2005) 48–49.

public order, possessing an explosive item, arm or ammunition and consorting with persons carrying arms or ammunition.[99]

The problem became how to achieve the goal while lobbying for death penalty repeal and was ongoing in London given that justice was built on procedures. After considering that the lobbying did not concern Kenya, the leader of British settlers in Kenya advised the colonial office that quick justice required exceptional powers to magistrate in capital cases, complete suppression of appeal and review of sentences without waiting for advisory opinions.[100] Suggestions included the restriction of review by the governor and holding executions within 24 hours. These measures aimed to re-establish colonial domination and satisfy the vehement demands of local settlers for the tightest control of the Kikuyu.

The trial against *Mau Mau* suspects was unprecedented. The longest case barely took a month to try. Poor quality evidence did not prevent judges from imposing the capital penalty. Extrajudicial depositions were approved without prior assessment. Some of the accused were convicted on the basis of a testimony of a child[101] or that of a witness who appeared in different hearings, praised in one and judged unreliable and deceitful in another.[102] Judges doubted the accused even when they retracted confessions allegedly obtained by coercion and torture.[103]

The magistrates who sat on the Lari trial were inexperienced. Some were brought in due to their conservative tendencies. The idea of wrongful acquittals worried them more than wrongful convictions. The goal was hanging. During this marathon of justice 46 persons were hanged in Githunguri and 25 in Nairobi.[104] In Githunguri, the process for hanging one convict took 19 minutes. The body was then taken down so that the gallows could be reset and used for the next convict. In 1953 alone, Kenya officially executed 91 persons.[105] Many innocent persons were convicted and hanged alongside guilty criminals. Executions were carried out in a manner designed to reflect the 'might of British justice'.[106] Was there justice? It is generally agreed that 'in this woeful process … the law did not learn from its experience'.[107]

In Tanganyika, there was much debate around the extension of the death penalty to homicide provoked by witchcraft. In 1932, the view had been held that murderers of supposed witches deserved the death penalty. This inferred that the colonial administration did not believe in witchcraft and condemned murder.

---

99 Anderson (n 94) 152.

100 Elkins (n 98) 55–56.

101 CC 317/1952 'Kamau Ndirangu and Githuka Kagwe' at Nairobi, 10 April 1953, KNA MLA I/464.

102 Anderson (n 94) 151–176.

103 CC40/1953 'Karaya Njonji and three others' at Nairobi, 23 April 1953, KNA.

104 Anderson (n 94) 175.

105 Read (n 41) 126.

106 Anderson (n 94) 173.

107 ibid 164.

Yet in 1941, the Governor of Tanganyika expressed a sincere belief in witchcraft, justifying the commutation of the death sentence for the murderer.[108]

Undoubtedly, Tanzanians and Ugandans have been subjected to fewer British judicial injustices than their Kenyan neighbours. In East Africa, the death penalty was introduced first by *Shari'a* on the Eastern Coast and Zanzibar and secondly by Indian law. It is doubtful whether Kabaka, the King of Baganda negotiated with Britain to retain and impose the death penalty as an indigenous punishment.[109]

Certainly, British colonisers manipulated it as they wished and extended its use to crimes which were dealt with in other ways. Still, the use of the death penalty during the period of British colonisation appears to have been inconsistent and discriminatory depending on the shape given to a particular territory. Kenya was considered to be the New England and white settlers, mostly farmers, enjoyed greater political influence there than they would have in Uganda and Tanganyika.[110] This explains the brutality with which the colonisers reacted to the *Mau Mau* anti-colonial movement and the thousands of hangings of Kikuyu after a flawed judicial process.[111]

The Death Penalty in British Southern Africa

Southern Africa is, geographically speaking, the expanse of land that extends up from the Cape to East Africa and Central Africa. Three colonisers occupied the area, namely Germany in Namibia (before South Africa took over under the League of Nations mandate), Great Britain in Zambia, Zimbabwe, Malawi, Swaziland, Botswana, Lesotho and South Africa and lastly Portugal in Mozambique and Angola.

Though Great Britain controlled the majority of territories, its legal principles only had a limited scope. The East African Colonial Office Model Penal Code was extended to Northern Rhodesia (Zambia) and Nyasaland (Malawi) and received the same attention there that it did in East Africa.[112] The sole exception to this was that in 1937 capital crimes and witchcraft were expressly excluded from the jurisdiction of native courts in Northern Rhodesia and Nyasaland.[113]

Other British territories in the area remained under the powerful and persistent influence of Roman Dutch law. As early as 1904, Roman Dutch law was the substantive law applied in Lesotho, Botswana, Swaziland, Zimbabwe, Zambia

---

108 Read (n 41) 127.

109 ibid 97.

110 William Burnett Harvey, *Introduction to the Legal System in East Africa* (East African Literature Bureau, Kampala 1975) 361. See also Crowder (n 20) 126.

111 Elkins (n 98) 50 and 57.

112 Read (n 50) 6. See also HF Morris, 'A History of the Adoption of Codes of Criminal Law and Procedure in British Colonial Africa, 1876–1935' (1974) 18 *Journal of African Law* 6, 17–20.

113 Section 11 (1) (a) (b) of the Native Courts Ordinance of 1 October 1937.

and Namibia.[114] The interpretation of statutory laws introduced later were always tested against the standards of Roman Dutch law and adjusted accordingly.[115]

Lesotho made an exception. The British allowed customary law and Native courts to deal with all suits, actions or proceedings between Africans. The favour was later interpreted as carrying a policy of no interference in African matters. This policy, coupled with the passivity and inertia of the British coloniser, contributed to the maintenance of Basutho indigenous law, which was death penalty free.[116] Basutho indigenous law passed the test of time, surviving the colonial period and establishing itself as the only valid law of the Kingdom of Lesotho.[117] It eventually took primacy over the written law and in particular over section 17 of the Cape Proclamation Act 47 of 1871 that had introduced the death penalty.[118]

In Botswana the coloniser took a different approach, that of direct interference in African matters. Under the Order in Council of 10 June 1891, the Resident Commissioner in Botswana (Bechuanaland Protectorate) had permissive jurisdiction in African cases. He had the right to limited interference in death sentences that native chiefs imposed. There was a collegial court presided over by the Resident Commissioner and two other officers that was in charge of trying cases of murder.[119] However, it appeared that their power was very limited. In only two cases, one in 1893 and one 1897, did the European court impose the death penalty.[120]

In 1912, a special court was created to separate the Resident's judicial and administrative functions.[121] Until 1928 this court dealt strictly with serious offences perpetrated by Europeans. From then on, its jurisdiction extended over treason committed by Africans.[122]

As regards Swaziland, the Protocol of 5 October 1898 extended the jurisdiction of the Transvaal Landdrost's court over that country. The Protocol was an executive measure of a convention concluded five years earlier between Transvaal and Swaziland that put the latter under the protectorate of the former. The

114 AJ Kerr, 'The Reception and Codification of Systems of Law in Southern Africa' (1958) 2 *Journal of African Law* 82, 82.

115 For example section 13 of the High Court Act, 1891, cap. 8 (Southern Rhodesia), section 1 (1) of the Proclamation no 21 of 1919 (South West Africa), section 2 of the Swaziland Criminal Procedure and Evidence Act, no 4 of 1907.

116 WT McClain, 'Lesotho's Criminal Law: South African Common Law or a Lesotho Penal Code' (1985) 1 *Lesotho Law Journal* 239, 239 and 241.

117 ibid.

118 JR Crawford, 'The History and Nature of the Judicial System of Botswana, Lesotho and Swaziland: Introduction and the Superior Courts' (1969) 86 *South African Law Journal* 476, 480.

119 ibid.

120 ibid.

121 Section 1 (1) of the Proclamation Act no 40 of 1912.

122 Proclamation Act no 40 of 1912 read together with Proclamation Act no 11 of 1928.

Protocol limited the jurisdiction of native courts in criminal matters and gave the Landdrost's court jurisdiction over serious offences including homicide. In 1904, the Anglo-Boer war had stopped the Landdrost's court from hearing cases in the protectorate. As a result, a special criminal court of Swaziland with a collegial bench appointed by the Governor of Transvaal and empowered with jurisdiction over capital crimes was created. However, the execution of the sentence required the Governor's confirmation.[123]

In 1907, the jurisdiction of Swaziland courts in criminal matters was reframed in line with Bechuanaland judicial organisation. The court of the Resident Commissioner had the power to impose capital punishment for Africans. Europeans were tried before the special court unless they consented to the jurisdiction of the Resident Court. The special court, whose bench included an advocate from the Supreme Court of Transvaal and two assistant commissioners, had jurisdiction over treason, murder, culpable homicide and all other serious offences perpetrated by Europeans.[124]

As in South Africa, the statutory death penalty existed for treason and murder in Botswana and Swaziland and extended to rape in Lesotho.[125] The court retained its discretionary power if it was satisfied that there were mitigating circumstances. The clash between customary law and Cape law often called for the judge to be more flexible in Botswana and Swaziland.[126] Thus, to create the appearance of a fair and just process, assessors (whose role was actually more advisory than substantial)[127] were associated with the court in cases involving Africans. Nothing could prevent the magistrate from imposing the death sentence even when there were strong disagreements.[128] In fact, some tribal laws (such as the Tswana law) imposed the death penalty for murder, while neighbouring tribes compensated homicide with girls or cattle.[129]

Roman Dutch Criminal law, as it existed in the Cape of Good Hope in 1891, was extended to Zimbabwe,[130] while Namibia received it as it was on 1 January 1920.[131] Later, English law influenced the legal philosophy of these countries. They departed from the principles of old Roman Dutch law in a number of criminal matters.

---

123 Crawford (n 118) 484.

124 ibid 485.

125 Robert D Leslie, 'Lesotho, Botswana and Swaziland' in Alan Milner (ed), *African Penal Systems* (Routledge and Kegan Paul, London 1969) 182.

126 Crawford (n 118) 478.

127 Joseph S Warioba, 'The Role of Assessors in Criminal Trials in Tanganyika' (1966) 1 *Journal of the Denning Law Society* 234, 234–240.

128 Anderson (n 94) 176.

129 Isaac Schapera, *The Bantu-Speaking Tribes of South Africa* (George Routledge and Sons, London 1937) 209.

130 Article 13 of the High Court Act, 1891, cap. 8 as quoted in Kerr (n 114).

131 Section 1 (1) of the Proclamation no 21 of 1919 as quoted in Kerr, ibid. This section was interpreted with approval in *R. v. Goseb* 1956 (2) S.A. 696 (S.W.A.).

Infanticide, homicide resulting from provocation and suicide ceased to be capital crimes. There was no death penalty for juvenile offenders or pregnant women.[132]

Nevertheless, judicial practice indicates that there was no interest in the death penalty. In Southern Rhodesia (Zimbabwe), the judiciary doubted the mandatory nature of the death penalty. In the *Sanka* case, the court stated that 'death is a possible but not a necessary sentence'.[133] This simple statement conveys the discretionary nature of the death penalty, a power to which courts resorted on various occasions for excluding the death penalty even in cases of proven murder.[134] To justify the exclusion of the death sentence, courts have resorted to mitigating circumstances such as intoxication, provocation[135] and youth.[136] Furthermore, the law in Southern Rhodesia was applied to Africans and to Europeans in the same way. This happened often mainly when the offender claimed the benefit of being a European. In the *Biljon* case, the Southern Rhodesia High Court clarified that '... it would indeed be putting back the clock and would be disturbing to the native mind if the impression gained ground that the commission of this crime by a European could be treated with comparative impunity'.[137]

By 1960, the death sentence had likely been imposed in only two 1938 cases, namely *Chikokonya* and *Longone*, in Southern Rhodesia.[138] There is no record that these sentences were executed. On the contrary, Northern Rhodesia and Nyasaland, which were under the full influence of English law, often resorted to capital punishment. By 1960, Northern Rhodesia had sentenced 49 people to death and executed 26. Nearly 53 per cent of its death sentences were carried out. Nyasaland had executed nine persons out of the 25 sentenced to death or an average of 36 per cent.[139] This is itself an indicator of the distance between Roman Dutch law and English law in Southern Africa.

The Death Penalty in British West Africa

There is no clear indication of the date of importation of English law in West Africa. Countries received it on different dates and in different ways.[140] Sierra Leone was the first British settlement in West Africa. Freetown and the suburbs were repositories of free Africans and West Indians slaves liberated by the British

132 Leslie (n 125) 182.

133 *Rex v. Sanka* [1923] R&N 20 (SR).

134 *Rex v. Sales* [1936] R&N 55 (SR) at 55–56, *Rex v. Sikonia* [1937] R&N 54 (SR) at 54–56.

135 *Rex v. Mahoko* [1949] R&N 6 (SR) at 6–7.

136 *Rex v. Gideon* [1951] R&N 11 (SR) at 11–12.

137 *Rex v. Van Biljon* [1938] R&N 180 (SR).

138 *Rex v. Chikokonya* [1938] R&N 122 (SR) at 122–125 and *R v. Longone* [1938] R&N 131 (SR).

139 UN Doc E/67 IV.15, 1968, p. 44.

140 Ollenu (n 15) 9.

government. English common law was the only law they knew. It superseded the savage and barbaric customs of indigenous people. Therefore, they extended its scope over their territories. The local bar defied several attempts to codify the criminal law. Accordingly, English law, as it existed in the eighteenth to nineteenth centuries (credited with more than 200 capital crimes),[141] was imported to Sierra Leone.[142]

This law was coupled with a certain dose of racial discrimination. The prosecution of non-natives for capital crimes ought first to be subjected to the Governor's fiat.[143] Fortunately the first interpretation of this exception in the *Sard* case led the court to conclude that its application would obstruct the course of justice as the 'effect would be to give no court jurisdiction in cases in which a non-native is charged with a capital offence in the Protectorate except upon a fiat of the Governor'.[144]

Before 1959 (two years before the independence), Sierra Leone had tried four cases of murder. Two defendants were sentenced to death[145] and the other two had their charges reduced to manslaughter.[146] In excluding the charge of murder, the death penalty was automatically excluded. It is evident that the death penalty was not a favoured punishment in Sierra Leone. Like Liberia, Sierra Leone was very attached to the idea of freedom and liberty.

The colony of Ghana was created in 1874 and it was strongly advised that while waiting for the adoption of a criminal code, the English common law be applied.[147] The Queensland penal code inspired the Ghanaian criminal code of 1892.[148] While it was recommended that all of British West Africa adopt the code, only Ghana took action. Its large list of capital crimes and the harshness of its punishments created a high number of opponents to its adoption in Ghana. Morris remarks that the African intelligentsia of the west coast was profoundly suspicious of the code and they bitterly opposed it.[149] Indeed, the code was suspected of imposing heavy punishments and creating easy opportunity for applying arbitrary measures.

In practice however, the Ghanaian courts demonstrated little inclination towards death sentences. Capital punishment lay dormant in the statute until the 1950s. Death sentences passed down and executed in Ghana (Gold Coast) in the period 1950–1955 are given in Figure 4.3.

---

141 Leon Radzinowicz, *A History of English Criminal Law and its Administration from 1750*, vol 1 (Stevens and Sons, London 1948) 4–5.

142 Morris (n 112) 10–13. See also Elias T Olewale, *Ghana and Sierra Leone: The Development of their Laws and Constitution* (Stevens and Sons, London 1962) 304–305.

143 Section 36 of the Protectorate Courts Jurisdiction Ordinance, no 16 of 1932.

144 *Rex v. Sard* (1935) A.L.R. 395 at 400–401.

145 *Kanu, Seisay and Koroma v. Regina* (1959) A.L.R. 331 at 336.

146 *Rex v. Sard* (1935) A.L.R. 395 at 400–401 and *Yebema v. Regina* (1959) A.L.R. 235 at 237.

147 Morris (n 112) 7.

148 'Legislation-Ghana' (1961) 5 *Journal of African Law* 157, 157.

149 Morris (n 112) 6.

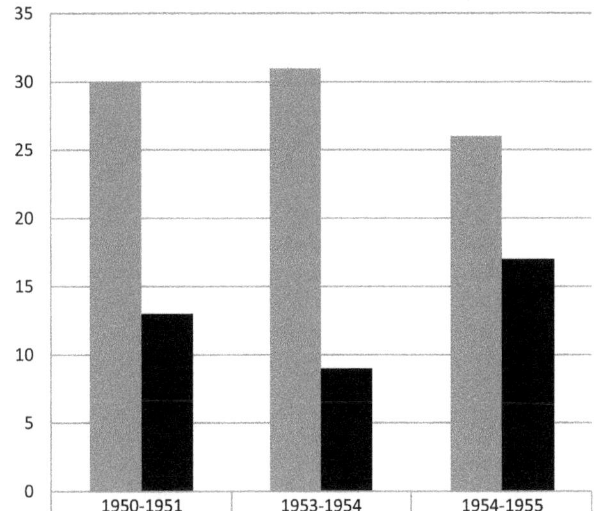

	1950-1951	1953-1954	1954-1955
Confirmed death sentences	30	31	26
Persons executed	13	9	17

Figure 4.3 The practice of the death penalty in Gold Coast (1950–1955)
Source: Robert B Seidman and JD Abaka Eyison, 'Ghana' in Alan Milner (ed), *African Penal Systems* (Routledge and Kegan Paul, London 1969) 75.

Even though justice was still modelled on the British concept of deterrence,[150] reviews of sentences by the executive and clemency saved almost half of the convicts. From 1950 to 1955 only 30 per cent of those convicted of capital crimes were executed. It is worth noting that before and even after the 1950s, courts frequently used their discretionary power to reduce a charge of murder to manslaughter so as to exclude the possibility of imposing the death sentence.[151]

Until 1950, the courts dealt more with economic crimes, largely the theft of cocoa nuts and the smuggling of mineral stones. Does this imply the absence of murders in Ghana or is it an indication of the coloniser's disinterest in such crimes and their punishments? Paragraph 3 of the Bond of 1884 had already provided for a dual system of English law alongside customary law in homicide cases. The absence of recorded cases in law reports leads to the conclusion that capital crimes did not interest the colonisers. Native courts dealt with them. Under British rule, legal problems between Africans fell within the bounds of native law.[152]

150 ibid 66.

151 *Rex v. Kwamina Afferi* (1926) G.C.L.R. 197 at 201.

152 Kodzo AP Kludze, *Chieftaincy in Ghana* (Austin and Winfield, Lanham 2000) 433.

However, from 1948, criminal law and its punishments (mainly the death penalty) played a huge role in the fight to quell social and political unrest in Ghana.[153] The sudden rise in death penalty cases corresponded to the use of capital punishment against political agitators to prevent them spreading the ideology of liberation and contaminating the populace.

British barristers holding offices as magistrates in Nigeria applied English common law from 1886 onwards, although that law was confined to foreigners.[154] The first principle of Regulation X provided that in 'criminal cases to which a foreigner is a party, the general principles of law and procedure shall be, as far as is practicable, similar to those in usage in Great Britain or other European States …'.[155] Section 2 of the regulation extended the application of the death penalty to foreigners. To avoid 'international complication', London had to confirm any such punishment before its execution. Those sentenced to death remained on death row until British authorities confirmed the death sentence.[156] 'Foreigners' were citizens from 'civilized states' other than those from Britain. British settlers in Lagos were therefore allowed to impose the death penalty on natives. The only safeguard for Africans was that the execution had to be reported by post in London.[157]

In 1900, British authorities reiterated that the common law of England applied in Nigeria.[158] Consecutive alteration and abrogation of the existing legislation would leave it intact.[159] Until 1904, there were only two capital crimes: treason and murder. Later, the British proposal to introduce the Ghana penal code in Lagos produced a storm of protest as it created new crimes and punishments. The penal code adopted for Northern Nigeria in 1904 resulted from a symbiosis of different codes largely based on the Queensland penal code and textbooks.[160] Its revised version was extended to the whole country in 1916.[161] The practice of the death penalty in colonial Nigeria was, however, negligible up to 1948. The law reports indicate that not one single capital case was confirmed before then. Paradoxically,

153 Henrietta JAN Mensa-Bonsu, '"Political Crimes" in the Political History of Ghana: 1948–1993' in Henrietta Mensa-Bonsu et al., *Ghana Law since Independence: History, Development and Prospects* (Black Mask, Accra 2007) 239.

154 The Charter of the Royal Niger Company of 10 July 1886.

155 Section D (1) of Regulation X: the General Principles of the Administration of Justice to Foreigners as reproduced in Henry C Gollan, 'Modes of Legislation in the British Colonies: Northern Nigeria' (1905) 6 *Journal of Comparative Legislation* 129, 130.

156 Section D (2) of Regulation X: the General Principles of the Administration of Justice to Foreigners as reproduced in Gollan, ibid.

157 Section C (3) of Regulation X: the General Principles of the Administration of Justice to Foreigners as reproduced in Gollan, ibid.

158 Section 34 of the Protectorate Courts Proclamation of 1900.

159 Protectorate Courts Proclamation of 1900 as modified by the Supreme Court Proclamation of 1902, and later repealed by the Provincial Courts Proclamation of 1902.

160 Morris (n 112) 9.

161 HF Morris, 'How Nigeria Got its Criminal Code' (1970) 14 *Journal of African Law* 137, 153.

from 1948 to 1960 death sentences increased to a level of, in some years, 90 per cent of homicide cases (see Figure 4.4).

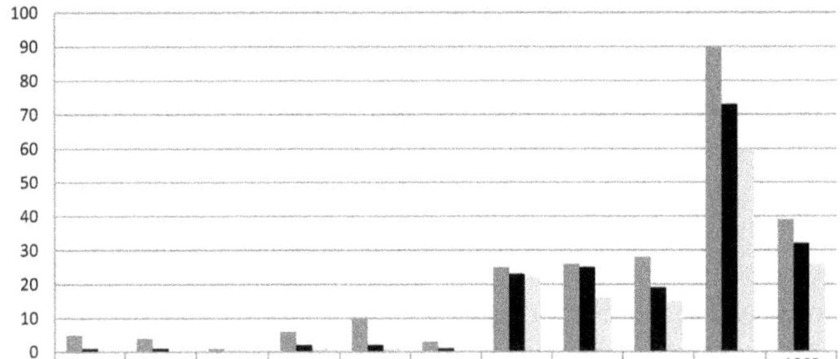

	1941-1942	1943-1944	1945-1947	1948-1950	1950-1953	1954-1955	1956	1957	1958	1959	1960 (until 1st Oct.)
Criminal cases	5	4	1	6	10	3	25	26	28	90	39
Homicide cases	1	1	0	2	2	1	23	25	19	73	32
Confirmed death sentences	0	0	0	1	1	0	22	16	15	60	26

Figure 4.4 The practice of the death penalty in colonial Nigeria (1941–1960)
Source: Nigerian Law Report (1881–1955) and Supreme Court of Nigeria Law Reports (1956–1960).

The fact that murder was the highest grade of Native and *Shari'a* courts' jurisdiction explains the absence of capital cases before 1947.[162] These courts were often perceived as being better able to reach the truth than a British court. They were more familiar with native modes of thought. This also complied with the indirect rule policy.[163] The death penalty had always existed under both indigenous law and *Shari'a* in Nigeria for witchcraft, murder, adultery, profaning gods and habitual theft. Methods of execution included hanging, stoning, killing by identical means or burying alive. Unfortunately, Native courts kept no record of capital cases during the colonial rule.

On occasions, however, Western judges resorted to legal technicalities such as insufficient evidence, provocation, irregular procedure and so on to impose more lenient punishments in cases that would otherwise attract capital punishment. This practice was common between 1881 and 1942. The case of *Lamidi Balogun*, a lorry driver who collided with a cyclist illustrates this. The cyclist was heavily injured and fell unconscious. The driver carried the injured cyclist and his bike to a bush some miles away from the scene of the accident, washed all traces

162 *Regina v. Ibrahim and two others* (1954) 20 N.L.R. 137.

163 C Clifton Roberts, *Tangled Justice: Some Reasons for a Change of Policy in Africa* (Macmillan, London 1937) 136.

of blood away with petrol and ordered his assistants to keep the secret. During several interrogations, he made no mention of the cyclist. The cyclist was found during a police search and died a few minutes later at the hospital. The prosecutor insisted that the driver's conduct after the accident amounted to malice, itself leading to a charge of murder. However, the court stated that the driver was only suppressing all signs of the accident and injury to the cyclist and was not expecting unconsciousness to result in the cyclist's death.[164]

In the *Francis Ojifo* case, the accused ran after the soon-to-be-deceased man who fell into a drain. The accused fatally stabbed the victim in the left side under the ribs. In considering whether there was provocation, the court stated that educated and civilised persons should be distinguished from uneducated primitive peasants, whose passion is uncontrollable. The court went on to state that 'possibly a more civilized and enlightened person might be able to curb his anger, but in the case of a more primitive and unenlightened person, [any reasonable man] would in all probability act as the accused did'.[165] Accordingly, the accused was convicted of manslaughter.

In 1944, the court convicted *Nwonwu Nshi* of manslaughter. The accused had murdered the police officer who was attempting to arrest him for theft with an irregular arrest warrant. The judge excluded the charge of murder on the grounds that the deceased's defective arrest warrant excluded any possibility of premeditation in the part of the accused.[166]

This situation prevailed until 1951 when a group of co-perpetrators who had submitted a suspected wizard to an ordeal test who died afterwards were sentenced to death.[167] The court had reasons to avoid the above legal technicalities. It was influenced by the ruling of the East African Court of Appeal, which systematically rejected the defence of provocation in cases of murder against witches.[168] It is also worth noting that in 1951 political unrest had driven the courts to use law to make people obey. Political events in Kenya and Ghana were sufficient to justify supposedly intimidating punishments. From 1954, modern courts and particularly the newly created National Supreme Court of Nigeria started dealing with cases that previously fell within Native courts' jurisdiction. Their decision revealed the true picture of modern justice. The highest ever number of death sentences was passed (nearly 92 per cent of all murder cases) in 1956.

There is no explanation for the shift. However, courts discovered that imposing the death penalty was legitimate, timely and justified. In 1957, out of 15 cases of murder, only one was reduced to manslaughter. Fourteen others (93 per cent) were

164 *Rex v. Lamidi Balugon* (1942) 16 N.L.R. 75 at 75–80.

165 *Rex v. Francis Ojifo* (1942) 16 N.L.R. 63 at 63–66 and *Rex v James Ojifo* (1944) 17 N.L.R. 99 at 102.

166 *Rex v. Nwonwu Nshi* (1944) 17 N.LR. 103 at 107.

167 *Rex v. Uko and Another* (1951) 20 N.L.R. 16 at 16.

168 See for example the ruling in *Rex v. James Adekanmi* (1946) 17 E.A.C.A. 99 at 101.

sentenced to death. The 1959 political unrest became the excuse for increasing the number of death sentences against political fanatics. These defendants were often tried and sentenced to death as a group.[169]

The court systematically overruled its previous decisions as regards the death penalty and rejected defences of provocation, insanity, youth and violation of criminal procedure. It referred consideration of mitigating circumstances to the Privy Council or to the Executive.[170] On refusing leave for appeal in the *Abdu Kadiri* case, the court added that 'we desire to say that, in our view, there are strong extenuating circumstances in this case, the more so if regard be had to the applicant's youth and condition in life. This will, no doubt, be taken into account by the Executive Authority at the appropriate time'.[171] In ruling so, the court departed from both its practice and that of the East African Court of Appeal, which had repeatedly excluded the death penalty for juvenile offenders.[172]

The Legacy of English Colonial Law

In British-controlled zones, colonial law remained a means to bend Africans to their master's will. For this reason, the law had to be flexible enough to meet the ever-changing realities on the ground. Any deviation from colonial instructions justified harsh punishments, and if necessary, harsher than the law prescribed. The Southern Africa region, which fell primarily under Roman Dutch law, escaped the harshness of English colonial administration.

The right to equal treatment before the law was not suited to deal with a childish, primitive and savage race characterised by a passion for crimes. Discrimination and racism were ingredients of English law. Britain only started lessening the appearance of inequality before the law but without outlawing inequality. 'The "lower orders" of society had to believe that the law was, by and large, unbiased.'[173] During colonial times, discrimination between aristocrats and commoners, men and women, juniors and elders was in vogue in England as among settlers in colonies. They only shared the common illusion of belonging to 'a superior race'.[174] Therefore, English law was not expected to fit the condition of an unsophisticated African. Accordingly, there was no need to find convincing evidence to ensure that the offender was a criminal. For example, instructions were even issued in East Africa to try 'cases according to substantial justice without regard to technicalities

169 *Queen v. Amoo* (1959) S.C.N.L.R. 272 at 278.

170 *Queen v. Kadiri* (1958) S.C.N.L.R. 25 at 26–27.

171 ibid 27.

172 *Rex v. Mvula s/o Irove* (1944) 11 E.A.C.A. 112 and *Rex v. Kulabirawo* (1947) 14 E.A.C.A. 116.

173 Brett Shadle, 'White Settlers and the Law in Early Colonial Kenya' (2010) 4 *Journal of Eastern African Studies* 510, 511.

174 Will Jackson, 'White Man's Country: Kenya Colony and the Making of a Myth' (2011) 5 *Journal of Eastern African Studies* 344, 344–368.

of procedure'.[175] Avoiding technicalities meant that 'proving the offence according to the ordinary rules of evidence should be disregarded' in order to impose a 'sharp, swift and effective punishment'.[176]

Crimes against Europeans and political crimes – or supposedly so – inferred the savage nature of people who rejected the obvious truth of the superiority of the white race and the goodness entrenched in the civilising mission of colonisation. Society needed, therefore, to be cleaned of any germ of opposition and if necessary by way of capital punishment. The law had therefore to ensure that the African remained subordinate and white interests were protected. In practice, the law set up three dimensions of criminality: intra-African crimes, intra-white crimes and anti-white crimes. In all colonies where the coloniser had the opportunity of extending and effectively applying its rule, an anti-white offence called for a mandatory capital punishment whereas legal technicalities applied to other categories. This justified the increase of capital punishment during anti-colonial revolts in Nyasaland, Kenya and Ghana. In theory, the French colonial policy was no different.

The Death Penalty in French Colonial Africa

The history of French colonial law and policy in Africa remains the most complex of all the colonisers'. Public institutions and the government were regularly restructured; individual colonies were created, modified, abolished and at times recreated.[177] At the same time, excessive tergiversation in Paris between the executive and the legislative regarding who should be regulating colonial affairs prevailed.[178] However, these problems did not hinder the centralisation of legislative power that became their governing principle during the entire colonial period. This meant that the body of laws applicable in French colonies in Africa emanated from the metropolis. Accordingly, French criminal law as it was exported to Africa largely contained nothing adapted to the local environment. It was a projection of what was in vogue in France.

All major French legal principles and methods of interpretation were transplanted to the colonies. This was not necessarily because of a lack of imagination but rather for reasons of assimilation.[179] Regardless of the motive behind this centralisation, former French colonies and protectorates in Africa have until now failed to wipe out the colonial system.

175 Shadle (n 174) 514.

176 ibid 514–515.

177 Jeswald W Salacuse, *An Introduction to Law in French-Speaking Africa, vol I: Africa South of the Sahara* (The Michie Company, Charlottesville 1969) 10.

178 ibid 13–16.

179 Michel Jeol, *Droit public Africain* (Berger-Levrault, Paris 1967) 14.

Therefore, a study of the death penalty in former French colonies cannot fail to acknowledge that legal and criminological developments in France strengthened the distaste for the death penalty in French colonial Africa. Paradoxically, a study of this kind is in essence a study of the French penal system itself as progressively shaped by new thoughts leading to changes in attitudes towards capital punishment until most African countries achieved their independence in the 1960s.

The Scope of the Death Penalty in French Colonial Law

Senegal was the first to become a French colony in Africa. This is because of its commercial ties with France, which had been in place since 1368. In the nineteenth century, politics led to West Africa becoming a strategic zone for France. In 1822, France exported its judicial organisation to Senegal with the sole exception that two natives sat on the bench of both the tribunal of first instance and the Council, which was at most a court of appeal. These courts had jurisdiction over serious criminal cases.[180] In 1877, France exported its penal code of 1810 (as it had been amended) to Senegal through specific legislation.[181]

Undoubtedly, the French penal code of 1810 was not the best of the Napoleonic codes. In addition to its structure being awkward because it dealt with punishments before offences, it was substantially based on pre-revolutionary ideologies. This was reflected in the harshness of its punishments for a considerable range of offences.[182] Before the French Revolution of 1789, there were nearly 100 capital crimes in French penal law. This was reduced to 32 in 1791.[183] The adoption of the 1810 penal code was not good news. The code had totally ignored the Parliamentary debate on abolition and it had widened the number of capital crimes from 32 to 36.[184]

Article 7 of the 1810 penal code made the death penalty its most severe punishment.[185] The method of execution was beheading through a ritual process that elicited more excitement in France than it did in all neighbouring countries.[186] Article 12 of the code expressly referred to the guillotine. It provided that 'Every

---

180 Eugene Hild, *L'organisation judiciaire en Afrique Occidentale Française* (Emile Larousse, Paris 1912) 65–67.

181 *Bulletin d'Outre-Mer*, 1877, p. 326.

182 Catherine Elliot, *French Criminal Law* (Willan Publishing, Devon 2001) 9.

183 Pierre Bouzat, *Traité de droit pénal et de criminologie, Tome I: Droit pénal general* (Dalloz, Paris 1970) 439.

184 ibid.

185 Article 7 of the Code Pénal Français (Loi décrétée le 12 février 1810 et promulguée le 22 février 1810) in Hyppolyte F Rivière, *Codes français et lois usuelles* (A. Maresq Aine 1970).

186 Jean Imbert, 'La peine de mort et l'opinion au XVIIIème siècle' (1964) 19 *Revue de science criminelle et de droit pénal comparé* 509, 509.

person condemned to death will be beheaded'.[187] The guillotine was the most famous technology developed in the context of judicial killing since 1792 and was praised as 'the progress of French civilization'.[188]

The code reinforced the dehumanising process that parricide criminals went through. Amputation of the hands preceded the execution. Amputation and the death penalty were among the harsh punishments that survived the revolution.[189] The only clothing authorised for parricide criminals was a shirt, they were to be barefoot and their head covered with a black veil as they walked towards the place of execution.[190] In 1832, new amendments introduced compulsory public exposure of the condemned before execution and a public reading of the execution warrant.[191] Families intending to bury their relatives were not entitled to record the event.[192]

Furthermore, the code largely remained mute on breastfeeding women and mentally disturbed people. There was only a short reference to pregnant women. Their executions were suspended until delivery, provided the woman had declared her pregnancy.[193] She was only given just enough time to deliver. It remained within the state's discretion to determine the day of execution. Nothing stopped this from being the same day of delivery.

Another concern was the rigidity regarding the execution of mentally disturbed offenders. Article 64 that made *dementia* a criminal defence did not cover people who became mentally disturbed after committing the crime.[194] Their mental disturbance had to be concomitant with the crime. Otherwise, the offender would not escape criminal responsibility.

The code of 1810 was a pitiless legislation that aimed to enforce individual obedience. The death penalty was a potential punishment for all kinds of offences: political offences, offences against life, offences against bodily integrity, economic crimes and offences against public welfare. Book III dealt with political offences that were punishable by death. These were treason, spying, *lèse-majesté*, attempting to overthrow the government, provoking a civil war, mutiny, destroying public property (vessels, stores, buildings and so on) by means of military weapons and commending mutiny groups.[195]

Voluntary homicide in its various forms, namely aggravated murder, assassination, parricide, poisoning and infanticide, constituted the second group

187 '[t]out condamné à mort aura la tête tranchée'. See article 12 of the Code Pénal Français (n 185).

188 Robin Bidwell, *Morocco under Colonial Rule: French Administration of Tribal Areas 1912–1956* (Frank Cass, London 1973) 267.

189 Bouzat (n 183) 438.

190 Article 13 of the Code Pénal Français (n 185).

191 Loi du 28 Avril 1832.

192 Article 64 of the Code Pénal Français (n 185).

193 Article 27 of the Code Pénal Français, ibid.

194 Article 27 of the Code Pénal Français, ibid.

195 Articles 75–79, 86–86 and 91–97 of the Code Pénal Français, ibid.

of capital crimes.[196] Murder was considered to be aggravated when it occurred in conjunction with another offence.[197] An example of this would be a robber getting rid of a witness. When the offender resorted to torture or barbaric acts in carrying out the murder, the crime shifted from murder to assassination and was punishable by death.[198]

As regards economic crimes, counterfeiting, forgery and theft were capital crimes.[199] During the same century, special laws extended the death penalty to the mistreatment of children with intention to kill, arson of an inhabited premises, sequestration accompanied with torture, perjury and desertion of a soldier to the enemy. Navy and railways police laws also imposed the death penalty for barratry, piracy and intentionally provoked fatal accidents.[200]

Contrary to public opinion and the majority views of liberal philosophers who had adopted ideas of Cesaria Beccaria,[201] attempts were punished as heavily as successfully-executed crimes.[202] Article 82 of the code specifically reiterated that attempt to commit treason and spying were capital crimes.[203] This applied to both repeat offenders and accomplices.[204]

Moreover, efforts to abolish the death penalty in France before and during colonisation failed. Conservatism added to political unrest and wars had already convinced many abolitionist pioneers to reintroduce capital punishment.[205] In 1791, the French Parliament rejected, for false pretexts,[206] Lepelletier de Saint-Fargeau's first proposal of abolition in peacetime. Certainly, the rejection of the proposal gave deputies sufficient time for abolitionist arguments to mature. Four years later (1795), Parliament approved the abolition of the death penalty after a proclamation of general peace. Unfortunately, this conditional abolition was not acknowledged by the judiciary, which maintained the *status quo*.[207] In 1801, Parliament ended the regime of ambiguity in adopting a unique article that stated: 'The death penalty will remain of application in cases it is provided for by the law until otherwise decided.'[208]

Efforts to abrogate the 1810 penal code repeatedly failed until 1994. Isolated amendments updated it to fit with new social realities and chiefly softened its repressive regime. The 1832 amendment was the first to have a significant

196 Article 302 of the Code Pénal Français, ibid.

197 Article 304 of the Code Pénal Français, ibid.

198 Article 303 of the Code Pénal Français, ibid.

199 Articles 132 and 381 of the Code Pénal Français, ibid.

200 Bouzat (n 183) 439–440.

201 ibid 92 and Imbert (n 186).

202 Article 2 of Dispositions Préliminaires du Code Pénal Français (n 185).

203 Article 82 of the Code Pénal Français, ibid.

204 Article 56, para 7 and article 59 of the Code Pénal Français, ibid.

205 Bouzat (n 183) 441.

206 Imbert (n 186).

207 ibid 525.

208 Loi du 8 Nivose an X (29 décembre 1801) as quoted by Imbert, ibid.

impact on the code. It humanised its repressive regime by introducing judicial mitigating circumstances and abolishing capital punishment for economic crimes. To strengthen this reform, article 5 of the 1848 Constitution abolished the death penalty for political crimes as well.[209] In 1901, the death penalty was abolished for infanticide when perpetrated by the mother. By 1941, infanticide was no longer a capital offence.

Other amendments were made to polish up this softening process but none dared to extend the scope of abolition. This reticence is justified by the fact that crimes perpetrated during war and post-war delinquency required tough punishments.[210] In France and in the French colonies, the death penalty remained a valid punishment for the majority of ordinary but 'serious' crimes such as parricide, assassination, poisoning, mistreatment of children with intention to kill, sequestration accompanied by torture, arson of an inhabited building and perjury when it had had the effect of condemning an innocent person to death.[211] In 1937, the death penalty was extended to punish the kidnapping of children when this was followed by the child's death and to military desertion, piracy, barratry and the provoking of train or boat accidents.[212]

This was how the death penalty existed in French law until 1981 when France repealed the death penalty. Although African colonies received French law differently, its substance remained almost unchanged. However, in practice the *jurés* and the executive played a memorable role in saving the condemned from the guillotine. Some French presidents, especially Felix Faure, Loubet and Fallieres, systematically pardoned all those condemned to death.[213]

The Expansion of the French Penal Law in Africa

French Guinea received the Senegalese penal legislation in 1892.[214] Dahomey and Ivory Coast received it in 1894.[215] Introducing colonial law in this way meant that amendments to the penal law in one country could not affect the law in another country. This complex system ended in 1901 when a decree re-extended the Senegalese penal legislation to Dahomey, French Guinea and Ivory Coast.[216] This meant that a single piece of legislation could amend laws throughout the whole of

209 Ancel and Marx (n 6) 632.

210 ibid.

211 Bouzat (n 183) 439.

212 ibid 440.

213 ibid. See also Michel Forst, 'The Abolition of the Death Penalty in France' in *The Death Penalty: Abolition in Europe* (Council of Europe Publishing, Strasbourg 1999) 105–116.

214 Article 23 of the Decree of 11 May 1892, PENANT (1892).

215 See respectively article 23, para 3 of the Decree of 26 July 1894, PENANT (1894) and article 23, para 6 of the Decree of 16 December 1896, PENANT III, 17 (1897).

216 Article 17, para 10 of the Decree of the 6 August 1901, PENANT III, 117 (1901).

French West Africa. The 1901 decree was modified in 1902 and 1904 (although this was never enforced) but the substance of the reception provision remained untouched.[217] The 1902 decree was thus the basic reception statute of the French penal law for the whole of West Africa. France did not acquire new territories but formed new colonies within the territorial boundaries of its original four colonies.

This technique was very pragmatic. It bore fruitful results in French Equatorial Africa and in territories entrusted to France by virtue of the League of Nations mandate and United Nations trusteeships. The trading, refuelling and missionary stations created in Gabon had resulted in the control of the whole interior of Central Africa, which was renamed French Congo. It received the Senegalese penal legislation in 1878.[218] The 1903 law organising the Congo justice system reinforced the Gabonese decree.[219] In 1910, French Congo became a federation of French Equatorial Africa comprising Gabon, Congo, Chad and Central African Republic. Each country applied the Senegalese penal legislation. Cameroon and Togo were not colonies rather territories under United Nations trusteeship. Legislation in force in French Equatorial Africa before 1 January 1924 was extended to Cameroon, while legislation in force in French West Africa before the 22 May 1924 became applicable in Togo.

In Algeria, France directly extended its penal code and *Code d'Instruction Criminelle* in 1830. These laws were applicable to Europeans and Arabs alike. Similar to the British in Kenya, the French managed Algeria as a French province. Any method of maintaining the native's obedience was justifiable. French justice in Algeria was oppressive and repressive.[220] Algeria applied the colonial penal legislation until 1966.[221]

The French penal code and *Code d'Instruction Criminelle* were introduced in Tunisia in 1913 and 1921 respectively. Independent Tunisia later found no interest in modifying its penal law and kept it intact for decades.[222] The situation in Morocco was different where the scope of French penal law was very limited. France failed to expand its penal legislation on *indigènes* that were used to the *Makhzen*.[223] Moroccans maintained a mixed law based on *Shari'a*, native customs, individual statutes, individual cases and judicial discretion. The course of the death penalty continued as it had existed before French influence.

217 Article 17, para 11 of the Decree of the 15 April 1902 PENANT III, 122 (1902). See also Salacuse (n 178) 24.

218 Article 14 of the Decree of 1 June 1878, *Bulletin des Lois* (12 Ser), pt. II at 553.

219 Article 17 of the Decree of 17 March 1903 PENANT III, 118 (1903).

220 Salacuse (n 177) 192.

221 ibid.

222 ibid 504.

223 The *makhzen* is conceived as a social ideology and particularly as a life style or a way of acting that is resorted to when the state cannot fulfil its mission. See Rachida Cherifi, *Le makhzen politique au Maroc: hier et aujourd'hui* (Afrique-Orient, Casablanca 1988).

The Policy of the Death Penalty in French Colonial Africa

Until 1946, the French coloniser resorted to dual penal justice. The personal jurisdiction of criminal courts was limited to French citizens and those assimilated. The majority of *indigènes* were subjected to the authority of administrative authorities. Two distinct institutions, namely the *tribunaux indigènes* and *jurisdictions pénales spéciales*, were successively resorted to for delivering penal justice to these *indigènes* whose inferior status did not allow them to enjoy the justice administered to citizens and those assimilated.[224]

The *Code d'indigénat* is the most criticised French colonial policy in Africa.[225] The *tribunaux indigènes* had jurisdiction over indigenous offences (anthropophagi, violation of tombs, forced marriage – corresponding to *rapt* in French – and abduction)[226] and over disciplinary offences (unauthorised meetings, travelling without a pass, disrespect towards Europeans, offensive language and so on).[227] Punishments for these offences included imprisonment, sequestration, forced displacement of the offender, forfeiture of property and, the most controversial, a collective fine or banishment.[228] Administrative authorities were entitled to create offences and punishment or extend the existing punishments to new offences.

The indigenisation of law was part of an effort to maintain pre-colonial law, while bringing it closer to European civilisation. It was indigenous justice as rethought, organised and supervised by the coloniser who never stopped reframing and altering it. The codification of indigenous law resulted in its transformation and most likely in its suppression.

This French policy attracted strong criticism from scholars and rightly so. The *Code d'indigénat* allowed for a flagrant violation of the principles of legality and individual responsibility, that were dear to French law.[229] Its only merit was the absence of the death penalty in its provisions. Until their repeal in 1946,[230] the *tribunaux indigènes* had never had the power to try capital cases. The French *Cour de Cassation* insisted that the death penalty was not part of the power entrusted to administrative authorities under the *Code d'indigénat*. In 1943, a self-appointed *Controlleur Civil* in Tunisia decreed that henceforth economic crimes and vandalism were capital crimes and criminals would be tried as if they were caught in *flagrante delicto* before courts martial. This meant a speedy procedure. A few

224 Jean Châtelain, 'Le régime disciplinaire et pénal des populations indigènes' (1947) 1 *Revue juridique et politique de l'union française* 84, 84–85.

225 Roger Germain, *La politique indigène du Bugeaud* (Larose, Paris 1955) 288–289.

226 Châtelain (n 224) 86.

227 Germain (n 225) 291.

228 ibid 292; Châtelain (n 224).

229 J Chabas, 'La sanction pénale des actes réglementaires pris par les représentants du gouvernement dans les départements et les territoires d'outre- mer' (1948) 2 *Revue juridique et politique de l'union française* 29, 29–36.

230 Decree of 30 April 1946, *Journal Officiel*, 1 mai 1946, at p. 3680.

days later, a Tunisian tribunal in Sousse imposed the death penalty for pillage on four thieves and directed the gendarmes to carry out the sentence immediately. It is certain that the tribunal had no material jurisdiction over pillage just as it was not competent to decide who should execute the death penalty or when the execution should take place.[231]

The *Cour de Cassation* ruled that the death sentence was illegal as the tribunal had assumed power beyond its jurisdiction. The *Cour de Cassation* was seized for orienting French jurisprudence.[232] Even when trying indigenous people, French courts were bound to observe French law.[233] Under French law, neither simple theft nor keeping stolen property were capital crimes unless accompanied by aggravating circumstances.[234]

Moreover, Muslim courts in Tunisia and Algeria (the Cadis) had completely lost their jurisdiction over capital crimes from 1842.[235] Such crimes fell within the jurisdiction of French courts regardless of the offender's origin or religion.[236] The only exception to this was Morocco. According to a 1913 *Dahir*, only the Sultan could impose the death penalty, a punishment that had become rare. Moroccans resisted the introduction of the guillotine until 1928. In interpreting the 1913 *Dahir*, the French *Cour de Cassation* stated that within the French Empire, French tribunals had jurisdiction over all crimes.[237]

These efforts were in line with the coloniser's policy of assimilation, which was perfected with the abrogation of the *indigénat* system. This created an environment favourable to the expansion of French penal law to all individuals liable for petty or serious offences. The *Cour de Cassation* played a major role in keeping uniformity of the law as applied by different colonial entities. An appeal to the *Cour de Cassation* became recommended in all serious cases and compulsory in all capital cases.[238] Thus, in ordering the execution of the death penalty within 24 hours, the Tunisian judge deprived the offenders of their rights to appeal and breached the fundamental rules that presided over the functioning of criminal tribunals in French territories.

231 Cour de Cassation (Chambre Criminelle) 12 juillet 1946.

232 ibid.

233 Article 39 of the Decree of 26 September 1842.

234 Article 381 of the Code Pénal Français (n 185).

235 Germain (n 225) 297–299. Hocine Bouzaher states that the decree became operational from the 17 July 1843. See Hocine Bouzaher, *La justice répressive dans l'Algérie coloniale 1830–1962* (Houma, Algiers 2004) 49.

236 Article 42 of the Décret du 26 septembre 1842 (Tunisia) and article 49 of the Décret du 28 février 1841 (Algeria).

237 Cour de Cassation (Chambre Criminelle) 6 octobre 1955.

238 Cour de Cassation (Chambre Criminelle) 12 juillet 1946.

The Example of French Justice in Algeria

French colonial justice left behind a bitter legacy in Algeria. Petty offences were severely punished. Algerian tribes were regularly sentenced to long-lasting collective fines for arson of forestry or revolt.[239] The 63 million franc fine imposed on all the Kabyles in 1887 caused lasting suffering. Many were forced to sell their lands and livestock as a result of the punishment. The consequence was long-term impoverishment.[240] Capricious governors would even hand down the death penalty for trivial offences. In 1831, the Governor passed a decree punishing public noise with death when the convicted person was serving a sentence of banishment and returned to Algeria.[241] It is likely that the noise that incurred the punishment was made during prayer. In 1941, another decree made it a capital crime to walk in the night while armed. All these crimes came under the court martial's jurisdiction.[242]

The hardship of these French laws was exacerbated with the Algerian Revolution against which France reacted by applying special laws that introduced unprecedented procedures and increased death sentences.[243] In addition to a plethora of emergency measures and extrajudicial executions,[244] the French administration reviewed 50 articles of the penal code, the code of criminal procedure and the code of military justice to contain the revolt. Article 59 of the new penal code specifically extended the death penalty to members of 'criminal associations'.[245] This provision targeted members of political and social movements. The mere suspicion that a person belonged to such a political movement became sufficient to justify the death penalty.

Mohamed Bouras, founder of the Algerian Muslim Scouts, was sentenced to death in 1941 for allegedly spying on behalf of Germany.[246] In 1945, courts martial imposed a death sentence on 99 persons convicted of treason and ordered the immediate execution of 22 Algerians.[247] In 1946, the death sentence was imposed on 10 Algerians for the same crime. The executive refused to grant mercy. The sentence was immediately carried out.[248] In 1955, a peasant was sentenced to death and executed on the mere suspicion that he belonged to a political movement. In 1956, Boudjema Souidani was sentenced to death in absentia for having burnt

239 Germain (n 225) 291.

240 Olivier Le Cour Grandmaison, 'The Exception and the Rule: On French Colonial Law' (2006) 212 *Diogenes* 34, 46–47.

241 Article 2 of the Decree of 25 June 1831. See also Bouzaher (n 236) 72.

242 Article 8, para 3 of the Arreté de Bageaud of 6 March 1841. See also Bouzaher, ibid 77.

243 Salacuse (n 178) 192.

244 Bouzaher (n 235) 56 and 197.

245 ibid 55.

246 ibid 140.

247 ibid 143.

248 ibid 143–144.

a farm.[249] The court interpreted arson on a farm belonging to a French settler as being politically motivated.

France failed to acknowledge that the harshness of these punishments increased tensions. Algerians saw those executed as martyrs of liberty. Simultaneously, a mere assault justified a death sentence. In 1957, three people were sentenced to death for assault.[250] Statistics for the period 1958–1962 indicate the extent to which France realised too late that extending the death penalty only served to weaken the colonial administration (see Figure 4.5).

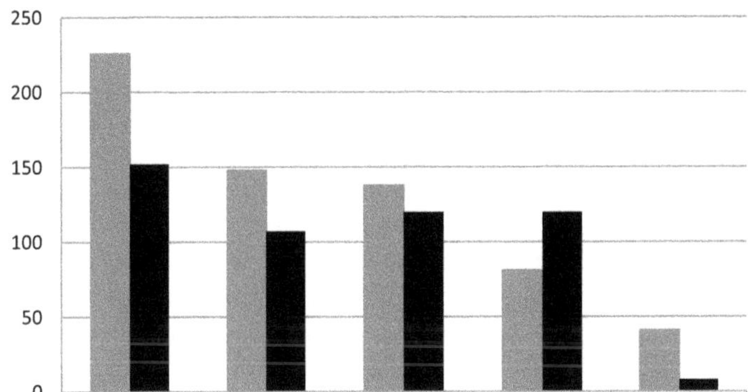

	1958	1959	1960	1961	1962
Number of cases	226	148	138	81	41
Death sentences	152	107	120	120	8

Figure 4.5 The death penalty for the five years before independence in Algeria
Source: Hocine Bouzaher, *La justice répressive dans l'Algérie coloniale 1830–1962* (Houma, Algiers 2004), 224.

People were often sentenced in a group. Only mercy, itself rare in the last five years of colonisation, saved the few who escaped hanging. Of the 272 requests for mercy in 1960, 200 were upheld. In 1961, out of 271 requests for mercy, 162 were granted and in 1962, out of 63 requests 33 were confirmed.[251] A French Parliamentary Commission reported that the system failed to meet the requirement of justice or efficiency.[252]

249 ibid 148.
250 ibid 148.
251 ibid 60.
252 ibid 49.

Despite the scarcity of comprehensive statistics in Algeria (as is the case in most French speaking countries), it appears that French policies in Algeria were not all that different from British policies in Kenya. Colonial laws were weapons against disrespect. *Le Courrier d'Oran* of 24 May 1882 observed that France had no other choice in the face of revolt than to adopt Moses' approach to Medianist Arabs. Moses executed all males and gave the remaining to his soldiers. 'The approach may look cruel to the eyes of people with short view, [however], it was rather intelligent.'[253]

This situation prevailed until specific territories achieved their independence. Two general standards were upheld: betrayal of French principles as contained in French law (legislation, case law and doctrine) was not tolerated and the death penalty (even for petty offences) was to be complied with when it served the purpose of colonial domination.

Contradiction in the French Legacy as Regards the Death Penalty

There is no doubt that, as regards the death penalty, France introduced the worse legislation in Africa. It exported anomalies and harsh punishments as they existed in the penal code of 1810. The movement of abolition that had started in France before the adoption of the code, however, prevented France from marrying the practice to theory in its colonies. The *Cour de Cassation* effectively played its role as the French justice referee in precluding French colonial authorities from abusing the *Code d'indigénat* that conceded them unlimited powers for petty offences. We should also acknowledge that the French executive often commuted death sentences to the extent that Dahomey, Ivory Coast and Togo preceded France to become *de facto* abolitionists.[254]

Nevertheless, that remained only so as long as the colonial enterprise was not shaken. Revolutionary movements brought the coloniser back to his original instinct. Armed with a pitiless penal code and emergency laws that empowered administrative authorities to create offences at their discretion, French colonial authorities in Algeria used capital punishment to eliminate freedom fighters, impose fear and extort obedience.

Judicial practice in French colonies, therefore, discloses opposing trends. On the one hand barbarian justice attempted to secure the Empire at any cost. On the other hand, judicial practice influenced by the French abolitionist movement accordingly limited the use of capital punishment. The latter was also the kind of justice practised by the Belgian coloniser.

253 ibid 19.

254 UN Doc E/67 IV.15, 1968, p. 69, at 252. For France see Forst (n 214).

Belgian Colonisation and the Death Penalty

Belgium did not tolerate a system inconsistent with its civilising and humanitarian policy. Therefore, criminal law played a dual role of maintaining order and installing colonial domination. A more human system progressively suppressed and replaced the primitive, savage and inhuman indigenous law. Belgian law was not, however, of unique origin. France occupied Belgium until 1815. Early attempts to amend the French penal code of 1810 systematically failed until 1867. Although the Belgian penal code was not a remake of classical doctrines present in the French code, subsequent amendments failed to do away with the underlying French criminal policy and were limited to softening the conditions of criminal responsibility and the harshness of punishments.[255] Congo received the Belgian penal code in 1888.[256]

Henceforth, serious offences and severe punishments such as the death penalty[257] fell within the jurisdiction of written law. Indigenous law was confined to petty offences. Belgium later extended the laws enforced in Congo to Ruanda-Urundi, which was successively placed under a League of Nations mandate[258] and United Nations trusteeship.[259] Article 3 of the law of 1925 extended all laws and decrees in force at that date in Congo to the newly acquired territory of Ruanda-Urundi.[260] Ruanda-Urundi simply received the new penal code of 1940 adopted for Congo.[261]

The Death Penalty in Belgian Colonial Law

The 1867 Belgian penal code provided the death penalty as its most severe punishment. Beheading in public and without record was the method of execution. It was prohibited to execute pregnant women and to carry out an execution on a public holiday. A church minister of choice could assist the offender and the family

255 Ancel and Marx (n 6) 177–180.

256 John Crabb, *The Legal System of Congo-Kinshasa* (The Michie Company, Charlottesville 1970) 63.

257 Article 87 ter of the Code Pénal du Congo-Belge tel que promulgué par le Décret du 26 mai 1888.

258 Exécution de l'article 22 du Traité de Versailles du 28 juin 1919 à travers la Décision de la Société des Nations du 31 août 1923 confirmant à S.M. le Roi des Belges le mandat sur le territoire de l'Est Africain, *Bulletin Officiel du Ruanda Urundi (B.O.R.U.)*, 2ème année, no 1, p. 1.

259 Chapters XII and XIII of the Charter of the United Nations (1945) AJIL Supp.190 (1945) CTS7.

260 Loi du 21 août 1925 portant union du territoire du Ruanda-Urundi et de la colonie du Congo Belge, *B.O.R.U.*, 3ème année, no 1, p. 10/178.

261 Code Pénal du 30 janvier 1940 in Léon Strouvens and Pierre Piron, *Codes et lois du Congo-Belge* (Larcier, Brussels 1948) 111–146. The Code was extended to Ruanda-Urundi by the Ordonnance du Ruanda-Urundi no 43/Just du 18 mai 1940, *B.O.R.U.*, 1940, p. 86.

could demand his body. Capital crimes were political offences, all categories of aggravated murder (assassination, parricide, infanticide, poisoning) and murder facilitating theft, extortion or shielding a criminal.[262]

In Congo, the exported legislation was tailored to the new territory's needs. In the 1888 Congolese penal code, offences were not classified on the criterion of the severity of the punishment. Even the 1909 reform proposal emphasised the need to introduce new offences, extend judges' power and tighten up the conditions around nominating judges over the need to restructure offences. According to the proposal, 'a long term imprisonment and mainly displacement of the offender who leaves the village where he was born [were] sufficient and satisfactory punishments'.[263]

Although the death penalty was a potential punishment, offenders enjoyed automatic appeal in all capital cases and the right to request mercy from the King of Belgium. No execution was carried out unless the king had refused mercy.[264] Hanging was the method of execution for civilians whereas soldiers faced a firing squad.[265] No specific provision prohibited recording the scene of an execution until 1936.[266] Later carrying out the death penalty on pregnant women also became prohibited. Public executions were outlawed as well. The executioner was further required to establish a record of the execution.[267]

The Congolese penal code punished accomplices and perpetrators differently. An accomplice in a capital crime was sentenced to a maximum of ten years' imprisonment.[268] The attempting and actual commission of an offence were placed on the same pedestal.[269] There was no clear justification for this severity. In Belgium, attempts (except those related to political offences)[270] carried lesser penalties than perpetrated offences, accomplices were not punished in the same way as perpetrators and there was no death penalty for junior offenders.[271] The only other place this kind of severity existed was in the French penal code of 1810. Prosecuting attempts this way was simply a revival of the famous French classical doctrine.

The legislator's lack of interest in political crimes indicates distaste for the death penalty. Even in Belgium, most death penalty provisions for political crimes

---

262 Articles 7–11, 101–103, 113–115, 118, 394–397 and 475 of the Loi du 8 juin 1867, *Moniteur Belge* du 9 juin 1867.

263 Arsène Detry, *Contribution à la reforme de la législation criminelle du Congo Belge* (La Meuse, Liège 1909) 29.

264 Mineur Garçon, *Commentaire du code pénal Congolais* (Larcier, Brussels 1947) 35.

265 Articles 5 and 6 (formerly articles 87 and 88 of the 1888 Decree) of Code pénal du 30 janvier 1940 (n 263). To be read with the Décret du Gouverneur Général du 9 avril 1898 later modified by Ordonnance no 11/37 du 24 janvier 1948.

266 Circulaire du 14 mai 1898 and Décret du 3 août 1936.

267 Articles 2 and 3 of the Ordinance of 24 January 1948.

268 Article 23, para 3 of the Code pénal du 30 janvier 1940 (n 261).

269 Article 4, para 2, of the Code pénal du 30 janvier 1940, ibid.

270 Article 120 of Loi du 8 juin 1867 (n 262).

271 Articles 52, 69 and 77 of the Loi du 8 juin 1867, ibid.

were introduced through special amendments during the First and Second World Wars.[272] The Congolese penal code started with life-threatening crimes. Here, only assassination and poisoning were capital crimes.[273] Assassination was defined as premeditated murder. The Elisabethville (Lubumbashi) Court of Appeal stressed that assassination required premeditation as a personal aggravating circumstance. Premeditation was not automatically extended to co-perpetrators and accomplices.[274] This distinction was very important. The court limited a blind application of the death penalty. Furthermore, *guet-apens* was not one of the defining elements of assassination. This meant that, since *guet-apens* often presupposes premeditation in practice,[275] the state's failure to prove premeditation excluded the charge of assassination. In other words, setting an ambush was not literally part of the crime of assassination. In the 1810 French penal code, *guet-apens* was part of the offence.[276] The Congolese code did not create infanticide and parricide as specific voluntary homicides.

Moreover, there was no death penalty for economic crimes. The death penalty remained discretionary for rape or arson. When the victim was dead, the court had the option of imposing death or life imprisonment.[277] Only two political crimes attracted the death penalty, treason and high treason. Article 182 which protected allies, did not create another crime of treason. It borrowed the incrimination in article 181, when an allied state was the victim.[278] There was only one single article in the military penal code that provided for the death penalty. It was provided for cowardice, treason, desertion in wartime and murder perpetrated by a junior soldier on his commander.[279]

The Congolese penal code was not as harsh as other colonial legislation in neighbouring countries. In Congo, judicial practices also revealed that courts did not make the death penalty an instrument of oppression

The Practice of the Death Penalty in Léopoldville (1935–1957)

A study of colonial jurisprudence in Congo and Ruanda-Urundi took place from 1887 to 1953.[280] It is unhelpful, however, as it provides no records of capital cases. It dealt with native courts, which had no jurisdiction over capital crimes.

272 A comparative interpretation of articles 101–103, 113–115, 118 of Loi du 8 juin 1867, ibid.

273 Articles 45 and 49 of the Code pénal du 30 janvier 1940 (n 261).

274 Elisabethville, 4 February 1943, at p. 43.

275 Likulia Bolongo, *Droit pénal spécial Zaïrois* (L.G.D.J., Paris 1985) 65.

276 Article 296 of the Code Pénal Français (n 185).

277 Articles 44, 85, 108 and 171 of the Code pénal du 30 janvier 1940 (n 261).

278 Articles 181 and 182 of the Code pénal du 30 janvier 1940, ibid.

279 Article 21 of the Décret du 22 décembre 1888 as amended by the Décrets du 24 novembre 1890, 12 mai 1943 and 29 avril 1944.

280 Jean Sohier, *Répertoire général de la jurisprudence et de la doctrine coutumière du Congo et du Ruanda-Urundi jusqu'au 31 décembre 1953* (Larcier, Brussels 1957).

This gap was expected to be covered by cases published in the *Revue Juridique du Congo Belge*. However, this source fails to provide a comprehensive picture even for Congo itself.[281] The only available record of the practice of the death penalty during Belgian colonisation is for Léopoldville, which was one of largest cities in colonial Africa. The court of Léopoldville had territorial jurisdiction over the entire south-western region of Congo, which covered six judicial circumscriptions (Léopoldville, Cataractes, Bas-Congo, Lac Léopoldville II, Kwango and Kwilu).[282] The practice of the death penalty in this court may be indicative of judicial trends towards the death penalty in Belgian territories.

Table 4.1 Capital crimes in Léopoldville (1935–1957)

	Assassination	Poisoning	Murder for facilitating theft	Arson that provoked death	Rape that provoked death
1935–1937	9	11	8	–	–
1938–1942	13	8	5	3	10
1943–1947	6	2	4	7	12
1948–1952	2	13	5	6	3
1953–1957	0	0	6	3	2

Source: Jean Sohier, *Essai sur la criminalité dans la province de Léopoldville* (Académie Royale des Sciences Coloniales, Brussels 1959), 34.

Table 4.1 lists only capital crimes. The death penalty was mandatory for assassination and poisoning. It was discretionary for murder when the crime was accompanied by aggravating circumstances. The code made no distinction between attempted crimes and actual perpetrated crimes. The conclusion here is that the rate of capital crimes was very low. For example, between 1953 and 1957, no crime occurred that called for the mandatory death penalty. This also implies that death sentences were rare.

The death penalty was indeed rarely imposed during Belgian colonisation (see Figure 4.6). Jean Sohier argues that life imprisonment was the sanction for the majority of assassinations.[283] During the Second World War, judges became more and more severe, insensitive to mitigating circumstances and driven by barbaric

281 *Revue Juridique du Congo-Belge* (1956–1960).

282 Jean Sohier, *Essai sur la criminalité dans la province de Léopoldville* (Académie Royale des Sciences Coloniales, Brussels 1959).

283 ibid 37.

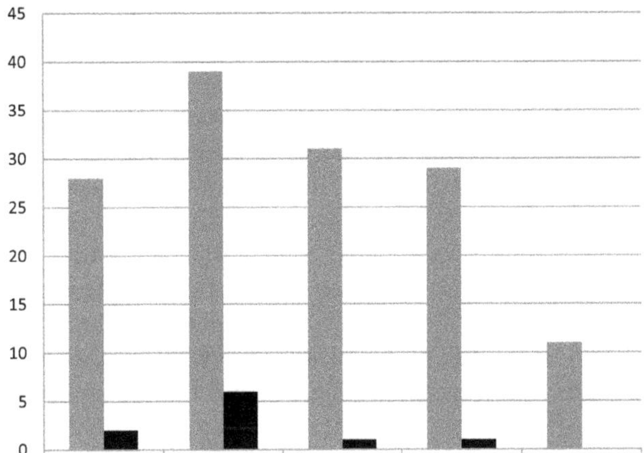

	1935-1937	1938-1942	1943-1947	1948-1952	1953-1957
Number of capital cases	28	39	31	29	11
Number of death Sentences	2	6	1	1	0

Figure 4.6 The death penalty in Léopoldville (1935–1957)
Source: Jean Sohier, *Essai sur la criminalité dans la province de Léopoldville* (Académie Royale des Sciences Coloniales, Brussels 1959), 38.

motives.[284] This statement is exaggerated, however, compared to the practice in British and French colonies. Despite discriminatory language in their judgments within which they referred to Africans as savage, with crude mentalities, Belgian judges detested the death penalty. The bitterness of the war and the revolt for independence did not affect their attitude.[285] After the war, the death penalty was almost abandoned. Jean Sohier states: '[s]ince the end of the war, judges are visibly repugnant to impose the death penalty despite the more and more extensive use of the royal right to grant mercy'.[286]

A single death sentence was imposed from 1948 to 1957. It is said that the heinous nature of the crime left the judges no option other than to impose the death penalty. A boy tortured his grandmother to death because he suspected her of witchcraft. The old women tried unsuccessfully to run away. The boy pursued and beat her to death. The two death sentences of 1935–1937 were imposed on thieves who had murdered their victims.[287]

284 ibid.
285 ibid.
286 ibid.
287 ibid 36.

Courts punished murder with aggravating circumstances more severely than assassinations. Indeed, judges had unilaterally made the death penalty discretionary for assassination. It is important to remember that Belgium had not used the death penalty since the nineteenth century. This fact explains the disgust of the colonial judges who visibly opposed the death penalty. If judges were reluctant to impose the death penalty on perpetrated crimes, it begs the question: would they impose it for attempts? None of the 53 cases of recorded attempted capital crimes between 1935 and 1957 was punished with death. The most severe punishment meted out was life imprisonment, which itself was seldom imposed for attempts.[288]

Arsène Detry was right when he stated that '[o]ur colony that originated in a genial conscience, unique in its genesis and formation, deserves a unique penal legislation. The latter, so different from examples of other people, as remarkable in its essence as in its application, reminds the doctoral principle of the historian Tite Live "[f]or doing better, turn the back to the crowd".'[289]

Conclusion

European law and judicial practice as regards the death penalty varied depending on the coloniser and the colony. Undoubtedly, the number of capital crimes, the methods of execution, including the ritual execution of parricide criminals and the quasi-absence of safeguards for offenders make the French penal code of 1810 the harshest legislation that African countries received. The severity of the penal code cannot, however, be paralleled to that of the *Code d'indigénat*. Although built on arbitrariness, the latter contained no provision on capital punishment.

The last decade of French presence in Africa corresponded with the progressive abandon of the death penalty in France. Out of 95 death sentences between 1950 and 1961, only 21 had been executed in France.[290] In French colonies except Algeria, the use of the death penalty was tempered. The development of moral values in the metropolis had a positive impact in the colonies to the extent that the executive systematically granted mercy in Dahomey and Ivory Coast.[291] Reluctance to impose the death penalty also existed in Belgian colonial courts. The Belgian colonial penal code was even more advanced, for it limited the death penalty to only a few offences. Belgian judges also expressed distaste for the death penalty, even during political and social revolt, which was the excuse other colonial powers used to increase capital offences and exceptional measures and to systematically impose the death penalty.

---

288 ibid 51–53.

289 Detry (n 263) 14–15.

290 Roger Merle and André Vitu, *Traité de droit criminel: problèmes généraux de la conscience criminelle, droit pénal général* (7th edn, Cujas, Paris 1997) 890.

291 UN Doc E/67 IV.15, 1968, p. 43, at 144.

Nevertheless, the death penalty was a common practice in British colonial courts and its abuse appeared to be legally authorised. Weighing atrocities perpetrated by English courts in Africa requires different scales, however. Kenya was a settlement, while other territories were either protectorates or colonies. The reaction of the coloniser depended therefore on the nature of the political administration within one specific territory. A settlement was compared to an overseas British territory, where settlers would do the undoable to stay. The British coloniser introduced biased, inconsistent and arbitrary judicial practices.

In Kenya, Africans were given the death penalty if their victim was European. Raping or attempting to rape white females earned a mandatory death penalty,[292] while mitigating circumstances reduced similar crimes to adultery or defilement if the victim was African. Voluntary homicide against Europeans was murder. It became manslaughter when perpetrated against Africans. In the 1950s, the *Mau Mau* insurrection lit this powder keg. Justice became a tool used to eliminate the *Mau Mau* movement and eventually its Kikuyu members in face of the failure of politicians, the police force and the army. Everywhere, the coloniser reacted to political demands with the death penalty, which had now become a political instrument of repression, oppression and suppression.

In its essence, colonisation was motivated by personal, unilateral and egoist interests.[293] To achieve their goals, the colonisers denied Africans common humanity and depicted them as beasts of burden and savages – a mentally retarded and childish race. The death penalty was not imposed on humans but rather on those who were less than human, 'to keep "bolshie" Africans in their place'.[294] It is unfortunate that these policies of domination have not yet been wiped away in many African countries. The African postcolonial era saw dictatorial regimes resorting to similar techniques to keep the 'independent people' obedient.

---

292 Uganda and Tanganyika resisted introducing the death penalty for rape. See Read (n 41) 105–106.

293 Albert Sarrat, *Grandeur et servitude coloniales* (Sagitaire, Paris 1931) 107–108.

294 Paul Nugent, *Africa since Independence: A Comparative History* (Palgrave Macmillan, New York 2004) 11.

Chapter 5
The Death Penalty as a Political Instrument in Africa

Introduction

The United Nations began to battle against the death penalty in November 1959.[1] Apart from Liberia and Ethiopia, only eight African countries were independent at that time.[2] By 1960, commonly known as the year of African independence,[3] another 17 countries had achieved independence.[4] This left almost 28 countries, the last of which to achieve independence were Eritrea and South Sudan. Western Sahara is still struggling to obtain what will now be its second independence.[5] The political independence that these African states eventually achieved was characterised by a strong sense of authoritarianism, which embodied personal, unilateral and egoist interests.[6]

All independent African countries had the death penalty at the time of their independence. Even former Portuguese colonies that were death penalty free under colonial rule had the death penalty entrenched in their legal systems at independence. Guinea Bissau introduced the death penalty upon achieving independence in 1974.[7] Angola and Cape Verde both reserved a death penalty provision in their constitutions in the year of their independence (1975).[8] São Tomé and Príncipe and Mozambique achieved independence in 1975 and then introduced the death penalty in their legal systems in 1979.[9]

1 UN Doc A/RES/1396 (XIV),1959.

2 Sudan, Libya, Ghana, Egypt, Morocco, Tunisia, Guinea and South Africa.

3 Paul Nugent, *Africa since Independence: A Comparative History* (Palgrave Macmillan, New York 2004) 7.

4 Cameroon, Togo, Mali, Senegal, Madagascar, the Democratic Republic of Congo, Somalia, Niger, Benin, Burkina Faso, Cote d'Ivoire, Chad, Central Africa Republic, Congo Brazzaville, Gabon, Nigeria and Mauritania.

5 AHG/RES 92 (XV), 1978 and AHG/RES 102–103 (XVIII), 1981.

6 Nugent (n 3) 8.

7 Hands off Cain, *Guinea Bissau*, 2011.

8 Agencia AngolaPress, *Angola Constitution Bans the Death Penalty*, 19 May 2010 and 'La peine de mort: Cap Vert', at www.peinedemort.org/National/pays.php?pays=136 (accessed 7 May 2011).

9 See respectively 'Les pays qui deviennent abolitionist de droit pour tous les Crimes', at www.peinedemort.org/National/Afrique-abolition.php (accessed 11 May 2011) and Amnesty International, *Human Rights and the Police*, April 1998, AI Index: AFR 41/01/98.

The Legacy of the State Killing Policy

In each case, the death penalty was applied to the same crimes and executed in the same manner as that practised by the colonial powers. Table 5.1 gives details of the death penalty in countries that were independent by 1962.

Table 5.1 The death penalty in Africa between 1958 and 1962

No	Country	Capital crimes	Average number of executions (1958–1962)	Minimum age	Methods of execution
1	Algeria	Treason, Murder, Torture, Kidnapping, Aggravated theft	None	Not specified	
2	Benin	Espionage, Treason, Murder	Not available	Not specified	Beheading
3	Burkina Faso	Arson, Espionage, Murder, Treason	None	Not specified	Beheading
4	Burundi	Treason, Murder, Kidnapping, Armed robbery, Rape	Not available	18	Hanging/ Civilians Shooting/ Soldiers
5	Cameroon	Arson, Espionage, Murder, Robbery, Treason	5	18	Shooting
6	Central Africa Republic	Espionage, Treason, Murder	None	16	Shooting
7	Chad	Murder	2	18	Shooting
8	Ivory Coast	Arson, Espionage, Murder, Robbery, Treason	None	Not specified	Beheading
9	Democratic Republic of Congo	Espionage, Treason, Assassination	1.4	18	Hanging
10	Egypt	Arson, Espionage, Murder, Treason	23	17	Hanging/ Civilians Shooting/ Soldiers

No	Country	Capital crimes	Average number of executions (1958–1962)	Minimum age	Methods of execution
11	Ethiopia	Arson, Espionage, Treason, Murder	Not available	21	Hanging/ Civilians Shooting/ Soldiers
12	Gabon	Arson, Espionage, Murder, Rape, Treason	None	21	Shooting
13	Ghana	Murder, Treason	6	17	Hanging
14	Guinea	Espionage, Murder, Treason	(Less than) 1	18	Shooting
15	Liberia	Murder, Treason	None	12	Hanging
16	Libya	Espionage, Murder, Treason	2	18	Hanging/ Civilians Shooting/ Soldiers
17	Madagascar	Arson, Espionage, Murder, Robbery, Treason, Rape	None	Not specified	Shooting
18	Mali	Arson, Burglary, Espionage, Murder, Robbery, Treason	Not available	18	Hanging/ Civilians Shooting/ Soldiers
19	Mauritania	Premeditated murder, Treason, Torture	Not available	Not specified	
20	Morocco	Arson, Espionage, Murder, Treason	5	18	Shooting
21	Niger	Burglary, Espionage, Treason, Murder, Rape	None	18	Shooting
22	Nigeria	Murder, Treason	51	18	Hanging
23	Rwanda	Treason, Murder, Rape, Indecent assault, Superstitious practices	None	18	Hanging/ Civilians Shooting/ Soldiers
24	Senegal	Espionage, Treason, Rape, Murder	None	18	Shooting

No	Country	Capital crimes	Average number of executions (1958–1962)	Minimum age	Methods of execution
25	Sierra Leone	Murder, Rape, Treason	Not available	18	Shooting
26	Somalia	Murder, Rape, Treason	2	Not specified	Shooting
27	South Africa	Burglary, Murder, Rape, Robbery, Treason	100	18	Hanging
28	Sudan	Espionage, Murder, Treason	Not available	21	Hanging/ Civilians Shooting/ Soldiers
29	Tanganyika	Murder, Treason	25.4	18	Hanging
30	Togo	Arson, Burglary, Espionage, Murder, Treason	None	18	Beheading Shooting
31	Tunisia	Espionage, Treason, Murder	2.2	18	Hanging/ Civilians Shooting/ Soldiers
32	Uganda	Espionage, Murder, Treason	29	18	Hanging

Source: Clarence H. Patrick[10] except for Algeria,[11] Burundi,[12] Mauritania[13] and Rwanda[14]

Conducts that were not crimes or which were not punished with death before colonisation remained capital offences after independence. In addition, some North Africa states extended the list of capital crimes when they adopted radical Islam. For example, the primary capital crimes in Mauritania were premeditated murder, treason and torture. From 1980 onwards, the death penalty under *Shari'a*

10 Clarence H Patrick, 'The Status of Capital Punishment: A Worldwide Perspective' (1965) 56 *Journal of Criminal Law, Criminology and Police Science* 397, 397–411.

11 Hands off Cain, *Report on Algeria*, 2010.

12 Human Rights Watch, *Background on 2008 Burundi Penal Code*, December 2008, at p. 4.

13 Hans Göran Franck, *The Barbaric Punishment: Abolishing the Death Penalty* (Martinus Nijhoff Publishers, The Hague 2003) 110.

14 Augustin Buzora, *La peine de mort en droit Rwandais* (Mémoire de Licence, Université Nationale du Rwanda, Butare 1990) 54–55.

was extended to rape, apostasy and homosexuality.[15] In Rwanda and Burundi, the colonial penal code that was enforced until more than two decades after independence extended the death penalty to indecent assault, rape and superstitious practices in Rwanda[16] and to kidnapping, armed robbery and rape in Burundi.[17]

The 1977 Rwandan penal code was supposed to suppress the colonial ideology. It in fact drew on the classical doctrines of the French penal code of 1810.[18] Worldwide progress on the issue of the death penalty in the 1970s was completely ignored. The death penalty was extended to non-homicide crimes such as political offences, military offences and offences against public faith,[19] assault with aggravating circumstances, armed robbery, voluntary arson that provoked death, destruction and degradation of objects followed by death, indecent assault that provoked death, witchcraft, rape that provoked death and sequestration followed by acts of torture that provoked death.[20] The code's underlying Napoleonic ideology was reinforced in subsequent amendments until the death penalty was abolished in 2007.[21]

Moreover, African countries adopted varied tendencies in legislating and applying the death penalty. Former French and Belgian colonies retained the death penalty as a mandatory punishment without alternative punishments, save when the offender had successfully demonstrated mitigating circumstances. This application of the death penalty was the consequence of restrictive interpretation of criminal law within the civil law system.[22] Proving that they had inherited a certified copy of the French penal law, France's former colonies followed the French model of categorising and punishing crimes dealing first with political crimes.[23]

---

15 Franck (n 13).

16 Buzora (n 14) 54–55.

17 Human Rights Watch, *Background on 2008 Burundi Penal Code*, December 2008, at p. 4.

18 Articles 26, 28–33, 151–155, 158, 159, 164, 312–317 and 403 of the of the Décret-loi no 21/77 du 18 août 1977 portant Code Pénal Rwandais tel que modifié et complété à ce jour, *Journal Officiel*, no 13 bis, 1978. This code was abrogated by Organic Law no 01/2012/OL of 2 May 2012 instituting the Penal Code, *Official Gazette*, no special of 14 June 2012.

19 Articles 151–200, 209, 238, 240, 282 and 459–487 of the Décret-loi no 21/77 du 18 août 1977 portant Code Pénal Rwandais tel que modifié et complété à ce jour, *Journal Officiel*, no 13 bis, 1978.

20 Articles 324, 349, 359, 360, 388, 404 ter, 442 and 444 of the Décret-loi no 21/77 du 18 août 1977 portant Code Pénal Rwandais tel que modifié et complété à ce jour, *Journal Officiel*, no 13 bis, 1978.

21 Organic Law no 31/2007 of 25 July 2007 relating to the abolition of the death penalty, *Official Gazette*, no special of 25 July 2007.

22 UN Doc E/67 IV.15, 1968, p. 14.

23 FIDH, *Tchad, la peine de mort entre opportunisme sécuritaire et règlement de compte*, Rapport, Mission International d'Enquête, no 404, septembre 2004, at p. 9.

The death penalty was also mandatory for murder in the former British colonies of Somalia, Gambia, Malawi, the Sudan and South Africa.[24] Some countries literally imported English law. Uganda drew on legislation from two centuries earlier using the definition of treason found in section 1 of the English Treason Act of 1795. In addition to the broadly described 'levying war', it was a capital crime to imagine, invent, devise or intend any act, matter or theory followed by expressions, uttering or declarations of such compassing, imagining, inventing, devising or intending by any overt act in order by force of arms to overturn the government.[25]

Shooting became the commonly preferred method of execution, particularly for military offences. Pre-colonial methods of execution (drowning, strangling and burning) were deemed primitive, inhuman and barbaric.[26] Benin and Burkina Faso were alone in applying decapitation. Public execution was prohibited save in Cameroon, the Central African Republic and Liberia. Ethiopia, Guinea, Mali, Malawi[27] and Morocco[28] remained ambivalent. The prohibition of media and public attendance as regards the process and the scene of execution went hand in hand.[29]

In the 1960s, three Anglophone countries executed the largest number of death sentences. South Africa executed 392 out of 592 death sentences. The Sudan followed this with 354 executions out of 547 death sentences. Surprisingly, Somalia was third, with eight executions out of 15 death sentences. Each carried out more than 50 per cent of the death sentences that were pronounced.[30] It is worth noting that under indigenous law the death penalty did not exist in the Sudan or Somalia. It was first introduced by *Shari'a* and strengthened by colonial regimes. Even under Islamic law, the Somali and Sudanese still redressed murder with *diyya*. Foreign legal influences shaped the law and the mentality of these people. Generally speaking, only Francophone countries developed a consistent custom of commuting death sentences. Table 5.2 lists countries that executed less than 50 per cent of death sentences in the period 1959–1960.

24 UN Doc E/67 IV.15, 1968, p. 14.

25 Section 25 (a) and (b) of the Penal Code Amendment Act, 1966. The phrase 'levying war' was also inserted in section 39 of the Tanzania Penal Code. See JJR Collingwood, *Criminal Law of East and Central Africa* (Sweet and Maxwell 1967) 78–81.

26 Buzora (n 14) 8.

27 Patrick (n 10) 398–404.

28 UN Doc E/67 IV.15, 1968, p. 26.

29 UN Doc E/67 IV.15, 1968, pp. 26–27.

30 UN Doc E/67 IV.15, 1968, p. 43.

Table 5.2 Countries that executed less than 50 per cent of death sentences (1959–1960)

No	Countries	Death sentences	Sentence quashed on appeal	Convict escaped	Commuted sentences	Mercy	Executions
1	Ivory Coast	16	–	–	16	–	–
2	Dahomey	3	–	2	1	–	–
3	Togo	1	1	–	–	–	–
4	Gambia	2	–	–	2	–	–
5	Ghana	179	14	–	111	–	54
6	Morocco	43	–	–	29	–	14
7	Zanzibar	14	–	–	9	–	5
8	Malawi	25	–	–	16	–	9
9	Nigeria	590	–	–	339	–	251
10	Tanganyika	289	17	–	128	–	144

Source: UN Doc E/67 IV.15, 1968, at p. 43.

Morocco is the only former French colony that continued the practice of the death penalty and Gambia is the only country within Anglophone Africa that made an exception, pardoning death sentences. Gambia had refrained from executing the death penalty since colonial times. After 30 years had passed without any executions, it became one of the first *de facto* abolitionist countries in Africa.[31] This is also evidence that colonial rule was perceived differently in Africa. Gambia received the same Colonial Office Model Penal Code as Malawi, Tanganyika and Zanzibar. These last three were credited with executing an average of 33 per cent of death sentences.

In former British colonies, the death penalty was imposed as the ultimate punishment and without accessory embellishments (torture, fine, special or general confiscation). However, African civil law countries imposed the deprivation of civil rights as a subsidiary punishment to the death penalty. Morocco and Benin additionally punished offenders convicted of state crimes with general forfeitures.[32]

31 UN Doc E/67 IV.15, 1968, p. 43.
32 UN Doc E/67 IV.15, 1968, p. 20.

In 1975, Guinea Bissau was the only African state on the list of *de jure* abolitionists for ordinary crimes before its withdrawal from the final list because the information relied on was from an unofficial source.[33] Guinea Bissau eventually abolished the death penalty in 1993. Mozambique was also mistakenly qualified as a *de jure* abolitionist since 1867, a date that corresponds to the abolition of the death penalty for ordinary crimes in Portugal.[34] Former Portuguese colonies simply did not have the death penalty in their colonial statutes. They all introduced capital punishment in their constitutions at the time of or early after their independence.

By 1978, the abolitionist movement had elicited different responses from countries throughout Africa. The majority of African countries remained indifferent. Others progressively decided not to impose the death penalty or, if it was imposed, to commute the sentence. These are countries that felt that 'capital punishment is unfortunate but … [an] unavoidable necessity'.[35] These conditions prevailed until the Seychelles legally abolished the death penalty for murder in 1978.[36] Three years later, Cape Verde took a stronger stance and abolished the death penalty for all crimes.[37]

In Africa, abolition has often coincided 'with major social changes, a period of national reconciliation, and a desire to break with an oppressive and troubled past'.[38] In fact, the death penalty is intimately connected to political power. Like the colonial powers, governments have applied it to enforce their policies. This explains its insertion into constitutions of independent countries that never applied it during colonial times. Dirk Van Zyl Smit states:

> In many African countries, rulers retain the death penalty, even if they do not use it, because they fear that the time will come when using their power to implement the death penalty will be the only way to demonstrate their authority. This tendency may be most obvious in coup-ridden, politically unstable states. However, it is equally a problem in countries where there is a perception that the state is powerless to act with other means against crime and corruption.[39]

Most African countries punished political crimes with the death sentence. Chad would be an exception where murder was the only capital crime.[40] However, it is

33 UN Doc E/5616/, 1975, pp 3–4, Annex I.

34 Patrick (n 10).

35 UN Doc E/5616/, 1975, at pp. 4–5.

36 UN Doc E/1980/9, at para 21.

37 William A Schabas, 'African Perspectives on Abolition of the Death Penalty' in William A Schabas (ed), *The International Sourcebook on Capital Punishment* (Northeastern University Press, Boston 1997) 32.

38 ibid.

39 Dirk Van Zyl Smit, 'The Death Penalty in Africa' (2004) 4 *African Human Rights Law Journal* 1, 15.

40 Patrick (n 10) 398.

common knowledge that oppressive regimes often punish ordinary crimes with death sentences for political reasons. These are described as politically motivated crimes. Following independence, many illegitimate and tyrannical regimes in Africa used the death penalty in this way.

The Death Penalty as an Instrument of Oppression in Africa: Some Case Studies

Four different legal systems will now be used to illustrate how often the death penalty has been used as an instrument of political oppression in contemporary Africa: the Roman Dutch law (South Africa), the Franco-Belgian law (the Democratic Republic of Congo) and the English law and *Shari'a* (Nigeria).

The use of the death penalty in these countries has been the most outrageous on the continent. Although South Africa applied sophisticated laws and an organised judicial machinery and the Democratic Republic of Congo (formerly Zaire) and Nigeria adopted untimely military decrees and improvised military courts, they all pursued a similar goal, silencing and mostly eliminating dissident voices. Today, South Africa has distanced itself from these two countries in abolishing the death penalty.

The Death Penalty under Apartheid in South Africa

Pre-union Roman Dutch law is sometimes excessively described as primitive, anarchic, barbaric and ferocious.[41] It is worth bearing in mind that, in principle, it was recommended at the Cape that autochthones be treated humanely and governed politically, civilly and judicially on the same basis as Europeans. Severe measures were sometimes taken against thieves of cattle to redress ill treatment of the Hottentots. Respectable Roman Dutch founders such as Van der Linden had expressed their aversion to the death penalty.[42] In reality, injustice and harsher punishments intensified with the Union of South Africa.

The state killing policy in South Africa

Until 1917, there was no judicial agreement on the mandatory nature of the death penalty for murder, rape and treason. Common law was itself unclear as to whether the death penalty was mandatory for murder and different courts

---

41 David Dyzenhaus, *Hard Cases in Wicked Legal Systems: South African Law in the Perspective of Legal Philosophy* (Clarendon Press, Oxford 1991) 33 and George Devenish, 'South Africa from Pre-colonial Times to Democracy: A Constitutional and Jurisprudential Odyssey' (2005) 1 *Journal of South African Law* 551–552.

42 Johannes Van der Linden, *The Institutes of the Law of Holland* (Amsterdam 1806) as quoted in *State v Lionel Phillips and Sixty-Three Others*, 1896, reprinted (1900) 17 *South African Law Journal* 25.

had inherited different practices. More recent laws also allowed alternative punishments.[43] Whipping for offenders under 16 years of age and imprisonment with the possibility of release on parole existed in Transvaal and the Free State.[44]

The Criminal Procedure Act of 1917, which was designed to provide the union with a uniform system of law, introduced the mandatory death penalty for murder.[45] It also marked the beginning of the politicisation of the death penalty. The policy of brutality and racial inequality between whites and non-whites that 'resulted in tragedy of inordinate proportion for all people of colour'[46] was, however, more present during British colonisation[47] and became a regular practice with the Union.

At the Cape as in Natal, British settlers ensured that their laws technically contained no discriminatory racial policies. Racial assimilation through Anglicisation became one of the settlers' new policies. Africans were even granted the right to participate in parliamentary voting, although excluded as candidates. This seemed sufficient to flatter them that they enjoyed more rights than they did under Roman Dutch law. The Cape appeared then to be a successful model of colour-blind laws and racial equality to inspire America.[48] However, 'from the inception of the second British occupation … the very nature [of the Cape] government was inordinately autocratic in nature, and was initially epitomized by haughty character and imperious conduct …'.[49]

Retrogressive developments ensured white hegemony and thus British supremacy at the Cape and in Natal. Conditions for voting were increased and Africans of Transkei, Zulu and Indians became disenfranchised. Any resistance was bloodily quashed. Several thousand Zulu opposing the divide and rule policy were massacred during the Bambatho rebellion.[50] In daily life, discrimination and

43 First Offenders (The Cap) Act 10 of 1906, Criminal Procedure Code (Transvaal) Ordinance 1 of 1903 and the Criminal Law Amendment (Transvaal) Act 38 of 1909, Administration of Justice (Orange Free State) Supplementary Ordinance 1 of 1906, Criminal Law Amendment (Natal) Act 10 of 1910.

44 Section 259 Criminal Procedure Code (Transvaal) Ordinance 1 of 1903.

45 Section 338 of the Criminal Procedure Act 31 of 1917.

46 Devenish (n 41).

47 Under section 2 (a) of the Immigration Act 47 of 1902, any person who could not successfully write an application to the Minister in any European language was prohibited to enter the Cape and qualified as an undesirable immigrant. Article 3 generally but especially paragraph (g) excluded illiterate Europeans from its scope of application. Other examples of similar discriminatory legislations include The Sale to Native Act 28 of 1898 which simultaneously prohibited Africans from making traditional beer and buying and consuming Europeans liquors, The Native Dance Act 16 of 1891 whose article 1 provided that 'Abakweta and Intonjane dances [were] prohibited upon any land in any district where this Act [was] proclaimed' and The Passes for Natives Act 22 of 1867 that prohibited free circulation of Africans on their lands without a signed pass.

48 Devenish (n 41) 553–354.

49 ibid.

50 Devenish (n 41) 557.

segregation supplanted equality. The Governor declared that 'The Zulu people were to be territorially separated and thereby segregated politically, economically and socially from whites, so that they could be protected from corruption and exploitation'.[51] The struggle of the judiciary to maintain racial equality faced resistance from influential politicians. Later the Cape administration was referred to as 'at best incompetent, at worst barbaric and corrupt',[52] while Natal was called 'the wretched colony – the hooligan of the British Empire'.[53]

British discriminatory policies were not restricted to Africans. Inhuman military methods such as the concentration camp for Boer and African women and children and exposure to disease and starvation resulted in the death of roughly 30,000 white and 14,152 African inmates during the Anglo-Boer war. These events also shaped the future.[54] Harrison claims, 'it was not war, it was deliberate murder'.[55]

The war in which many Asians, Africans and coloured people fought on the British side left a legacy of intense bitterness and hatred that had an impact on South African politics for generations.[56] Non-Europeans joined the British side because '... the British portrayed themselves as a more accommodating people ... But this faith was betrayed after the war, when the British showed little sympathy for the future of non-Europeans throughout Southern Africa.'[57] The Union of South Africa inherited a legacy of white supremacy, discriminatory laws and segregationist policies, ultimately apartheid.[58]

White Afrikaners were also victims of frustration and unfair segregation. John Vorster, the then South African Prime Minister and later President under apartheid explained how in 1924 an English-speaking girl in his Eastern Cape High School became the reason that the whole school had to study in English:

> We had to take our classes, except for Afrikaans, in English because she could not follow Afrikaans. But they never asked us whether we could follow English; they just took it for granted.[59]

---

51 ibid.

52 ibid.

53 ibid.

54 Dyzenhaus (n 41).

55 David Harrison, *The White Tribe of Africa: South Africa in Perspective* (Ariel Books, London 1985) 40–49.

56 David Dyzenhaus (n 41) and Hulme T Siwundhla, 'White Ideologies and Non-European Participation in the Anglo-Boer War 1899–1902' (1984) 15 *Journal of Black Studies* 223, 223–234. It is worth noting that some burghers fought on the British side. See also Albert Grundlingh, *Boer Collaboration in the South African War of 1899–1902: The Dynamics of Treason* (Protea, Pretoria 2006) 221 230.

57 Siwundhla, ibid.

58 Devenish (n 41) 558–563.

59 Harrison (n 55) 56.

Racial segregation was a British policy. Important antecedents of racial segregation could be found in the British controlled zone, particularly in Natal,[60] where the apartheid policy was

> characterized by traumatic and tragic policies of progressive disenfranchisement of people of colour and institutionalized racism, enforced within a brutal and rigid system of law that was characterized by the erosion and eclipse of the rule of law effected by increasingly draconian security legislation, for which South Africa became notorious and was regarded as a political outcast.[61]

In 1920, a judge complained about the racist features of English law through the institutionalisation of juries. White-only juries were used to enforce racial discrimination. He was shocked when a jury found not guilty two whites who had broken the arm of an African and killed his child.

> This state of things has been going on for a century, ever since the English jury system was introduced into South Africa. With a people more vindictive than the coloured population of South Africa, justice would have been secured by extra judicial methods.[62]

English law had made the death penalty mandatory for murder. Flaws associated with the concept of malice resulted in extensive and analogical interpretations that drove the majority of Africans, most of whom were innocent, to the gallows.[63] The democratic government's inquiry concluded, 'in alarming numbers, most of those executed were later found to have been innocent'.[64] It is contended that 95 per cent of those who went to the gallows were Africans. Unjust laws, harsh punishments and unfair dismissals intended to suppress any revolt against inequality.[65] Inmates on death row ended up calling the Pretoria Maximum Prison 'The Head Office of Hanging'.[66]

---

60 Devenish (n 41) 564.

61 ibid.

62 George Morice, 'The Administration of Criminal Law in South Africa' (1920) 37 *South African Law Journal* 131, 137.

63 Clarkson H Tredgold, *Handbook of Colonial Criminal Law* (Juta, Cape Town 1904) 256 and Robert Turrell, *White Mercy: A Study of the Death Penalty in South Africa* (Praeger, London 2004) 5.

64 Department of Justice and Constitutional Development, Address of Minister Jeff Radebe, 22 September 2009 at the 3rd International Meeting of Ministers of Justice, Rome, Italy.

65 Turrell (n 63) 7.

66 Truth and Reconciliation Special Hearing, *95 Per Cent of Death Sentences Were Black* (McBride, Johannesburg 22 July 1997).

The judicial battle against the death penalty

The union inherited the death penalty from both English law and Roman Dutch law. Prior to 1917, courts were reluctant to impose it. In *R v. Blumenthal*,[67] it was held that for crimes other than murder, rape and treason, the death penalty had tacitly been abrogated by its disuse. The death penalty had also ceased to be mandatory for murder (see Figure 5.1).

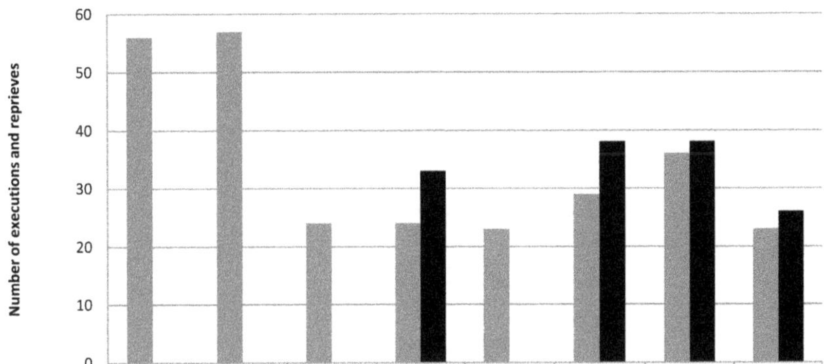

	1910	1911	1912	1913	1914	1915	1916	1917
Executions	56	57	24	24	23	29	36	23
Reprieves	0	0	0	33	0	38	38	26

Figure 5.1 Discretionary death penalty in South Africa (1910–1917)

Note: O represents data that are not available.

Source: South African Journal of Criminal Justice,[68] Robert Turrell[69] and Ellison Kahn[70]

There are no data on reprieves for 1910–1912 and 1914.[71] However, reprieves were more common than executions over the entire period. The death sentence was not imposed for rape and was rarely imposed for treason between 1910 and 1917. The only case in which the defendant was executed for treason was that of Jopie Fourie, who had rebelled against the South African invasion of Namibia in 1914.

67 1915 TPD 420.

68 'Statistics' (1992) 2 *South African Journal of Criminal Justice* 251, 251–254.

69 Turrell (n 63) 258–259.

70 Ellison Kahn, 'Crime and Punishment 1910–1960: Reflections on Changes since Union in the Law of Criminal Punishment and its Application' (1960) 191 *Acta Juridica* 191, 198–206.

71 ibid.; 'Statistics' (1992) 2 *South African Journal of Criminal Justice* 251, 251–254 and Turrell (n 63) 258–259.

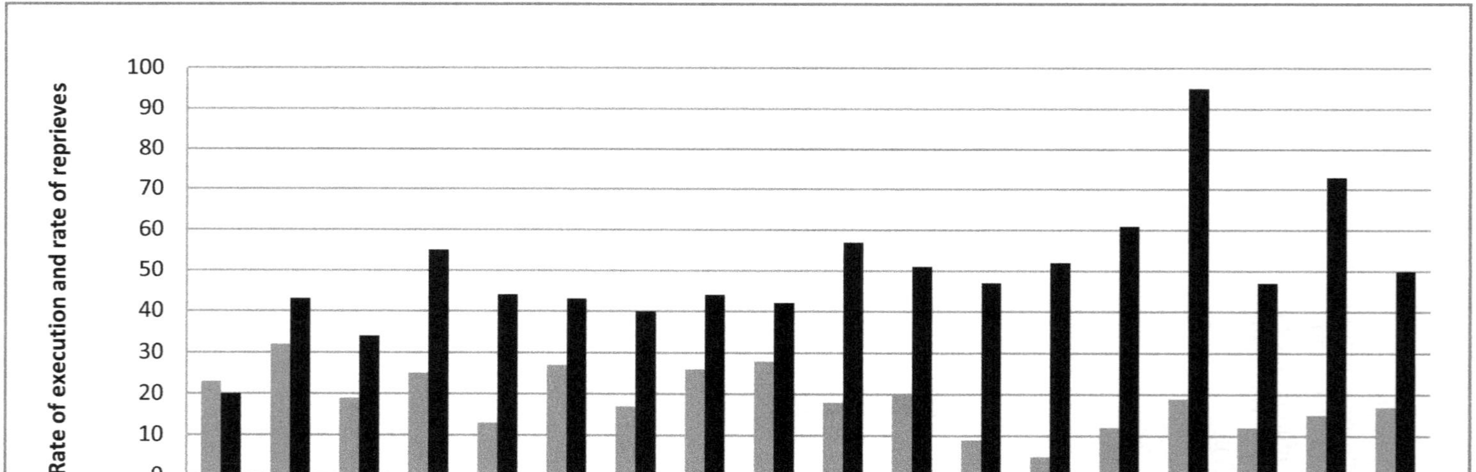

	1918	1919	1920	1921	1922	1923	1924	1925	1926	1927	1928	1929	1930	1931	1932	1933	1934	1935
Execution	23	32	19	25	13	27	17	26	28	18	20	9	5	12	19	12	15	17
Reprieves	20	43	34	55	44	43	40	44	42	57	51	47	52	61	95	47	73	50

Figure 5.2 Executions under mandatory death penalty in South Africa (1918–1935)

He was captured on 16 December 1914 in Rustenburg, was tried by a court martial for high treason and executed on 20 December 1914.[72]

It is a matter of controversy whether or not there was a decrease in executions after 1917. Professor Ellison Kahn submits that the situation evolved after 1917 and that there were less than 25 executions between 1923 and 1934.[73] Figure 5.2 opposes this view. (Source information for Figure 5.2: Ellison Kahn,[74] Robert Turrell,[75] Van Niekerk[76] and *South African Journal of Criminal Justice.*[77])

Despite the mandatory death penalty, there are three reasons used to justify the decreased level of executions from 1918 to 1935: public disapproval of the degeneration of criminal law, discretionary power of the juries to convict defendants of culpable homicide and the bureaucratic burden of reporting each capital case.[78] Though some may doubt the exclusion of the death penalty on subjective grounds such as its unpopularity with the public, or the additional reporting duties it imposed on the judicial administration, it is clear that there were fewer executions during this period than for the period 1910–1917. Prior to 1935, courts had no discretion and they were not statutorily entitled to consider mitigating circumstances.[79] However, the executive managed to keep the rate of executions lower than that of reprieves. A judge explained that he also invoked the vague term of circumstantial evidence introduced in 1917 to save people from the death penalty.[80]

Mitigating circumstances could exclude the death penalty between 1935 and 1946. Recommendation regarding extenuating circumstances was made as early as 1920. Some questioned whether or not, in addition to the exclusion of the death penalty for women and junior offenders, article 338 of the Criminal Procedure Act 1917 should integrate mitigating circumstances for other classes of criminals.[81] The courts had realised that the death sentence was not serving the purposes of justice at all. George Morice, a judge in Johannesburg, stated, 'at present, the passing of the death sentence is often no more than a farce'.[82]

African convicts saw courts as a transitional step towards their death. They did not trust judges' recommendations for mercy. A judge was shocked when a Swazi man for whom he recommended mercy asked permission to pack his belongings

72 Barend Van Niekerk, 'Hanged by the Neck Until you Are Dead' (1969) 86 *South African Law Journal* 457, 459.

73 Kahn (n 70) 200.

74 ibid.

75 Turrell (n 63) 258–259.

76 Van Niekerk (n 72) 458.

77 'Death Penalty in South Africa, the Statistics' (1989) 2 *South African Journal of Criminal Justice* 252, 252.

78 Kahn (n 70) 200.

79 Section 61 (a) the General Law Amendment Act 46 of 1935.

80 Morice (n 62) 132.

81 ibid 134.

82 ibid.

and bid farewell to his relatives. The judge felt obliged to reassure him via an interpreter that he would not be hanged.[83] This drove George Morice to call for a complete abolition of the death penalty:

> [Given] the cruelty of which [the death penalty] is enhanced by the special solemnities that sometimes accompany it, such as calling silence in the court and the medieval barbarity of the black cap[,] one feels inclined a blush for civilization when one has to pronounce such a sentence upon an unsophisticated native after explaining to him that it would probably not be carried out.[84]

However, it seemed premature to suggest abolition. Basing abolition on the poor understanding of an unsophisticated native who questioned the reasoning behind imposing a death sentence that would not be carried out was a weak foundation. George Morice strengthened his position by referring to the harm that the death penalty causes to humanity and asked for the discretionary death penalty to apply for murder so that 'there would be less likelihood of these perverse verdicts, which we meet with in cases of so called natural justice'.[85]

In 1933, the judges' conference requested an amendment in order to allow a discretionary sentence.[86] Instead, a new definition of homicide was provided. It split the crime in two. The death penalty remained mandatory for premeditated murder and became discretionary for culpable homicide.[87] This decision was politically motivated, although it was a return to Roman Dutch classification of crimes. General Smuts had compared statistics and found that 60 per cent of death sentences were carried out in the United Kingdom, while only 11 per cent of executions of death sentences in South Africa were implemented. He therefore decided to preserve the mandatory death penalty and carried this decision through Parliament.[88] In dividing the definition of homicide, the law divided justice: Europeans were prosecuted for culpable homicide and non-Europeans for murder.

Racial selection of the barbarian to be executed

Executions substantially decreased leading up to 1950. Mitigating circumstances were found to exist in 997 cases out of 1,507 for the decade 1936–1946. At the same time, 297 cases were reprieved, proving that judges had started taking control of the death penalty and that judicial recommendations for mercy were being

---

83 ibid.

84 ibid.

85 ibid 134–135.

86 Kahn (n 70) 200.

87 Section 61 (a) of the General Law Amendment Act 46 of 1935. See also Kahn (n 70) 200–201.

88 Ellison Kahn, 'How Did We Get our Lopsided Law on the Imposition of the Death Penalty for Common Law Crimes? And What Should Do We Do about It?' (1989) 2 *South African Journal of Criminal Justice* 137, 137 and 149.

upheld (see Figure 5.3: Source: Ellison Kahn[89] and Robert Turrell[90]). Executions were carried out in only 213 cases, a figure that represents 14 per cent of all death sentences.[91] South Africa excluded the death penalty in nearly 86 per cent of cases.[92] It was the only decade in which South Africa had the highest number of reprieves.

In 1958, the death penalty was extended to property and political crimes, unless perpetrated by juvenile offenders.[93] The government justified its return to nineteenth-century practices on the grounds of deterrence. In addition to murder, rape and treason, eight statutory offences became capital crimes: robbery with aggravating circumstances, housebreaking with aggravating circumstances, sabotage, undergoing communism training, advocating social change, kidnapping, child stealing and terrorism.[94] This extending of the death penalty's scope received a great welcome in the white community. The political opposition was enthusiastic about the decision and some judges attempted a retrospective application of the law.[95] The law was passed in 1958 and in February 1959, the first convict was executed.[96]

The period leading up to 1959 is also politically relevant. The National Party had won elections in 1948 and political unrest was brewing out of a desire for full independence from Britain. Every effort was made to move towards building a pure Afrikaner republic.

Figure 5.4 looks at the death penalty in South Africa between 1958 and 1989. (Source for Figure 5.4: Ellison Kahn,[97] Christina Murray,[98] Robert Turrell[99] and *South African Journal on Human Rights.*[100])

Murder was the most common reason for hanging and accounted for 97 per cent of executions between 1970 and 1985,[101] a period during which the recorded

89 Kahn (n 70) 202.

90 Turrell (n 63) 258–259.

91 Kahn (n 70) 202.

92 Turrell (n 63) 258–259.

93 Section 25 of the Criminal Law Amendment Act 16 of 1959.

94 See section 11 of the Internal Security Act 44 of 1950 for communism and advocating social change, section 21 of the General Law Amendment Act 76 of 1962 for sabotage, section 2 (1) of Terrorism Act 83 of 1967 for terrorism, section 1 (1) (i) read with section 227 of the Criminal Procedure Act 51 of 1977 for robbery and housebreaking with aggravating circumstances and for kidnapping and child stealing. For details see Ellison Kahn, 'What Is Happening to the Death Penalty?' (1981) 98 *South African Law Journal* 103.

95 *R v. Mazibuko* 1958 (4) SA 353 (A.D.).

96 Kahn (n 70) 204.

97 ibid 202.

98 Christina Murray, 'Hangings in Southern Africa: The Last Ten Years' (1986) 2 *South African Journal on Human Rights* 349, 350.

99 Turrell (n 63) 259.

100 'Hangings: Last Ten Years' (1985) 1 *South African Journal on Human Rights* 180.

101 Kahn (n 94) 103.

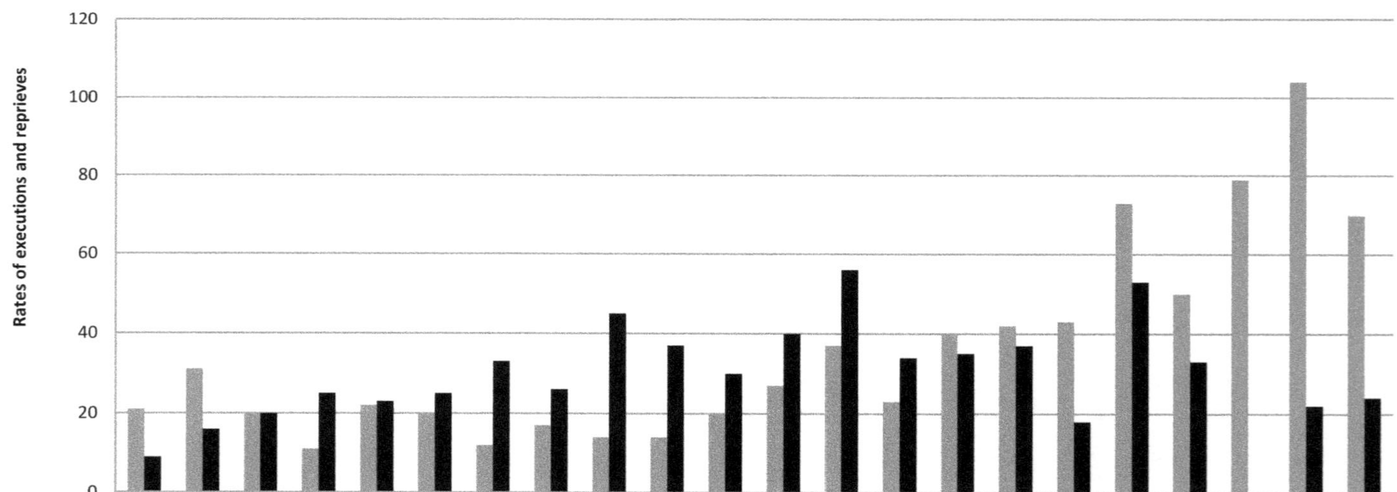

	1936	1937	1938	1939	1940	1941	1942	1943	1944	1945	1946	1947	1948	1950	1951	1952	1953	1954	1955	1956	1957	1958
Execution	21	31	20	11	22	20	12	17	14	14	20	27	37	23	40	42	43	73	50	79	104	70
Reprieves	9	16	20	25	23	25	33	26	45	37	30	40	56	34	35	37	18	53	33	0	22	24

Figure 5.3 The impact of judicial recommendations for mercy

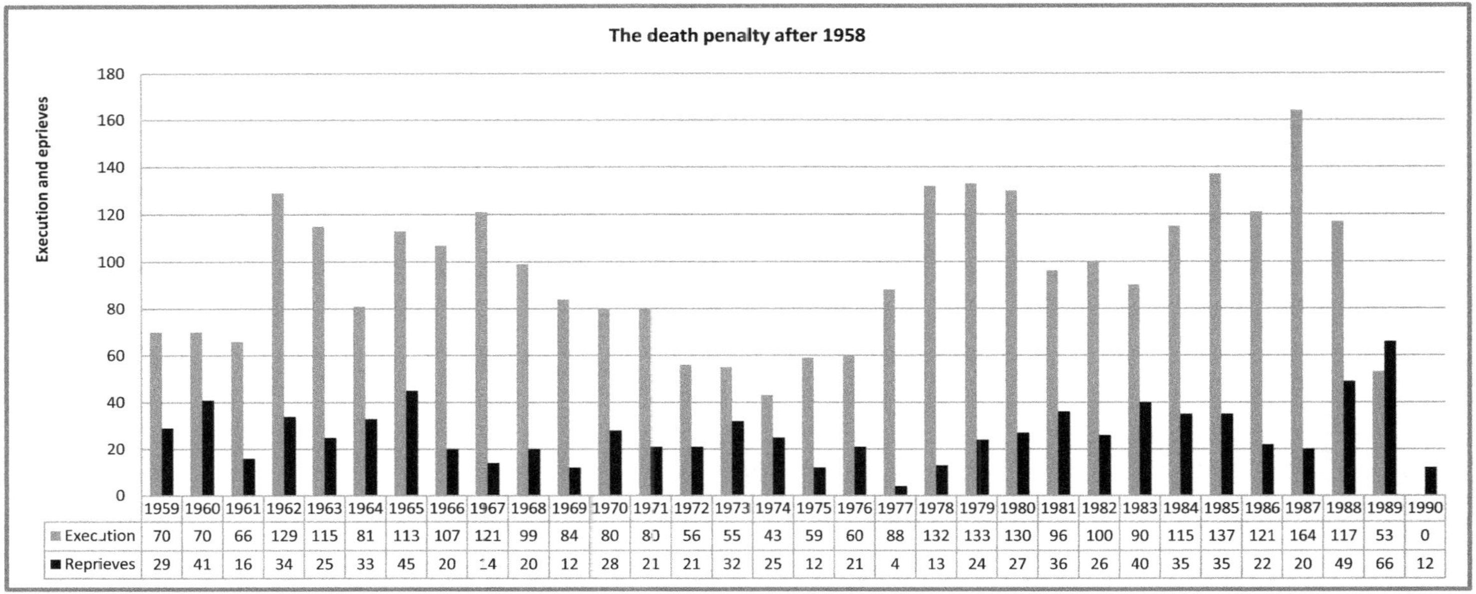

	1959	1960	1961	1962	1963	1964	1965	1966	1967	1968	1969	1970	1971	1972	1973	1974	1975	1976	1977	1978	1979	1980	1981	1982	1983	1984	1985	1986	1987	1988	1989	1990
Execution	70	70	66	129	115	81	113	107	121	99	84	80	80	56	55	43	59	60	88	132	133	130	96	100	90	115	137	121	164	117	53	0
Reprieves	29	41	16	34	25	33	45	20	14	20	12	28	21	21	32	25	12	21	4	13	24	27	36	26	40	35	35	22	20	49	66	12

Figure 5.4 The death penalty between 1958 and 1989 in South Africa

number of executions reached a peak. Sometimes murder was accompanied with rape or robbery.

In 1882, De Villier, the then Cape Chief Justice, had ruled that the death penalty for rape required extreme circumstances of atrocity that left the judge no other option.[102] The legislation on the death penalty for Africans who raped European females regardless of the circumstances originated in Natal. The 1887 Natal legislation, aiming to protect white females scared of Africans, introduced the discretionary death penalty for rape.[103] Political propaganda strengthened this racial discrimination. In 1896, a judicial report justified this law by stating that 'violating chastity, especially where the offender is a male of an inferior race, is keenly felt among white people as an irreparable wrong to the victim and her relatives and an outrage upon the white race'.[104]

Within the Union, rape became one of the most important racial crimes. The recorded figure of 170 executions for rape between 1919 and 1988[105] is a gross understatement. There were 123 executions for rape in the period 1911–1966.[106] Nearly 96 per cent of convicted rapists were Africans, coloured and Asians. Out of the 19 executions for rape that took place between 1911 and 1919, there was one coloured person. All the rest were Africans.[107] In 1955, the Minister of Justice declared that, since he had taken office, he had systematically refused mercy to natives convicted of raping white women because it was a special horror to be raped by an African man.[108] The rape of a white woman by an African became known as 'black peril'.[109]

Were whites ever hanged for any of the listed crimes? A complete lack of executions handed down to whites would infer both inequality and a policy of eliminating the African race. Whites committed murder and rape on non-whites four times more often than did non-whites on Europeans.[110] Professor Ellison Kahn states that it is not 'entirely accurate' to state that whites were not executed for inter-white crimes or for crimes perpetrated against Africans.[111] However, he found that until 1960, only three of 1,520 persons executed were whites. The first case dated back to 1949. There is no record of a single execution of a white offender before 1949. Compared to the number of Africans executed over the same period, three seems insignificant. This unequal treatment was most apparent in rape cases.

102 *R v. Nonosi* (1882) 1 Buch AC 154 at 155–6.

103 Section 1 of Law no 27 of 1887 (N).

104 Exton M Burchell and Peter MA Hunt, *South African Criminal Law and Procedure* (Juta, Cape Town 1970) 141, footnote 28.

105 ibid 141.

106 Van Niekerk (n 72) 459.

107 Kahn (n 88) and Kahn (n 70) 203.

108 *Rand Daily Mail*, 16 September 1955 as quoted by Kahn (n 88).

109 Lilian Chenwi, *Towards the Abolition of the Death Penalty in Africa: A Human Rights Perspective* (Pretoria University Law Press, Pretoria 2007) 18–20.

110 Van Niekerk (n 72) 471.

111 Kahn (n 70) 204.

Under the Immorality Act,[112] even consensual sexual intercourse between whites and natives was a criminal offence.

The first case of a European executed for rape was recorded in February 1960. The offender had raped his six-year-old daughter.[113] A few whites were executed beginning with the 1960s for two reasons: the need to balance racial figures on execution and the need to escape criticism based on the apparent political nature of executions and the observable trend of eliminating from society inferior whites who constituted an insult to white civilisation. The concept of degeneration helped eliminate whites who opposed apartheid. Several acts were passed to empty degeneracy of its then criminological content. 'It took a crucial political meaning. It was mobilized in ideological opposition to mass democracy and socialism. In South Africa, degeneracy was pressed into service in opposition to white working class.'[114] All South African pre-democracy political regimes referred to the concept 'degeneracy' against 'whites who posed a threat to the white race'.[115] Even there, the life of a white convict carried more value than that of other racial groups.

Nevertheless, the few cases that resulted in the executions of whites still fell within the racial ideology. Although the purpose of apartheid was white supremacy, it was still necessary to demonstrate to the public and to an increasingly demanding abolitionist movement that the death penalty was applied as an instrument of justice rather than a means of crushing the enemy. This judicial hypocrisy led white judges to send a few whites to the gallows as sacrificial lambs.

That should not veil the reality that in many instances white offenders prosecuted for murder were convicted for culpable homicide. Sometimes the charge of murder was reduced to culpable homicide for Africans too when the victim was an African. This policy resulted less from a sense of justice than from a general disdain for the lives of Africans. The non-imposition of the death penalty 'did not originate in a belief in the abolition of the death penalty but in a "relaxed, casual attitude towards violence if it did not involve the white community"'.[116] Killing a white would necessarily result in a charge of murder and a death sentence.

The unsophisticated native, the primitive, savage, dangerous barbarian was diminished in his humanity. The political system provided judges with comfortable laws and circumstances that justified the award of capital punishment on the basis of racial bias. 'Judges were able to sentence blacks to death because racism provided them with that essential psychological resource that diminished a black man's humanity.'[117] This is what explains the increase in executions from 1944. The death penalty was undoubtedly a weapon against political antagonists in an

112 No 5 of 1927.

113 *The Star*, 17 February 1960 as quoted by Kahn (n 70) 203.

114 Turrell (n 63) 96.

115 ibid 97.

116 ibid 8.

117 ibid 12.

attempt to shore up racial segregation. Murder was a political crime until the death penalty was abolished.

Abolition of the death penalty in South Africa

Four factors, when combined, always resulted in the death penalty. The person had to be poor, non-European, male and represented by a *pro bono* defence council.[118] The death penalty for murder was generally imposed on Africans, Indians and coloureds.[119] In South Africa, racial issues have always been perceived as highly political for both ordinary citizens and learned judges. Van Niekerk calls them the 'taboos of our land'.[120]

In the *Makwanyane* case, the court avoided addressing the link between the death penalty and race. It dealt with race together with poverty and other factors of arbitrariness.[121] The death penalty was outlawed not because it was a political instrument against non-whites but because it irreparably breaches the most fundamental human rights, the rights to life, to dignity and to not to be subjected to cruel, inhuman and degrading punishments.[122] This legal approach left the taboos mostly intact.

Academics blamed the court for avoiding the practical problems that South African society was facing. It should have analysed the racial question through the right to equality, which is entrenched in the South African constitution. 'In so doing, he [Chief Justice Chaskalson] avoided an assessment of the role the death penalty played in maintaining a system of racial oppression.'[123]

However, the court had clarified that it was not dealing with the desirability of the death penalty vis-à-vis the majority of South Africans. Rare would have been non-Europeans who desired the death penalty. On the contrary, the majority of white judges, lawyers and deputies favoured the death penalty. Parliamentarians stated that '[p]eople fear that the abolition of the death penalty will result in thousands of Non-whites overcome by their instincts, murdering [whites] in [their] beds ....'[124] These subjective considerations were dismissed in one sentence: '... in the matter before us the court had been called upon to decide an issue of constitutionality ....'[125]

It is unfortunate that today, retentionists are campaigning against the sanctity of the right to life. It is submitted that there cannot be respect for the sanctity of human life unless the murderer's life carries more weight than that of the

118 *S v. Makwanyane and Another* 1995 (3) SA 391 (CC), paras 48–49 per President Chaskalson.

119 Kahn (n 70) 206.

120 Van Niekerk (n 72) 463.

121 *Makwanyane and Another* (n 118) 49 footnote 78, paras 51–54 and 94 per President Chaskalson.

122 ibid paras 10, 21–24, 26, 57, 67 and 144 per President Chaskalson.

123 Turrell (n 63) 13–14.

124 Debates in Parliament, cols 2578–9 as quoted by Van Niekerk (n 72) 471.

125 *Makwanyane and Another* (n 118) para 303 per Justice Ackermann.

helpless and innocent victim.[126] Worries about the murder rate, which doubled between 1990 and 2000,[127] have led some academics to argue that thinking that criminals are deterred by effective prosecution is no less a legal hypocrisy than the belief that they were deterred by the death penalty:

> It is ironic that apartheid was characterized by empty phrases which were incompatible with the reality of everyday life and yet, with our new constitutional order, we are running the same risk. The burning question which remains is, whether South Africa has perhaps not again placed ideology over reality.[128]

Whatever the case may be, the state has no right to take the lives of citizens it has the duty to protect. It would be a step backward to reinstate the death penalty in a country that has experienced its outrages.

The Death Penalty in the Democratic Republic of Congo (formerly Zaire)

The colonial penal code survived in the Congo where there has not been much progress since 1960. A member of the Belgian administration remarked in 1969 that he would be surprised if laws and institutions in the Congo were not 'a marked survival of the structure established before independence'.[129] He was right. Subsequent amendments strengthened the repressive colonial regime. The latest amendment dates to 30 November 2004.[130]

The death penalty is provided for both ordinary and military crimes. Ordinary capital crimes range from homicides and political offences to property crimes. The military penal code contains more than 48 articles providing for capital punishment. The number of ordinary and military capital crimes causes the Congolese penal legislation to resemble colonial emergency laws. Since independence, politicians have resorted to capital punishment to stabilise their insolvent regime at the expense of innocent lives.

---

126 Carel R Snyman, *Criminal Law* (4th edn, Butterworths, Durban 2002) 30 and Stephane S Terblanche, *The Guide to Sentencing in South Africa* (Butterworths, Durban 1999) 528.

127 In 2003, the murder rate was about 11 times higher than in Germany and 20 times higher than in the United Kingdom, the two having the lowest levels in Europe. See Snyman (n 126) 29.

128 Jolandi Le Roux and Bernard Bekink, 'The Abrogation of the Death Penalty in South Africa: Participating in the Ongoing Debate' (2006) 62 *Journal for Contemporary Roman Dutch Law* 201, 201–214.

129 Antoine Rubbens, 'The Congo Democratic Republic' in Alan Milner (ed), *African Penal Systems* (Routledge and Kegan Paul, London 1969) 23 and 28.

130 Décret du 30 janvier 1940 portant code pénal congolais tel que modifié à ce jour (Mis à jour au 30 novembre 2004), *Journal Officiel*, 45ème année, no spéciale, 30 novembre 2004.

The death penalty as a draconian punishment in Congo

The death penalty by hanging for civilians and shooting for soldiers is the most severe punishment. The court may, however, impose life imprisonment if it is satisfied with mitigating circumstances. Civilians are entitled to conditional release after serving a quarter of their sentence. They must serve at least five years' imprisonment if they are sentenced to life imprisonment. The regime for soldiers' conditional release is more onerous. The length of imprisonment before conditional release is discretionarily determined by the court.[131]

Although the condemned is entitled to mercy, he or she has no right to introduce a plea for mercy. The prosecutor is required to introduce such a plea to the head of state for all death sentences. This is an unfair procedure. The prosecutor is the defendant's adversary at the trial. Furthermore, the head of state's decision is based on the recommendation of the prosecutor, which has often proved to be against mercy. This incoherence led President Mobutu to keep inmates on death row for decades. The death penalty is executed inside the prison unless the government decides otherwise.[132] Table 5.3 provides a synopsis of the ordinary capital crimes in Congo.

Table 5.3 A synopsis of ordinary capital crimes in Congo

Ordinary crimes	Circumstances	Legal provisions of the penal code	Punishment
Assassination	Premeditation	Articles 44 and 45	Death
Murder	Simple murder	Articles 44 and 45	Death
Murder	To facilitate theft or obstruct justice	Article 85	Death
Poisoning		Article 49	Death
Creating armed groups	For endangering human beings or their property	Articles 156–158	Death is imposed for the mere fact of creating or supporting the association

131 Articles 5, 6, 18 and 35 of the Décret du 30 janvier 1940 portant code pénal congolais tel que modifié à ce jour (Mis à jour au 30 novembre 2004), *Journal Officiel*, 45ème année, no spéciale, 30 novembre 2004, articles 26, 27 and 28 of the Loi No 024/2002 du 18 novembre 2002 portant code pénal militaire, *Journal Officiel*, no spéciale, 20 mars 2003 and article 1 of the Arrêté du Gouverneur General du 9 avril 1898.

132 Article 2 of the Arrêté du Gouverneur Général du 9 avril 1898.

Ordinary crimes	Circumstances	Legal provisions of the penal code	Punishment
Superstitious practices	If death, physical incapacity or an incurable disease are the consequences	Article 57, paragraphs 2 and 3	Death
Illegal arrest or arbitrary detention	If accompanied by torture that caused the death	Article 67, paragraph 2	Death sentence is discretionary
Rape	Which resulted in the victim's death	Article 71	Death sentence is discretionary
Indecent assault	Which resulted in the victim's death	Article 71	Death sentence is discretionary
Armed theft		Article 171	Death
Treason	Perpetrated by a Congolese	Articles 181–184	Death
Espionage	Perpetrated by foreigners	Article 185	Death
Attempt to massacre or to commit pillage	With intention to commit massive killings, devastation or pillage	Article 200	Death
Sedition organised by an armed group	Commanders and subalterns bear the same responsibility	Article 204	Death
Using a weapon in an insurrectional movement	Article 207 paragraph 1 does not clearly indicate the nature of the weapon	Article 207, paragraph 2	Death
Directing or organising an insurrectional movement	The outcome and circumstances are immaterial	Article 208	Death

Source: Décret du 30 janvier 1940 tel que modifié et complété à ce jour (Mis à jour au 30 novembre 2004).[133]

The independent legislator has kept in line with the colonial code. Amendments have simply linked offences that presented strong similarities[134] or have hardened the repressive regime for certain crimes. The Congolese penal legislation does not, however, make infanticide and parricide separate offences. They are dealt

133 *Journal Officiel*, 45ème année, no spécial, 30 novembre 2004.

134 For example articles 44 and 45 relating to murder and assassination were combined in article 1 of Ordonnance-loi no 68/193 du 3 mai 1968, M.C. no 14 du 15 juillet 1968, p. 1324.

with as murder or assassination. Furthermore, there is no mandatory death penalty for illegal arrest or detention, rape or indecent assault that provoked the victim's death. The court discretionarily evaluates the aggravating circumstances and can impose life imprisonment. It should be noted that the most alarming provisions of the death penalty are found in the military penal code (see Table 5.4).

Table 5.4 A synopsis of military capital crimes in Congo

Military crimes	Circumstances	Legal provision in the military penal code	Punishment
Simple desertion	Deserting with weapons or ammunitions	Article 49, *in fine*	Death
Desertion to the enemy or desertion in the presence of the enemy	Soldier or civilians member of the crew of military navy or aircraft	Articles 50 and 51	Death
Cowardice	Running away in front of the enemy or using irregular methods for avoiding the danger	Article 57	Death
Capitulation or defeatism	Commander ordering to stop the fight or withdrawing before finishing ammunitions at his disposal	Article 58	Death
Abstaining from securing a fellow unit in danger or abstaining to fight the enemy with equal force	You must be the commander	Article 60	Death
Military plot during exceptional circumstances	If committed in war time or exceptional period for the security of the training or affect the decision of the military commander	Article 62	Death
Pillage	In wartime or in period of emergency laws	Article 65	Death
Forgery on the report of the commander or of the chief of staff	With intention to endanger national security or destruction of military materials or military unit	Article 72	Death
Military revolt	In wartime or in front of the enemy	Article 90	Death

Military crimes	**Circumstances**	**Legal provision in the military penal code**	**Punishment**
Rebellion		Articles 91 and 92	Death
Insubordination	In wartime or in front of the enemy	Article 94	Death
Violence against guards	In wartime, under emergency laws, police operation or in front of the enemy	Article 101	Death
Violence against civilians	In wartime or during exceptional periods	Article 103	Death
Abandoning an assigned position	In wartime or under special circumstances	Article 116	Death
Abandoning a military vessel or aircraft or leaving troops behind	You must be a commander or pilot in wartime or in front of the enemy	Article 119 and 120	Death
Abandoning the position	In wartime or in front of the enemy	Article 121	Death
Treason	In wartime, the military code applies to both civilians and soldiers	Article 128 and articles 181–184 of the ordinary penal code	Death
Espionage	For foreigners	Article 129 and articles 181–185 of the ordinary penal code	Death
Sabotage	For serving foreign powers or organisations	Article 133	Death
Giving misguiding information	In wartime	Article 134	Death
Attack by a military group		Article 135	Death
Directing or participating in an insurrectional movement		Articles 137–139	Death
Taking commanders in hostage		Article 140	Death
Inciting the army to surrender to the enemy		Article 143	Death
Demoralising the army	In wartime	Article 146	Death
Jeopardising national defence	In war time or in a special period	Article 148	Death
Terrorism	If it provoked death	Article 158	Death

Military crimes	**Circumstances**	**Legal provision in the military penal code**	**Punishment**
Genocide and crimes against humanity	When any of them is indivisible of other military or ordinary offences	Articles 161–175	Death
Evading prisoners		Article 179	Death
Enrolling on the enemy's side		Article 190	Death
Exactions against civilians	If accompanied with torture or any offence	Article 191	Death
Forced labour for civilians, sequestration accompanied by torture, embezzlement, theft and unlawful destruction of military materials		Articles 192, 194 and 202	Death

Source: Loi No 024/2002 du 18 novembre 2002 portant code pénal militaire.[135]

Aggravating circumstances that justify the death penalty are war, public disorder, an emergency period, torture and the victim's death. The harshness of the military penal code may however be tempered by the discretionary power that this law concedes to judges as regard sentencing. Article 27 of the military penal code provides that the military court may impose a sentence of life imprisonment or any other term of imprisonment in alternative to the death penalty provided it indicates the minimum period before which the offender cannot be eligible to conditional release. The practice shows that judges have ignored this salutary window mainly when they are sentencing crimes that are labelled to be of political connotation. It is argued that although it was expected that the Military Court would not impose the death penalty in the case of the assassination of President Laurent Desire Kabila, military judges decided to maintain the status quo. Their decision has now kept the supposed killers of Laurent Desire Kabila on death row for years.[136]

Genocide and crimes against humanity are capital crimes whether perpetrated in peacetime or in wartime. Articles 173–175 of the military penal code do not provide for any punishment against war crimes. There might have been a material mistake in the drafting of the code of 2002. War crimes were capital crimes under

135 *Journal Officiel*, no spéciale, 20 mars 2003.

136 Lievin Ngondji Ongombe, 'L'impact de la peine de mort dans le processus de l'adoption de la loi de mise en œuvre du statut de Rome en République Démocratique du Congo', in Kai Ambos, Ottilia A. Maunganidze (eds), *Pouvoir et Poursuite: Défis et Opportunités pour la Justice Pénale Internationale en Afrique Sub Saharienne* (Konrad Adenauer Stiftung, Göttingen, 2012) 76.

the *Code de justice militaire* of 1972.[137] In ratifying the Rome Statute of the International Criminal Court, the Congo also committed itself to punishing all crimes within the court's jurisdiction.[138]

There are other unanswered questions, however: why are international crimes located in a military penal code, tried before military tribunals and punished with death sentences? The military penal code provides that military tribunals only have jurisdiction over genocide, crimes against humanity and war crimes when they are connected to or indivisible from other crimes.[139] These are often crimes connected to others such as murder, assassination, poisoning, torture and so on. The consequence of militarising these crimes is that civilian offenders have appeared before military courts.[140] To appear before a court whose procedure is limited by disciplinary procedures jeopardises defenders' rights. Military tribunals are no less than professional courts. Soldiers are prosecuted for having failed to perform their duties.

The wording of the law does not make genocide, crimes against humanity and war crimes military crimes. They are wrongly brought under the jurisdiction of military justice. While desertion is a professional offence, genocide, crimes against humanity and war crimes are the most serious and heinous crimes. They have nothing in common with the military profession.

There is, therefore, only one possible justification for this shortcut. The Congo ratified the Rome Statute on 11 April 2002. Meanwhile, amendments of the 1972 military penal code were pending in Parliament. It eventually appeared justified to insert international crimes amongst military crimes rather than amending the ordinary penal code or initiating a separate law.

The death penalty at the service of politics

The Congo is one of the most troubled countries on the continent. Coercion, arbitrary arrests and prolonged illegal detention, violence, eliminating political activists, massacres of civilians and students, and more recently intertribal and interethnic killings have characterised it since its independence.[141] Unfortunately, 'even before 1960, documentation on criminal statistics was difficult to find and since independence it has not usually been readily available'.[142] Congo is one of

137 Ordonnance-Loi no 72/60 du 25 septembre 1972 portant code de justice militaire, *Journal Officiel*, no 6 of 25 septembre 1972.

138 Article 12 (1) of the Rome Statute of the International Criminal Court of 17 July 1998, UN Doc A/CONF. 183/9, 17 July 1998.

139 Article 161 of the Loi no 024/2002 du 18 novembre 2002 portant code pénal militaire, *Journal Officiel*, no spéciale, 20 mars 2003.

140 *Military Prosecutor v. Khawa Panga Mandro*, RMP N0227/PEN/2006, ILDC 524 (CD).

141 Thomas Turner, 'Zaire: Flying High above the Toads: Mobutu and Stalemated Democracy' in John F Clark and David E Gardiner (eds), *Political Reform in Francophone Africa* (Westview Press, Oxford 1997) 248.

142 Rubbens (n 129) 26.

the Sub-Saharan countries that has developed a practice of not disclosing data on capital punishment.[143] It applied the death penalty in such a way as to terrorise and intimidate the population.[144]

Les pendus de la pentecote were the first victims of Mobutu's regime. Four persons (Evariste Kimba, Emmanuel Bamba, Alexandre Mahamba and Jerome Anany) were hanged six months after Mobutu's putsch of 24 November 1966. The Minister of Information had reported that they would receive a death sentence for high treason and be hanged. He later alleged that he was only speaking in the conditional tense. The court martial, created the day after the 1966 Pentecost,[145] took 90 minutes for hearings and five minutes for deliberation.[146] The defendants were executed at the current Kasa-Vubu Bridge in Kinshasa. Later Mobutu declared that '… it was necessary to strike by example … so that people may not dare again'.[147]

Two years later, Mobutu granted a tenuous amnesty to his former rebel opponent, Pierre Mulele, for the purpose of peace and reconciliation. The latter sailed on a presidential boat from Brazzaville and received a heroic welcome in Kinshasa. In a public meeting at the Park de la Revolution on 2 October 1968, Mobutu declared that Pierre Mulele committed crimes against the nation. He was arrested before the end of the speech and tried by a military tribunal at the Kokolo military camp. The court delivered the judgment on 8 October and on 10 October 1968, the radio announced that Pierre Mulele had been sentenced to death and executed by shooting.[148] A year earlier, Moise Tchombé, the then secessionist President of Katanga and prime minister of Congo, had received a death sentence in absentia for high treason during the famous trial of *Les procès Tshipola*. He escaped hanging before he mysteriously disappeared in Algiers, where President Houari Boumedienne had opposed his extradition to Kinshasa.[149] His co-defendants, the *gendarmes Katangais*, were convicted of treason as well and executed.

The *Coup monté et manqué* trial of 1 September 1975 tried more than 30 persons accused of treason, assassination, creating military gangs, inciting soldiers

143 The number of African countries willing to disclose their data on the death penalty is striking. Out of 46 countries, only seven participated in the 1975 report (UN Doc E/5616), the number increased to nine in 1980 (UN Doc E 1980/9), then dropped to five in 1985 (UN Doc E/1985/43/Corr1) before falling to only two countries, namely Mauritius and Cape Verde, in 1990 (UN Doc E/1990/38/Rev.1). In 1996, six countries responded (UN Doc E/CN.15/1996/19) but again the number gradually decreased to five in 2000 (UN Doc E/2000/3), four in 2005 (UN Doc E/2005/3) and two in 2010 (UN Doc E/2010/10).

144 Turner (n 141) 248.

145 Ordonnance no 66/338 du 30 mai 1966 portant création du tribunal militaire d'exception.

146 Conférence Nationale Souveraine, *Période allant de 1965 à 1971*, Dossier 1, août 1992, at p. 6.

147 ibid 12.

148 ibid Dossier 3, at p. 35.

149 ibid Dossier 4, at pp. 38–46.

to insubordination and disclosing military secrets. Four officers and three accomplices were sentenced to death. They spent 20 months on death row before receiving mercy on President Mobutu's forty-ninth birthday.[150] The *Conférence Nationale Souveraine* concluded that Mobutu perpetrated crimes against humanity in 1978 when he massacred the entire village of Mulembe in Idiofa. He had accused the villagers of reincarnating Pierre Mulele's ideology. On this basis, 14 survivors of the massacre were sentenced to death and executed.[151] After the 1978 *procès du siècle* that brought 90 persons to trial for treason and terrorism, and 13 of those to the gallows the next morning, Mobutu declared that he would no longer accept human rights pretexts for reprieving death sentences.[152]

Summary executions were also a regular practice beside military trials. In retentionist countries, *de facto* and summary executions may exceed the total number of world reported judicial executions.[153] Without naming individual cases, the following were massacred: students of the Kinshasa University in 1969, peasants of Kabare and Idjwi in 1985, Kinshasa protesters in 1988 and 1990, students of the Lubumbashi University in 1990, peasants in Mbuji-Mayi in 1991, Christians in 1992 and more.[154]

The 1992 *Conférence Nationale Souveraine* found that President Mobutu used the death penalty as a threat against his political opponents.[155] At that time, the conference suggested taking four steps that would lead to a complete abolition of the death penalty: envisaging the abolition of the death penalty within five years

150 Ordonnance no 79/238 du 13 octobre 1979 portant grâce présidentielle. See also Conférence Nationale Souveraine, *Coup d'etat monté et manqué de 1975: rapport de synthèse*, Dossier 5, août 1992, at pp. 59–69.

151 Conférence Nationale Souveraine, *Massacre d'Idiofa en janvier 1978*, Dossier 7, août 1992, at pp. 73–80.

152 Conférence Nationale Souveraine, *Procès dits des terroristes*, Dossier 8 bis, août 1992, at pp. 89–102.

153 UN Doc E/1980/9 at para 84.

154 See alternatively Conference Nationale Souveraine, *Periode allant de 1965 a 1971*, Dossier 2, août 1992, at pp. 15–25, Conférence Nationale Souveraine, *Massacres dits de l'Ile d'Idjwi (Sud-Kivu) 1985*, Dossier 10, août 1992, at pp.110–112, *Massacre dits de Kabare*, Dossier 11, août 1992, at pp. 113–116, *Massacre du Pont Kasa-Vubu, dimanche 17 janvier 1988*, Dossier 12, août 1992, at pp. 117–125, *Soulèvement populaire protestant contre la Hausse des prix: 01 Décembre 1990*, Dossier 12 bis, août 1992, at pp. 126–132, *Massacres (des Chrétiens) des 16 février et 01 mars 1992*, Dossier 13, août 1992, at pp. 133–137, *Massacre des etudiants de l'Université de Lubumbashi dans la nuit du 11 au 12 Mai 1990*, Dossier 14, août 1992, at pp. 138–169, *Massacre de Mbuji Mayi du 13 au 17 avril 1991*, Dossier 15, août 1992, at pp. 170–178.

155 Conférence Nationale Souveraine, *Période allant de 1965 à 1971*, Dossier 1, août 1992, at p. 12.

from 1992, restricting the imposition of the death penalty to assassination, raising public awareness of abolition and improving penitentiary administration.[156]

In the 1990s, Mobutu started commuting death sentences and began to envisage abolition. However, political instability, civil war and massive crimes reversed this trend.[157] During the 1996 war, both sides applied capital punishment for different purposes: Mobutu to punish treason and Laurent Kabila to discipline soldiers. For example, in January 1997, the Kisangani military tribunal imposed death sentences on 14 government soldiers for cowardice and desertion and one civilian for disclosing a military position to the enemy.[158] In May 1997, Laurent Kabila resorted to speedy trials and executions as well. Soldier Kanyongo Kisase's trial for murder took only a few hours. He was refused both appeal and mercy and executed on 22 October 1997.[159] In 1998, Laurent Kabila's second year in office, the Congo executed 100 persons.[160] There were 236 executions between 1996 and 2000.[161] In 2002, President Joseph Kabila declared a moratorium on executions under the Congolese Charter of Human Rights. However, the Special Rapporteur on capital punishment doubted both the decision and the binding character of the charter.[162]

Indeed, Joseph Kabila hanged more people than did his predecessor. In a list of the number of executions per country between 1999 and 2003, the Congo occupied fifth position.[163] It had been thirteenth between 1994 and 1998. Statistics indicate that there were 350 executions between 1999 and 2003.[164] Although some consider that the last execution dates back to 2003,[165] death sentences[166] and secret executions continued. It was reported that 15 persons were secretly executed on 7

156 Nyabirungu Mwene Songa, *Traité du droit pénal général Congolais* (Editions Universitaires Africaines, Kinshasa 2007) 369.

157 Roger Hood, *The Death Penalty: A Worldwide Perspective* (3rd edn, Oxford University Press, New York 2002) 41.

158 Amnesty International, *Zaire: Killings and Other Human Rights Violations by Security Forces*, 1997, at p. 8, AI Index: AFR 62/06/97.

159 Amnesty International, *DRC: Deadly Alliances in Congolese Forests*, 1997, at p. 31, AFR 62/33/97.

160 UN Doc E/2005/3 at 46 table 2. Although data are presented for the period 1994–1998, it is indicated that they all count for 1998. See UN Doc E/2000/3 at p. 12.

161 Hood (n 157) 92.

162 UN Doc A/57/437 at 36.

163 UN Doc E/2005/3 at 46 table 2.

164 ibid.

165 Anjan Sundaram, 'Congolese Minors Sit on Death Row', *IPS*, 26 April 2006 at http://ipsnews.net/news.asp?idnews=33017 (accessed 8 July 2010).

166 Nadine Kavira, 'Kalemie: affaire Féfé et consorts, peine de mort pour trois prévenus', Augustin Kinienzi 'Procès Franck Ngyke: peine capital pour tous le prévenus', *Le Potentiel*, 5 April 2007.

January 2003.[167] The Congo is reported to have executed 215 persons between 2002 and 2006.[168]

Towards the abolition of the death penalty in Congo

The law and the courts have played the game of politics in bringing a huge number of soldiers and civilians to the gallows regardless of their age or sex through a process that has ignored all standards of fairness. The promised abolition of military courts only happened after the Constitution of 18 February 2006.[169] The Constitution is also interpreted as containing abolitionist provisions because it proclaims an unrestricted right to life and dignity.[170]

Therefore, death sentences imposed from 18 February 2006 should be deemed to be unconstitutional.[171] However, according to article 150 of the Constitution, judges impose the penalties available in the penal code. Penal provisions cannot be abrogated tacitly. That lays the blame with the lawmaker who does not enact a penal code consistent with the Constitution. Meanwhile, the only remedy for the condemned would be an appeal to the constitutional court. Nevertheless, the condemned has few chances of having the case heard. Article 139 of the Constitution provides for an *a priori* judicial review of constitutionality of laws, initiated by a few top political organs. In sum, a penal law that outlaws the death penalty in Congo remains the only efficient abolitionist mechanism.[172]

Furthermore, it remains unclear whether States Parties to the Rome Statute of the International Criminal Court such as the Congo may impose severer punishments than the court itself would. This stems from the problem of precedence between article 77 and article 80 of the Rome Statute. It is argued that the rationale of article 80 was a political compromise intending to attract ratifications;[173] or a concession to countries viscerally or culturally attached to the death penalty.[174] It follows that article 80 read together with article 17, which makes the International Criminal Court a complementary tribunal to domestic courts, gives power to domestic judges to impose the death penalty.[175] Congolese

167 Home Office (United Kingdom), *Democratic Republic of Congo*, 2004, at 5.29.

168 Roger Hood and Carolyn Hoyle, *The Death Penalty: A Worldwide Perspective* (4th edn, Oxford University Press, New York 2008) 149.

169 Article 149, para 3 of the Constitution de la République Démocratique du Congo du 18 février 2006 telle que révisée par la loi no11/002 du 02 janvier 2011, *Journal Officiel de la République Démocratique du Congo*, no 3, 1 février 2011.

170 Article 16 read together with article 61 the Constitution de la République Démocratique du Congo du 18 février 2006, ibid.

171 Nyabirungu (n 156) 371.

172 ibid 370–371.

173 William A Schabas, *The International Criminal Court: A Commentary on the Rome Statute* (Oxford University Press, New York 2010) 921.

174 Nyabirungu (n 156) 369.

175 Nadia Bernaz, *Le droit international et la peine de mort* (La Documentation Française, Paris 2008) 268.

courts have, however, taken an opposite direction. When trying crimes within the jurisdiction of the Rome Statute, Congolese military courts have excluded the death penalty as provided for by the Military Penal Code and referred to article 77 of the Rome Statute.[176]

They confirm the fact that the ambiguous position of Congo during the negotiations of the Rome Statute meant it joined Cuba, Japan, Kenya and Senegal whose silence implied that they have substituted the death penalty for imprisonment.[177] It is not clear that Congolese military judges were aware of the negotiation process. They might, however, have acknowledged the abolitionist signal that the Rome Statute has sent in excluding the death penalty for the most serious crimes. Congolese judges have interpreted their country's ratification of the Rome Statute as a subscription to the principle of article 77 rather than to the exception contained in article 80. This somehow confirms that the window open by article 80 is not an excuse for countries to impose the death penalty.

The worst mistake of our time has been resorting to the death penalty in the belief that its use protects the paramount interests of the state or fundamental rights. The case of the Democratic Republic of Congo demonstrates that this is an illusion. Stability is not achieved by cheapening the lives of citizens. While governments think they are quelling political dissidents by resorting to repressive punishments, their actions create chaos and an infinite circle of violence. Thus, the values protected under articles 16 and 61 of the Congolese Constitution that proclaim the sanctity of life and the ratification of the Rome Statute of the International Criminal Court call on Congo to abolish the death penalty.

The Death Penalty in Nigeria

The death penalty has a long history in Nigeria. It existed already under indigenous law and *Shari'a*. With the English law influence, the sentencing policy of these pre-colonial laws progressively fell in line with the new legal order. Indigenous and Muslim judges started applying punishments similar to those of English courts.[178]

After independence, the task became easier. A uniform penal code applied all over Nigeria. For the sake of harmony, lessons on criminal law and procedure were initiated in the Northern Province, which was a bastion of *Shari'a* and native

176 *Military Prosecutor v. Khawa Panga Mandro*, RMP N0227/PEN/2006, ILDC 524 (CD), paras 20 and 113 and *Military Prosecutor v. Bongi Massaba*, RP No 018/2006, ILCD 387 (CD2006), paras 61, 66–68 and 117.

177 Countries that declared to prefer the death penalty during negotiations of the Rome Statute of the International Criminal Court include Ethiopia, Saudi Arabia, Lebanon, Rwanda and Trinidad and Tobago. See William A Schabas, *The Abolition of the Death Penalty in International Law* (3rd edn, Cambridge University Press, Cambridge 2002) 253 (footnote 110) and 258.

178 Alan Milner, 'Sentencing Patterns in Nigeria' in Alan Milner (ed), *African Penal Systems* (Routledge and Kegan Paul, London 1969) 268–269.

courts until independence.[179] The survival of pre-colonial courts and the extension of the penal and the criminal procedure codes to the entire country created a jurisprudence that was neither indigenous nor Islamic nor modern.

Indigenous and Islamic judges had, however, adopted attitudes similar to those of English lawyers.[180] Unfortunately, the political turbulence that characterised Nigeria post-independence led to the militarisation of criminal law. The military junta systematically overthrew civilian rulers and took the law in hostage. As a component of criminal law, the death penalty became an instrument that silenced opposing voices.[181] This exacerbated the latent but existing religious and ethnic antagonism. Nigerian Muslims found refuge in Islamic law and called for an Islamic state with wider application of *Shari'a*, which itself is not death penalty free.[182] With the arrival of democracy and the strengthening of a civil society advocating locally and internationally for the abolition of capital punishment, the federal state of Nigeria was split into abolitionists and retentionists.

The death penalty at the service of politics

As did most of the former British colonies, Nigeria introduced fundamental rights into its Constitution at independence. Prior to independence, it was put under the jurisdiction of the European Convention for the Protection of Human Rights and Fundamental Freedoms by a 1959 order in Council.[183] In 1963, independent Nigeria reproduced a whole chapter on fundamental rights in its first Constitution inspired by the text of the European Convention. Since then, the rights to life (article 2 of the European Convention), to dignity and to not be subjected to cruel, inhuman and degrading treatment (article 3 of the European Convention) have become part of Nigerian law.[184] Articles 18 and 19 of the 1963 Constitution respectively reproduced nearly exactly articles 2 and 3 of the European Convention.[185]

The European Convention's drafting history and the state of international law in the 1950s make article 2 of the European Convention one of the most

179 ibid 266.

180 Milner (n 178) 287.

181 Anthony Onyemachi Agwuele, 'Military Occupation, the National Question and the Rise of Ethnic Nationalism' in Toyin Falola (ed), *Nigeria in the Twentieth Century* (Carolina Academy Press, Durham 2002) 350 and 352.

182 John Hunwick, 'An African Case Study of Political Islam: Nigeria' (1992) 524 *Annals of the American Academy of Political and Social Sciences* 143, 143–155.

183 Nigeria (Constitution Amendment no 3) Order in Council, 1959 (S.I. 1959 No 1772, p. 3229, s. 69 and Sch) and section 3 of the Nigeria Independence Act, 1960 (8 and 9 Eliz, 2 Ch. 55).

184 For example sections 30 and 31 of the Constitution of the Federal Republic of Nigeria of 1 October 1979 and sections 33 and 34 of the Constitution of the Federal Republic of Nigeria (Decree no 24 of 1999).

185 Articles 2 and 3 of the European Convention on the Protection of Human Rights and Fundamental Freedoms, Rome 4 November 1950, E.T.S No 5 read with sections 18 and 19 of the Constitution of the Federation of Nigeria Act no 20, 1963.

conservative and anachronistic provisions on the death penalty. At the time it was drafted, in 1950, most European states were retentionist and the execution of Nazi criminals was still fresh in the collective memory. The European Convention is also unique in that it clearly sets up exceptions other than the death penalty to the right to life in article 2, paragraph 2 and in being silent, amongst other things, on juvenile offenders and pregnant women.[186]

In drafting its fundamental rights, Nigeria added three more exceptions:

a. the word mutiny was added after insurrection;
b. lethal force may also be used to prevent the commission of a criminal offence; and
c. under article 18 (3) of the Nigerian Constitution, the use of force by the government outside these prescribed cases is as well justified.[187]

The interpretation of exceptions to fundamental rights has been controversial. The Supreme Court of Nigeria maintains that the death penalty is constitutional since it only acts as an exception which is unmistakably part of the construction of the provision on the right to life.

> [The provision …] recognizes deprivation of life so long as it is pursuant to the execution of the sentence of a court in a criminal offence of which the accused has been found guilty in Nigeria.[188]

It is unfortunate that the Supreme Court does not elaborate further to find that exceptions to the right to life annihilate the whole value of the Constitution.

As regards extrajudicial exceptions, Grove argues that they are unacceptable.[189] The chapter on Fundamental Rights was intended to protect individuals against the actions of the majority dominating Nigerian political life. Since the legislative and the executive cannot pronounce the unconstitutionality of their excess, the duty of protecting individuals in applying and upholding the law, and principally the Constitution, is vested in the courts. However, the Supreme Court held that its role was not to speculate on what the law ought to be but to decide whether any exception to fundamental rights was 'reasonably justifiable in a democratic society'.[190] This is said to be an erroneous interpretation. Since the chapter was born out of the European Convention, the test is not reasonableness, but rather

---

186 Schabas (n 177) 260–265.

187 Section 18 (3) of the Constitution of the Federation of Nigeria Act no 20, 1963.

188 *Onuoha v The State* (1998) 13 N.W.L.R. 531 at 587–588.

189 DL Grove, 'The "Sentinels" of Liberty? The Nigerian Judiciary and Fundamental Rights' (1963) 7 *Journal of African Law* 152, 170–171.

190 *DPP v. Obi* (1961) 1 All N.L.R. 182.

necessity. 'Restrictions … are permitted only when they are "necessary" and not "reasonably justifiable".'[191]

The verbatim adoption of the European convention means that 'a person is deemed to have been deprived of his life constitutionally only if the force which was applied was no more than is absolutely necessary'.[192] Therefore, in retaining the test of 'reasonably justifiable' the court impliedly consented to reducing its power to review governmental action.[193] In other words, the Supreme Court should have noticed that in foreseeing extrajudicial exceptions to the right to life, the Constitution created artificial obstacles against any challenge to the constitutionality of governmental actions. The individual is often part of an unpopular minority mainly when his actions are appreciated through the wording of a constitution (such as the Nigerian Constitution) adopted by parliament rather than referendum. In this respect, the court should bear in mind that it performs its duties more correctly and efficiently when it concentrates more on individual rights and less on exceptions to those rights.

The main capital crimes are treason and culpable homicide, which comprises both murder and negligent homicide.[194] However, the death penalty may discretionarily be imposed also for brigandage followed by culpable homicide, participating in an ordeal trial that provoked death, false testimony from which an innocent person is executed, attempt to commit culpable homicide by a convict serving a prison sentence and abetment of suicide of a mentally disabled person or a child.[195] Among the safeguards are the prohibition of death sentences for juvenile offenders, pregnant women and mentally diseased persons.[196] Persons convicted of capital crimes also enjoy the right to appeal which is automatic when the death sentence emanates from a native court. The condemned may also apply for mercy.[197]

The use of capital punishment increased with military regimes. In fact, the 1966 military coup started a cycle of military dictatorship that by 2002 had lasted for 30 out of the 41 years of Nigerian independence.[198] The military junta attacked the Constitution by annihilating the chapter on fundamental rights, suspending the Constitution as a whole and by passing military decrees, which had primacy over

191 Alexander S De Smith, 'Fundamental Rights in the New Commonwealth-II' (1961) 10 *International Comparative Law Quarterly* 215, 222–223.

192 ibid.

193 Grove (n 189) 167.

194 Alan Gledhil, *The Penal Codes of Northern Nigeria and Sudan* (Sweet and Maxwell, London 1963) 466.

195 ibid 757.

196 UN Doc E/67 IV.15, 1968, at paras 185–186.

197 Gledhil (n 194) 757–758.

198 Agwuele (n 181). See also George Klay Kieh and Pita Ogaba Agbese, 'From Politics Back to the Barracks in Nigeria: A Theoretical Exploration' (1993) 30 *Journal of Peace Research* 409, 413–414.

any other law including the Constitution.[199] For example, Decree no 1 of 1966 that amended the Constitution provided that '… this Constitution shall not prevail over a Decree and nothing in this Constitution shall render any provision of a decree void to any extent whatsoever'.[200] A more authoritarian phrasing appears in section 3 (1) of Decree no 17 of 1966:

> The Government shall have power to make laws for peace and order of Nigeria with respect to any matter whatsoever. It shall make laws by decrees and no question as to the validity of this or any decree or edict shall be entertained by any court of law in Nigeria.[201]

Subordinating the Constitution to military decrees meant that the legality of those decrees could not be questioned. The certainty of the applicable law to a specific conduct was nullified. This enabled soldiers to penalise conduct that was previously not an offence by adopting retroactive penal laws. Such laws were often adopted in targeting 'the undesirable elements' that opposed the military junta. 'In other words, arbitrary, inconsistent and obnoxious laws were promulgated provided they met the needs of the incumbent dictator.'[202]

The federal police became an instrument of oppression focused on political opponents, terrorising the population and repressing agitators who were demanding the acknowledgement of minimum human rights and the suppression of military tribunals.[203] Among the military tribunals were the Recovery of Public Property Special Military Tribunal,[204] the tribunal created under the Robbery and Firearms Act,[205] Miscellaneous Offenses Tribunal[206] and the tribunal created under Exchange Control (Anti-sabotage) Act.[207] The military, assisted by policemen with no specialised knowledge in law, tried crimes within the jurisdiction of these tribunals, which were empowered to impose the death penalty. Until human rights activists pushed the military to set up the special appeal tribunal, there was no right to appeal under the Robbery and Firearm Tribunal.[208] Although the absence of official reports makes it impossible to give the actual rate of executions,[209] it

---

199 Chika B Onwekwe, 'Militarism versus Democratic Governance' in Toyin Falola (ed), *Nigeria in the Twentieth Century* (Carolina Academy Press, Durham 2002) 389–390.

200 Decree no 1 of 1966 (Nigeria).

201 Section 3 (1) of the Decree no 17 1966.

202 Onwekwe (n 199).

203 Agwuele (n 181) 352.

204 Recovery of Public Property (Special Military Tribunal) Act of 1990, Cap. 389.

205 Robbery and Firearms (Special Provision) Act of 1970 as amended by the Robbery and firearms (Special Provision) Act of 1990, Cap. 398.

206 Special Tribunal (Miscellaneous Offences) Act of 1990, Cap. 410.

207 Exchange Control (Anti- Sabotage) Act of 1990, Cap. 114.

208 Bolanle Awe, 'Conflict and Divergence: Government and Society in Nigeria' (1999) 42 *African Studies Review* 1, 12.

209 UN Doc E/1985/43, p. 10 at 29.

is common knowledge that under the firearms and robbery act, military tribunals made Nigeria one of the world leaders in execution. Figure 5.5 details the number of executions of the death penalty in Nigeria in the period 1961–1989.

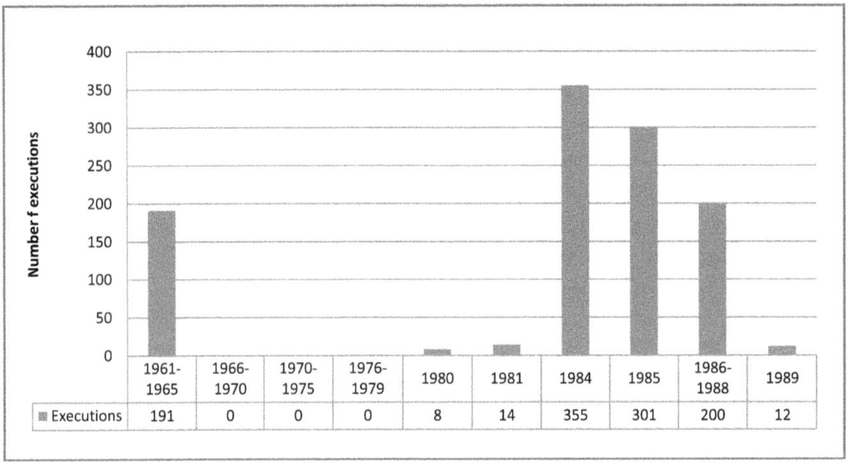

Figure 5.5 Executions of the death penalty in Nigeria (1961–1989)
NB: O represents data that are not available.
Source: Olubgeni Fatula[210] and Amnesty International.[211]

There were 251 executions between 1959 and 1960.[212] Despite the unavailability of data for 1966–1979, it is known that the majority of executed persons were convicted under the Robbery and Firearms Decree of 1970. Respite only occurred during periods of ephemeral civilian rule such as that of 1979–1983. In 1979, the civilian president restored the jurisdiction of the high court over armed robbery and the right to appeal was reinstituted. Consequently 'a relatively small number of executions took place'.[213] In 1983, the civilian government was overthrown. In 1984, special military tribunals were re-established and the right to appeal was again suppressed; cases were tried by the military and police officers.[214] That year Nigerians watched at least one execution per day. Article 11 (4) of the Robbery and

210 Olugbemi Fatula, 'Capital Punishment: To Be or not To Be in Nigeria' (2001–2004) 14 *Lesotho Law Journal* 97, 103.

211 Amnesty International, *Nigeria: Death Sentences for Murder*, 1991, AI Index: AFR 44/03/91.

212 UN Doc E/67 IV.15, 1968, at p. 43.

213 Amnesty International, *Nigeria: Death Sentences and Executions for Armed Robbery*, 1992, AI Index: AFR/44/04/92.

214 Robbery and Firearms (Special Provision) Decree No. 5 of 1984.

Firearms Decree (the 1984 version) reads, '[no] appeal shall lie from a decision of a tribunal constituted under this Act or from any confirmation or dismissal of such decision by the Governor'.[215]

In August 1985, a new military junta withdrew the death penalty under the Miscellaneous Decree that made drug offences, tempering with electric or telephone cables, tempering with pipelines and arson capital crimes. However, the death penalty was maintained without appeal for armed robbery. In 1986, the Military Governor of the state of Niger stated that 'people convicted of armed robbery should be executed by being wounded slowly so that they could die by instalments and thereby their death could take a longer time'.[216]

It is doubtful whether there were only 12 executions in 1989. The government had decided to carry out executions in secret from 1989.[217] There were at least 2,600 executions between 1970 and 1999, an average of 90 executions per year.[218] The wave of execution increased again in 1990 (see Figure 5.6).

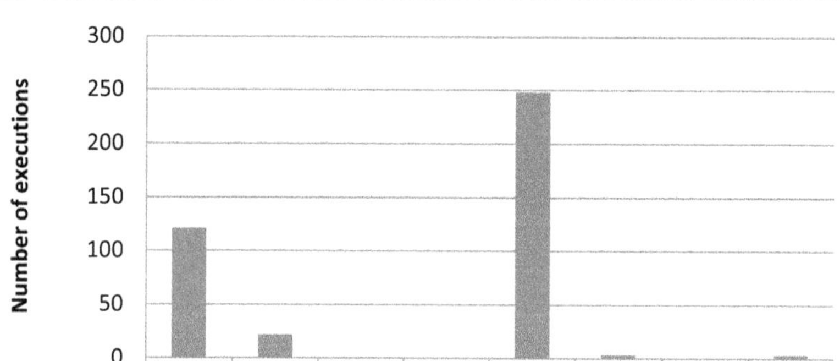

	1990	1991	1992	1993	1994-1998	1999-2003	2004-2010	2011-2013
Execution	121	22	0	0	248	4	0	4

Figure 5.6 Executions of the death penalty in Nigeria (1990–2013)
NB: O represents data that are unvailable save for 2004–2010
Source: United Nations[219] and Amnesty International.[220]

215 Section 11 (4) of the Robbery and Firearms (Special Provision) Decree No 5 of 1984.

216 Fatula (n 209) 104.

217 Amnesty International, *Nigeria: Death Sentences for Murder*, 1991, AI Index: AFR 44/03/91.

218 Amnesty International, *Nigeria: Imo State Death Penalty Puts Victims at Risk*, 7 May 2009.

219 UN Doc E/2000/3, p. 13 table 2 and UN Doc E/2010/10, p. 22 table 3.

220 Amnesty International, *Nigeria: Death Sentences and Executions for Armed Robbery*, 1992, AI Index: AFR/44/04/92 and Amnesty International, 'Nigeria Executions:

In 1990, of the 121 persons executed, 69 were convicted of treason for attempting a *coup d'état*.[221] Critics of this practice forced the military government to retreat and partially modify the law in 1990.[222] In 1991, the Nigerian Constitutional Rights Project seized the African Commission for Human and Peoples' Rights on provisions, which had not been improved by the 1990 amendment that limited the right to appeal, excluded appeal against the Governor's decision on mercy and organised a bench where soldiers were chaired by a civilian judge.[223] The Commission confirmed that Nigerian laws and courts have violated 'fundamental rights as described in article 7 (1) (a) of the African Charter [of Human and Peoples' Rights]. In this the fundamental rights in question are those to life and liberty provided for in articles 4 and 6 of the African Charter.'[224]

In analysing the fairness of the right to appeal, the Commission stated, '... to foreclose any avenue of appeal to "competent organs" in criminal cases bearing such penalties clearly violates article 7 (1) (A), and increases the risk that severe violations may go unadressed'.[225]

Accordingly, the government started commuting death sentences. In 1991, death sentences were commuted for eight persons convicted of treason.[226] In 1992, 13 death sentences in River State were all pardoned. However, in 1994, the rate of execution was alarming. One hundred persons were executed.[227] This period corresponded with post-electoral unrest that opposed General Sani Abacha and Moshood Abiola, who later supposedly died in detention. The African Commission reacted by calling upon 'African military regimes to respect fundamental rights'.[228] The military regime responded by giving its decrees primacy over the African Charter on Human and People's Rights, a position that local judges vividly combated.[229] The African Commission condemned gross violations of human rights, the exclusion of the African Charter on Human and Peoples' Rights and the disregard of ordinary courts by the military junta.[230]

"They Almost Executed Him Secretly"', 28 June 2013.

221 Amnesty International, *Nigeria: Death Sentences and Executions for Armed Robbery*, 1992, AI Index: AFR/44/04/92.

222 Robbery and Firearms (Special Provisions) Act of 1990, Cap. 398.

223 *Constitutional Rights Project v. Nigeria*, African Commission on Human and Peoples' Rights, Comm. No. 60/91 (1995).

224 ibid.

225 ibid.

226 Amnesty International has given two different figures of executions (15 and 20) for 1991. See alternatively Amnesty International, *Nigeria: Death Sentences for Murder*, 18 January 1991, AI Index: AFR 44/03/91 and Amnesty International, *Nigeria: Death Sentences and Executions for Armed Robbery*, 7 May 1992, AI Index: AFR/44/04/92.

227 Amnesty International, *Nigeria: Death Sentences and Executions for Armed Robbery*, 7 May 1992, AI Index: AFR/44/04/92.

228 ACHPR /Res.11 (XVI) 94: Resolution on Nigeria (1994).

229 *Abacha v. Fuwehinmi* (2000) 6 N.W.L.R. 228.

230 ACHPR /Res.11 (XVI) 94: Resolution on Nigeria (1994).

The battle with the African Commission worsened as death sentences without possibility of appeal were imposed against Ken Saro Wiwa and his eight co-defendants in 1995. The African Commission condemned the continued gross breach of human rights targeting human rights activists and political opponents.[231] The government carried out executions despite the protests of the Organisation of the African Unity and United Nations.[232] Unfair trials led to the arbitrary executions of 248 persons between 1994 and 1998. The last four years of Sani Abacha's regime placed Nigeria seventh in the world in a list ranking countries by number of executed persons.[233]

In 2004, Nigeria reportedly executed four people.[234] In 2005, Nigeria indicated that it was envisaging abolishing the death penalty.[235] It is doubtful whether Nigeria has in fact applied a moratorium on executions. The strength of the abolitionist movement has sometimes created a hypocritical political stance. Many retentionist countries claim *de facto* abolitionist status while executions continue in secret. In Kano, at least six persons were secretly executed in 2006.[236] This number increased to seven in 2007. Prison services have ensured that the condemned are relocated to other states before their execution.[237] Since 1984, executions have been at times carried out simply to decongest prisons.[238] The extension of the death penalty to new crimes such as kidnapping and homosexuality is also pending. Six states extended the death penalty to kidnapping in 2009.[239] The Governor of Imo State declared in July 2010 that he would not hesitate to sign death warrants against kidnappers.[240] There are concerns that homosexuality will also be made a capital crime in the south as has been the case for so-called acts of terrorism which were made capital crimes since the Boko Haram attacks in the country. Efforts to quell Boko Haram's terrorist activities have led the current Nigerian

231 ACHPR /Res.16 (XVII) 95: Resolution on Nigeria (1995).

232 A/RES/50/199 of 11 March 1996.

233 UN Doc E/2000/3, p. 13 table 2.

234 UN Doc E/2010/10 at para 27, footnote 70.

235 UN Doc E/2005/3 at 37.

236 Amnesty International, *Nigeria: Amnesty International, Human Rights Watch and Nigerian Civil Society Call on State Governments not to Resume the Execution of Prisoners*, 25 June 2010, AI Index: AFR 44/010/2010.

237 Amnesty International, *Nigeria: Government Misleads World about Death Penalty Record*, 17 December 2007, AI Index: PRE 01/004/2007.

238 Amnesty International, *When the State Kills ... the Death Penalty v. Human Rights* (Amnesty International Publications 1989) 186–187 and Amnesty International, *Nigeria: Amnesty International, Human Rights Watch and Nigerian Civil Society Call on State Governments not to Resume the Execution of Prisoners*, 25 June 2010, AI Index: AFR 44/010/2010.

239 Amnesty International, *Death Sentences and Executions 2009*, ACT 50/001/2010, at p. 23.

240 Kareem Ubgodaga, 'Death Penalty for Kidnappers', *PM News*, 27 July 2010.

leadership to resume executions. In 2013, Nigeria violated its moratorium and executed four people.[241]

It is unfortunate that the leadership has not realised that the death penalty has been politically instrumentalised in Nigeria. It is associated with oppression, dictatorship, unjust laws and unfair justice. This is well understood by those continuing its use even under *Shari'a*.

The politicisation of Shari'a *and the death penalty*

Under military rule the diffusion of political energy became a contributing factor to the politicisation of religion, or rather, the use of religion as a tool for creating a political constituency.[242] By 1977, drafters of the new Constitution had suggested the creation of a *Shari'a* Federal Court of Appeal. Although Christians opposed the idea on the grounds of equality, Muslim parliamentarians succeeded in having three judges exclusively vested in *Shari'a* related cases. The 1979 Constitution conceded also that states can establish *Shari'a* courts of appeal in personal status matters.[243] Muslims argued that refusal would mean that lay judges would have to try *Shari'a* cases. This was perceived as both discrimination and an attack on Islam.[244] While Christians suspected that Muslims intended to Islamise the whole of Nigeria, Muslims felt that their secular country was nothing more than 'a child, albeit bastard, of Christianity ... [which] has become a sinister but convenient mechanism to blackmail Muslims and impede the progress of Islam'.[245]

The radicalisation of Islam worried politicians. This divisive debate on *Shari'a*-related provisions resurfaced throughout the constitutional history of Nigeria until the current Constitution of 1999. For the sake of national unity, the 1999 Constitution maintained unaltered *Shari'a* provisions of the 1979 Constitution.[246] However, the 1999 restoration of civilian rule in 12 northern states sought to correct prejudices suffered by Muslims in adopting executive and legislative measures with the view of reversing the *status quo*. The new Constitution extended the jurisdiction of *Shari'a* courts in criminal law and reintroduced community participation in crime prevention and detection.[247]

241 UN Doc A/HRC/24/18, 1 July 2013, para 14, Amnesty International, Death penalty 2013: Small number of countries trigger global spike in executions, ACT 50/001/2014, 27 March 2014 and Fran Blandy, 'Homosexual Africans Face Prison, Intolerance and the Death Penalty', *The Telegraph*, 11 January 2010. In 2009, the Nigerian Parliament attempted to criminalise same-sex marriage under a civil law. See Human Rights Watch, *Nigeria Rejects 'Same Sex' Marriage Ban*, 26 January 2009.

242 Hunwick (n 182).

243 Andrew Ubaka Iwobi, 'Tiptoeing through a Constitutional Minefield: The Great *Shari'a* Controversy in Nigeria' (2004) 48 *Journal of African Law* 111, 115.

244 Hunwick (n 182).

245 Ibrahim, 'Politics of religion in Nigeria', p. 77 as quoted by John Hunwick (n 182).

246 Iwobi (n 243) 116–120.

247 ibid 121.

The claim for Islamic heritage was translated into the enactment of a *Shari'a* penal code that broke down the compromise that the 1960 penal code had introduced. In fact, flogging and the death penalty were retained in the north because they were also *Shari'a* punishments. The British outlawed repugnant punishments such as amputation of the hands and cross amputation of hand and foot and introduced new methods of executing the death penalty so as to get rid of crucifixion, decapitation and stoning. At the same time, the *qisas* punishment of retaliation was abolished.[248] The Zamfara *Shari'a* Courts Law of 1999[249] inspired the other 11 northern states.[250] It imposes the death penalty by stoning for adultery, rape, sodomy and incest when committed by married persons[251] and crucifixion for robbery if followed by murder.[252] Homicide cases are dealt with by way of retaliation. The victim is entitled to inflict the same pain on the perpetrator.[253]

For Nigerian Muslims, the introduction of *Shari'a* was a re-affirmation of their religious identity, after decades of religious tensions with Christians. They expected *Shari'a* to redress moral perversity, corruption, enrooted criminal law injustices and economic problems in the north.[254] Nevertheless, Nigeria has been rebuked for violating its international obligations. The death penalty by stoning violates the rights to life and to dignity,[255] and adultery, homosexual intercourse and apostasy are excluded from the range of capital crimes as envisaged under international law.[256] Capital crimes should be so serious that they threaten human life or bear 'lethal or other extremely grave consequences'.[257] The United Nations Human Rights Commission has urged Nigeria to outlaw the death penalty for sodomy and adultery.[258]

---

248 ibid 138–139.

249 Shari'a Courts (Administration of Justice and Certain Consequential Changes) Law, No 5 of 1999.

250 By 2002, the following states had adopted *Shari'a* criminal laws: Bauch, Borno, Gombe, Jigawa, Kaduna, Kano, Katsina, Kebbi, Niger, Sokoto and Yobe.

251 Sections 127 (b) for adultery, 129 (b) for rape, 131 (b) for sodomy and 136 (b) for incest of the Shari'a Courts (Administration of Justice and Certain Consequential Changes) Law, No 5 of 1999.

252 Section 153 (d) of Shari'a Courts (Administration of Justice and Certain Consequential Changes) Law, No 5 of 1999.

253 Section 200 of Shari'a Courts (Administration of Justice and Certain Consequential Changes) Law, No 5 of 1999.

254 Human Rights Watch, *'Political Shari'a'? Human Rights and Islamic Law in Northern Nigeria*, vol 16, No 9 (A), 2004, at p. 14.

255 Iwobi (n 243) 141–145.

256 William A Schabas, 'International Law and the Death Penalty: Reflecting or Promoting Change?' in Peter Hodgkinson and William A Schabas (eds), *Capital Punishment: Strategies for Abolition* (Cambridge University Press, Cambridge 2004) 48.

257 ibid 46.

258 A/HRC/8/3/Add.3, para 80.

Nigerian Islamic states point out that international instruments prohibiting *Shari'a* punishments are part of an international plot against Islam.[259] They find that the Torture Convention 'intended to make illegal most aspects of *Shari'a* Hudud as divinely ordained by Allah [thereby] violating the fundamental belief of all true Muslims in Nigeria in particular and the world in general'.[260] Therefore, the abolition of the death penalty is equated with the denial of freedom of worship and an attack against Islam.[261]

The first case of effective application of *Shari'a* appeared in the Katsina state. Sani Yakubu Rodi was accused of a triple murder. He pleaded not guilty and later changed his mind and pleaded guilty. The accused was assisted by his grandfather who refused to appeal on the grounds that it would defy God's justice. The accused was convicted and hanged on 3 January 2002.[262]

The practice of *Shari'a* courts attracted much attention when death sentences by stoning were imposed against Amina Lawal from Katsina and Safiya Husseini from Sokoto.[263] The two divorced women were accused of adultery, convicted and sentenced to death based on their confession and pregnancies, which satisfied the evidentiary requirements of *Shari'a*. The men involved had denied the charge. Amina Lawal had retracted her confession but the court did not allow this under *Shari'a*. Safiya Husseini asked the court to conduct a DNA test on the male culprit, but the court ruled that DNA tests were not provided for under *Shari'a*.[264]

This distortion of justice encouraged lawyers to appeal both cases. Amina Lawal's lawyer argued that the court had violated the Constitution. The court replied that it was not bound by the Constitution but by *Shari'a*. A second appeal sustained that the court erred in rejecting the *Shari'a* right of retracting confession. The majority of the appeal bench considered this second argument, but one dissenting judge remained convinced that the offender should be stoned. In the case of Safiya Husseini, the appeal court found that DNA testing was indeed outside the realm of *Shari'a* but also that the lower court had precipitously and retrospectively applied the *Shari'a* penal code.[265]

The Court of Appeal has so far played an enormous role in saving people that lower *Shari'a* courts have sent to the gallows. It generally quashes death sentences imposed for sexual offences. In one example, the court found that Sarimu

259 Iwobi (n 243) 140.

260 ibid.

261 Hood and Hoyle (n 168) 80.

262 Human Rights Watch, *'Political Shari'a'? Human Rights and Islamic Law in Northern Nigeria*, vol 16, No 9 (A), 2004, at pp. 32–33.

263 Human Rights Watch, *Nigeria: Woman Sentenced to Death under Shari'a*, 23 October 2001 and Human Rights Watch, *Nigeria: Court Should Reject Death Penalty*, 26 March 2002.

264 Human Rights Watch, *'Political Shari'a'? Human Rights and Islamic Law in Northern Nigeria*, vol 16, No 9 (A), 2004, at pp. 34–35.

265 ibid.

Mohammed Baranda, who was sentenced to death for rape, was insane at the time of the crime.[266] Similar legal technicalities also saved Attahiru Umaru and Jibrin Babaji, who were convicted of sodomy, Fatima Usman and Ahmadu Ibrahim, who were convicted of fornication, Umar Tori, who was found guilty of incest, and Yunusa Chiyawa, who was convicted of adultery.[267]

Shari'a courts are now perceived as instruments of oppression. The enthusiasm with which the northern states championed *Shari'a* has now caused some to suspect a hidden political agenda. Politicians 'championed *Shari'a* simply to boost their popularity. These officials have been willing to sanction serious abuses to enhance their political popularity.'[268] In attempting to redress this perception, the Niger state created a hybrid legal system where provisions from modern law would correct weaknesses in *Shari'a*. Other states (Kaduna and Kano) are very cautious in their application of *Shari'a* in serious cases.[269] This has created confusion as to what law is in force in the northern states.

The myth of divine justice is indeed nullified by the harshness of *Shari'a* punishments. The absence of sympathy, the limited skills of judges in *Shari'a* and the indifference of justice towards human weaknesses added to the judicial flaws have disillusioned those who believed that *Shari'a* would save society from the moral perversion, corruption and injustices that have characterised Nigerian society since independence.

Perspectives on abolition in Nigeria

Secret executions that regularly violate the country's self-imposed moratorium and Nigeria's opposition[270] or indifference towards the United Nations' moratorium on the use of the death penalty have led many to conclude that Nigeria is attached to the death penalty.[271] Until 2013, there were reasons to be optimistic. In 2010, Nigeria did not oppose the United Nations' moratorium. This change in attitude was expected to lead to a vote and likely to abolition in the near future. Positive initiatives, though isolated, had been observed within the country. Lagos was for example taking the lead in becoming *de facto* abolitionist. The return to the practice of executing prisoners on death row in 2013 surprised the world. It is believed however that Nigeria has sufficiently learnt its lesson. It is illusory to think that the death penalty will reduce the crime rate or weaken terrorism.

Indeed, several reasons peculiar to Nigeria call for abolition either through constitutional amendment or judicial decision:

---

266 ibid.

267 ibid.

268 ibid 2.

269 ibid 15.

270 A/HRC/8/3/ Add.3, para 80.

271 Amnesty International, *Nigeria: Government Misleads World about Death Penalty Record*, 17 December 2007, AI Index: PRE 01/004/2007.

a. Section 2 of the 1960 Constitution, which has since been copied in subsequent constitutions, remains a colonial provision that aimed to crush any resistance to colonial rule. The provision is itself built on the European Convention that, among other things, was rooted in Nazi atrocities and subsequent Nuremberg trials.
b. The practice of the death penalty is evidence that it failed to decrease rates of criminality.
c. Since independence, the Nigerian criminal justice system has failed to guarantee a fair process of justice where offenders would be tried by professional judges and represented by trained lawyers before independent and impartial courts. Offenders were denied their rights to appeal, judicial review and pardon. The absence of this process has suffocated justice to the extent that eventually more innocents than culprits were sent to the gallows.
d. Nigerian society has been torn apart by the politicised application of the death penalty by both military courts and *Shari'a* courts.
e. The discriminatory application of the death penalty based on the offender's state of origin or religion fractures the community more than it unites it. *Shari'a* does not serve justice when it applies in one area and not in another.

Conclusion

In the1960s, independent Africa inherited different criminal policies coloured with what had been the colonial practice in each territorial circumscription. To keep the 'independent people' obedient and at times silent, all African countries, including colonial *de facto* abolitionists, resorted to the death penalty. Surprisingly, new leaders of countries where the colonial power did not provide for it, namely Angola, Cape Verde, Mozambique and Guinea Bissau, found that the death penalty was an unavoidable necessity. The eagerness with which new countries legislated or simply continued the pre-existing colonial regime on the death penalty law demonstrates that African leaders continued the politicisation of the death penalty.

Political context shapes the use of the death penalty, whether imposed for political crimes or for ordinary crimes such as murder. A political context suffices even if the punishment is imposed on ordinary crimes. Illustrations from South Africa eloquently demonstrate how politicians manipulate the death penalty to their benefit and use it as a political weapon. The law of homicide that distinguished between murder and culpable homicide also decided who should visit the gallows. Murder that called for a mandatory death penalty targeted the non-white community; cases in which the criminal was a European or the victim was a non-European often carried the charge of culpable homicide.

A detailed study of the death penalty in the Democratic Republic of Congo and Nigeria concludes that these countries have made and continue to make the death penalty an instrument of political oppression without hiding behind ordinary crimes. The laws and practices related to the death penalty in the Democratic Republic of Congo and Nigeria illustrate the extent to which retentionist countries retain the death penalty for political reasons rather than in the pursuit of justice. Thus, the colonial practice of silencing dissident voices and political opponents has been at the vanguard of the use of the death penalty in these countries.

Unfairness and arbitrariness have been common denominators of the practice of the death penalty both in the Democratic Republic of Congo and in Nigeria. The judiciary served the interest of military junta as they successively replaced one another. Since the abolition of the death penalty in South Africa, unfair procedures and arbitrary laws have made Nigeria the most notorious executioner on the continent.[272] Periods of respite were interrupted by the introduction of religious laws, namely *Shari'a*, in northern states. There is no doubt that the reestablishment of *Shari'a* courts complied with the political agenda of the Muslim leaders that have dominated Nigerian politics and the army since independence. Save that the death penalty in *Shari'a* remains a matter of policy choice,[273] inconsistencies between the ruling of Muslim courts within one state and another and inconsistencies between the law of one state and the law applied on the next street in another state within one country are additional arguments that call for the abolition of the death penalty in Nigeria.

272 Hood and Hoyle (n 168) 80.

273 M Cherif Bassiouni, 'Death as a Penalty in the Shari'a' in Peter Hodgkinson and William A Schabas (eds), *Capital Punishment: Strategies for Abolition* (Cambridge University Press, Cambridge 2004) 185.

Chapter 6
Concluding Remarks on *De Facto* Abolition in Africa

Introduction

The most problematic aspect of studying the death penalty from legal and criminological perspectives remains categorising countries' practices.[1] It is easier to identify countries whose laws (constitution, penal laws or common law) do not provide for the death penalty than it is to identify abolitionists in practice. Countries without the death penalty in their legal systems are *de jure* abolitionists. Since criminal justice is built on the legality of offences and punishments, the absence of the death penalty in the legal system prevents the judge from imposing an imaginary punishment however heinous the nature of the offence or whatever the degree of damage and violence associated with the crime. Acting otherwise would mean that the judge has imposed an arbitrary punishment.

Countries where courts do not impose the statutory or common law death penalty or where the government systematically refrains from carrying out death sentences are known as abolitionists in practice, or *de facto* abolitionists. *De facto* abolition status remains problematic. How much time must elapse for a country to be acknowledged as *de facto* abolitionist and who decides that? To what extent are beneficiaries of the criminal justice system in a particular country guaranteed that the death penalty will not be imposed or executions will not be resumed? Finally, is imposing a symbolic death penalty not itself evidence that the death penalty is not a deterrent per se?

The Scope of *De Facto* Abolition in Africa

Until the 1960s, studies had not yet defined *de facto* abolition. The absence of a definition was a good excuse to dismiss the need for analysis.[2] The first attempt at a definition was made in 1960. *De facto* abolition became defined as 'a constant

---

1 Clarence H Patrick, 'The Status of Capital Punishment: A Worldwide Perspective' (1965) 56 *Journal of Criminal Law, Criminology and Police Science* 397, 405.

2 ibid.

and deliberate practice of pardoning condemned persons'.[3] This abolition stems from the malaise that the government has in executing a sentence which it would have repealed should it be empowered to do so. The legislator is blamed for failing to acknowledge that the context is distanced from the text. For example, in 1965, the Ivoirian legislator should have realised that the executive had systematically commuted all death sentences and abolished the death penalty.[4] Such general *de facto* abolition has often been an incentive towards the judicial non-imposition of the death penalty. Some courts cease to impose death sentences upon realising that their previous orders had not been executed.[5]

Use of the word 'deliberate' implied an official commitment to not carry out the death penalty. Hence, the absence of any official commitment is referred to as 'suspension' of executions and not *de facto* abolition.[6] As a consequence, none of the four African countries (Ivory Coast, Dahomey, Gambia and Togo) that spent at least five years without executing the death penalty was classified *de facto* abolitionist.[7]

In 1965, it was upheld that courts that refrained from imposing the death sentence would be labelled *de facto* abolitionist.[8] This initiative did not extend the scope of the existing definition; rather, another category of *de facto* abolition was introduced. In this case, the judge decides to outlaw the death penalty on a case-by-case basis. The government is thus prevented from executing the culprit even if it would wish to. This indicates a true commitment not to resume executions. Countries in this category should be qualified as 'real *de facto* abolitionist'. Judicial *de facto* abolition differs from the judicial recommendations for mercy that existed in South Africa, Morocco and Zanzibar.[9] For example, African offenders under apartheid rule in South Africa knew that judicial recommendations for mercy put them in an uncertain position.[10] Once a sentence is imposed, judges automatically lose the power to control the next step in the process.

In 1975, *de facto* abolition was referred to as 'abolition by custom'.[11] Although it took time to recognise the importance of the word 'custom', its use implied the progressive exclusion of the death penalty under customary international law or, at the very least, regional customary norms. It is submitted that despite the counterargument of human rights' cultural relativism, regional efforts that have

3 UN Doc E/67 IV.15, 1968, p. 29, at para 78.

4 ibid 97, table 1.

5 UN Doc E/5616, 1975, p. 8 at 19.

6 UN Doc E/67 IV.15, 1968, p. 69, at 252.

7 ibid para 144.

8 ibid para 63.

9 ibid 16–18.

10 George Morice, 'The Administration of Criminal Law in South Africa' (1920) 37 *South African Law Journal* 131, 134.

11 UN Doc E/5616, 1975, p. 6 at 19.

cemented a custom of abolition should be acknowledged as having achieved normative value in international law.[12]

Custom refers to constant, consistent and deliberate practices. However, until 1975, the length of time necessary to achieve the status of *de facto* abolitionist was unclear. Researchers had swung between 50, 40, 25 and 20 years or more without providing any justifications.[13] The consequence of this procrastination is that efforts made by some new countries in Africa, such as Gambia, Seychelles, Cape Verde, Ivory Coast, remained unacknowledged.

Progress was made in 1985 when abolition by custom and *de facto* abolition were differentiated. The first of these categories refers to a 40-year period without execution and the second addresses the issue of new states by introducing a new period of 10 years without executions. This was the first recognition of efforts that some new nations made to consistently refrain from executing the death sentence.[14] In 1990, the debate on the scope of *de facto* abolition ended.[15] Countries that have systematically and continuously refrained from either handing down or executing the death penalty for a period of at least 10 successive years were categorised *de facto* abolitionist.[16] However, the risk that they might resume executions hangs over the heads of those convicted like the sword of Damocles. Thus the trend is to consider that *de facto* abolitionists are those countries with a settled policy not to resume executions and those that have declared a moratorium on the use of capital punishment.[17] This is undoubtedly a third category of *de facto* abolition.

In 1990, five African countries, namely Ivory Coast, Djibouti, Madagascar, Senegal and Togo, were reported to be *de facto* abolitionist.[18] This figure is not insignificant given that at that point Liberia had resumed executions but Cape Verde, Mozambique, Namibia, Seychelles and São Tomé and Príncipe had become *de jure* abolitionist.[19] The movement evolved so fast that within two decades 22 countries in Africa had become *de facto* abolitionist.[20] Based on the

12 William A Schabas, 'International Law and the Death Penalty: Reflecting or Promoting Change?' in Peter Hodgkinson and William A Schabas (eds), *Capital Punishment: Strategies for Abolition* (Cambridge University Press, Cambridge 2004) 43.

13 UN Doc E/5616, 1975, at para 19 and Annexe I and UN Doc E/1980/9 at Annex, footnote a.

14 UN Doc E/1985/43 Legend.

15 UN Doc E/1990/38/Rev., at para 15.

16 UN Doc E/CN.15/1996/19, at paras 6–7; UN Doc E/2000/3, at paras 32–40; UN Doc E/2005/3, at para 3 (c) (i) and UN Doc E/2010/10, at para 3 (c) (i).

17 UN Doc E/2005/3, at para 3 (c) (i) and UN Doc E/2010/10, at para 3 (c) (i) and Roger Hood and Carolyn Hoyle, *The Death Penalty: A Worldwide Perspective* (4th edn, Oxford University Press, New York 2008) 17.

18 UN Doc E/1990/38/ Rev.1, Annex, table 3.

19 William A Schabas, 'African Perspectives on Abolition of the Death Penalty' in William A Schabas (ed), *The International Sourcebook on Capital Punishment* (Northeastern University Press, Boston 1997) 32.

20 See Appendix Table I and UN Doc E/2010/10, at p. 64, table 4.

number of years that have gone by without executions in these countries, they will undoubtedly become the next *de jure* abolitionists.

The Importance of *De Facto* Abolition in Africa

In the 1960s African countries knew that the deterrent effect of the death penalty was debatable. They kept the penalty as a threat until the imbalance between the number of death sentences and the number of executions carried out betrayed the malaise that the death penalty imposed on executive and judicial authorities. This disparity ended up creating a culture of non-executions, which was followed by complete abolition.

While elsewhere countries have begun by abolishing the death penalty for ordinary crimes or in peacetime,[21] such a progressive approach was rather rare in Africa. South Africa is alone in retaining the death penalty for treason in wartime.[22] However, in basing abolition on human rights arguments, the South African Constitutional Court likely intended complete abolition.[23] São Tomé and Príncipe, Seychelles, Ivory Coast and Mauritius first hesitated on the retention of the death penalty for mercenaries, political crimes or drug trafficking before making the move towards complete abolition. Current *de jure* abolitionists spent a considerable length of time not executing the death penalty prior to outlawing it for all crimes.[24]

The general public also learned that their criminal law had 'all the necessary legal prerequisites to ensure the all-round protection of the state and its citizens from criminal encroachments'.[25] The absence of an increase in criminality during a period of *de facto* abolition is an indication that the death penalty is no greater deterrent than other punishments. Using the death penalty as the only appropriate punishment would mean that the choice is between the death penalty and impunity. The choice is rather between the deterrent effects of different punishments, one of which is the death penalty.[26] The absence of the death penalty does not cause the law to fall into disrepute. Justice becomes ineffective when criminals are not apprehended and brought to trial.[27]

One would expect the current 22 *de facto* abolitionists to follow the path of *de jure* abolitionists in abolishing the death penalty for good and for all crimes. However, the reinstatement of executions in former *de facto* abolitionist countries

21 UN Doc E/2010/10, at para 13.

22 *S v. Makwanyane and Another* 1995 (3) SA 391 (CC), para 149 per President Chaskalson.

23 UN Doc E/CN.15/1996/19, at para 38 c*.

24 UN Doc E/CN.15/1996/19, at para 27. See also Appendix Table II.

25 UN Doc E/1990/38/Rev.1, at para 19.

26 *Makwanyane and Another* (n 22) para 123 per President Chaskalson.

27 ibid paras 123–124 per President Chaskalson.

in the 1990s and in 2013 and the continuing secret executions in countries that have declared a moratorium on executions are counter-arguments. In the absence of strong safeguards, *de facto* abolition remains fragile.

The Fragility of *De Facto* Abolition in Africa

De facto abolition depends on the political will of a particular government or the humanitarian trends of the judiciary during a particular period within a country that is legally retentionist. The non-deterrent effect of the death penalty is time tested while the public is prepared for legal abolition, the logical next step. There are countries, however, in which the course of events can cause an about turn. Instead of moving towards legal abolition, they resume executions. Changes in political regimes, rising rates of criminality, general insecurity, atrocious crimes such as war crimes, crimes against humanity and genocide have all been arguments for resuming executions.

Examples of sudden breaches of *de facto* abolition in Africa are abundant. Guinea was classified *de facto* abolitionist as far back as 1983; however, the government warned in 1995 that executions would be resuming as a way of addressing increases in criminality. In 2001, five criminals were executed.[28] In Mauritius, changes in the political regime in 1984 nullified their 24 years of *de facto* abolition by suddenly resuming executions. In Gambia, the first execution happened 16 years after independence.[29] Gambia then observed a moratorium for nearly three decades. It violated the moratorium on 26 August 2012 when President Yahya Jammeh ordered the execution of nine of the prisoners on death row.[30] In Comoros, an execution in 1996 was the first since the country achieved its independence.[31] After 15 years of *de facto* abolition, Burundi executed six people in 1997 for killing Tutsi civilians. Burundi's previous execution dated back to 1982.[32]

The 1989 execution of six criminals in Sierra Leone was the first since 1977. Sierra Leone refrained from executing any more death sentences until 1998 when 24 persons, allegedly members of the Armed Forces Revolutionary Council (AFRC),

---

28 UN Doc E/CN.15/1996/19, at para 29 and UN Doc E/2010/10, p. 13, footnote 54.

29 Amnesty International, *List of Abolitionist and Retentionist Countries*, AI Index: ACT 50/002/2009 at 9.

30 Zainabo Sylvie Kayitesi, *Report of the African Commission on Human and People's Rights Working Group on the Death Penalty in Africa: Viewed in 25 Years of Existence of the ACHPR* (Yamoussoukro, October 2012), at pp. 10–11, at www.achpr.org (accessed 5 January 2013).

31 UN Doc E/2000/3, at para 36 and UN Doc E/2010/10, p. 13, footnote 46.

32 UN Doc E/CN.15/1996/19, at para 29 and UN Doc E/2000/3, at para 37.

were executed for treason.[33] After the first *de facto* moratorium from 1960 to 1974, Benin observed a second *de facto* moratorium between 1974 and 1986 and then resumed executions.[34] In 1982 Morocco refrained from executing the death penalty and resumed executions in 1993.[35] Botswana[36] executed five persons in 1995 and in 1997 Zambia secretly executed eight persons. Both countries had gone for eight years without executions. Since then, secret executions have continued alongside public executions in Botswana.[37] A 1998 execution in Ethiopia was the country's first in seven years. Since then, it has become *de facto* abolitionist again.[38] Libya has been *de facto* abolitionist since 1977. It last violated this self-imposed moratorium in 2005 when five foreigners went to the gallows.[39]

Chad ceased to resort to capital punishment in 1991 with the abolition of courts martial. Afterwards, the government declared a *de facto* moratorium on executions. In June 2003, there was a debate in N'Djamena on *Les Etats Généraux de la Justice* during which the *Commission Justice et Justiciables* recommended legal abolition. Instead, in November 2003, the government resumed executions, apparently for political reasons. The Supreme Court justified the sentence based on the resurgence of insecurity in the streets of N'Djamena and the state of Chadian prisons, which can be compared to sieves.[40] The 2003 executions targeted the nine persons officially convicted of murdering Acheik Ibn Omar Assaid Idriss, a Chadian businessman of Darfur origin and close friend to President Idriss Deby. However, the condemned were also suspected of financing the Zaghawa rebellion, which is at the centre of recent conflicts in Darfur and has politically distanced N'djamena from Khartoum.[41]

In Rwanda, suggestions were made in 1995 that the only way of redressing the pain suffered by victims of genocide against the Tutsi was the execution of the perpetrators or, at least, of those who played a major role in the commission of the crimes.[42] Thus, the penalty held symbolic weight in that it was intended to redress the legacy of victims' sufferings and to pacify the hatred that could lead to more atrocities. The then government of Rwanda was so interested in the death penalty that it voted against the establishment of the International Criminal

33 Amnesty International, *Sierra Leone: Amnesty International Expresses Dismay at 10 Death Sentences for Treason*, AI Index AFR 51/009/2004.

34 UN Doc E/CN.15/1996/19, at para 29 and UN Doc E/2010/10, p. 13, footnote 54.

35 UN Doc E/CN.15/1996/19, at para 36g and para 48.

36 UN Doc E/1985/43/Corr.1, table 2.

37 Hood and Hoyle (n 17) 79 and Amnesty International, *Condamnations à Mort et Exécutions en 2013*, ACT 50/0001/ French, 27 March 2014, 8-9.

38 ibid 81.

39 ibid 68.

40 UN Doc E/67 IV.15, 1968, p. 14.

41 ibid.

42 Gérard Prunier, *The Rwanda Crisis 1959–1994: History of a Genocide* (Columbia University Press, New York 1995) 355.

Tribunal for Rwanda for the reason that, among other things, it was unable to impose the death penalty.[43]

The subsequent organic law no 31/96 of 30 August 1996 provided in its article 14 that punishments of the crime of genocide and crimes against humanity committed between 1 October 1990 and 31 December 1994 were those listed in the Rwandan Penal Code.[44] Article 14 of this law included a special provision on capital punishment for masterminds of genocide against the Tutsi. In 1998, 22 criminals convicted of genocide against Tutsi were executed. Rwanda courts continued to impose death sentences but criticism against the previous executions led the government to refrain from executing them. The country took the most important step in 2007 when it legally abolished the death penalty for any and all crimes committed in peacetime and in wartime.[45]

Countries that have legally abolished the death penalty usually do not reintroduce it and they should not.[46] However, this custom can be defied on the grounds of state sovereignty in criminal matters. This calls for safeguards against the reintroduction of the death penalty in both *de facto* and *de jure* abolitionist countries.

Safeguards Against the Reintroduction of the Death Penalty

It is not appropriate to categorise countries as abolitionist simply because they have gone a certain period without executions.[47] *De facto* abolitionists must have 'clearly indicated their intention to remove capital punishment from their legislation and to subscribe to international conventions which ban its reintroduction'.[48] Otherwise, they are a subcategory of retentionist states.

A moratorium is the only existing mechanism international law has provided for strengthening *de facto* abolition. A moratorium guarantees that the state representative on the trial commits not to request the death penalty. Few judges would impose a punishment that the prosecutor finds inappropriate. So far, out of the 22 *de facto* abolitionists, five (Algeria, Tunisia, Cameroon, Kenya and Zambia) have declared a moratorium on executions. Zambia maintains its *de facto* abolitionist status. In 2013, the Zambian President commuted 113 death sentences to life imprisonment. In December 2010, Burkina Faso, Congo Brazzaville and Madagascar joined Algeria and Benin in their support of the United Nations resolution on a moratorium on the use of capital punishment. The number doubled

43 Mark A Drumbl, *Atrocity, Punishment and International Law* (Cambridge University Press, New York 2007) 72.

44 *Official Gazette* no 17 of 1 September 1996.

45 Article 2 of the Organic Law no 31/2007 of 25 July 2007 relating to the abolition of the death penalty, *Official Gazette* no special, 25 July 2007.

46 UN Doc E/2010/10, at para 13.

47 UN Doc E/2000/3, at para 40.

48 ibid.

in 2012 when Central African Republic, Chad, Mali, Sierra Leone, South Sudan and Tunisia joined the list of countries that voted in favour of the United Nations moratorium on the use of the death penalty.[49] Other *de facto* abolitionists abstained from voting. The number of abstaining states has, however, decreased from 16 in 2010 to 10 in 2012.[50] The abstaining policy indicates that abstaining countries may resume executions anytime.

A moratorium resembles a promise more than an engagement. It can be defied if the judge remains empowered to impose the death sentence. The alleged secret executions in the Democratic Republic of Congo and Nigeria demonstrate that a moratorium is a partial and hypothetical measure that the court can ignore and impose a legal punishment. However, it is important for the *de facto* abolitionist category to exist as an incitement towards legal abolition.

In summary, there are no absolutes. Even *de jure* abolitionists can reintroduce the death penalty. There has been no such case in Africa apart from in Liberia, where there has been no execution since 2000. Liberia abolished capital punishment in 2005 and reintroduced it for gang rape the same year before substituting it with life imprisonment. Meanwhile Liberia acceded to the Second Optional Protocol to the International Covenant on Civil and Political Rights that prohibits the reintroduction of the death penalty.[51] In 2008, Liberia passed another law punishing armed robbery, terrorism and hijacking with the death penalty. The question of whether Liberia is retentionist or abolitionist remains unanswered. It is submitted that despite the 2008 law, Liberia remains *de jure* abolitionist under international law. This applied as well to Benin which joined the Second Optional Protocol in July 2012 before legally abolishing the death penalty. However, conflict between Benin's domestic law and international law lead Benin to repeal the death penalty provision in the criminal procedure code.[52] The principle extends to another nine *de jure* abolitionists that have ratified or acceded to the Second

49 UN Doc E/2010/10, at para 19, footnote 29; UN Doc A/67/457/Add.2, 20 December 2012 and UN Doc A/HRC/24/18, 1 July 2013, para 54.

50 Cameroon, Central African Republic, Eritrea, Gambia, Ghana, Kenya, Lesotho, Malawi, Morocco, Niger, Sierra Leone, Swaziland, United Republic of Tanzania and Zambia abstained from the vote for the United Nations moratorium on the use of the death penalty in 2010. In 2012, only Cameroon, Eritrea, Kenya, Lesotho, Malawi, Mauritania, Morocco, Niger, United Republic of Tanzania and Zambia were among the *de facto* abolitionists to abstain from voting. See alternatively UN Doc E/2010/10, at para 19, footnote 30 and UN Doc A/67/457/Add.2, 20 December 2012.

51 Second Optional Protocol to the International Covenant on Civil and Political Rights, aiming at the abolition of the death penalty, 15 December 1989, GA Res.44/128 (1990) 29 *ILM* 1464.

52 UN Doc E/2010/10, p. 14 at 24. For Benin, see Amnesty International, *Staying Power: Keeping Up the Fight for Human Rights in 2012 and Beyond*, vol 43, January–February 2013 and UN Doc A/HRC/24/18, 1 July 2013, para 5.

Optional Protocol, namely Cape Verde, Djibouti, Guinea Bissau, Madagascar, Mozambique, Namibia, Rwanda, Seychelles and South Africa.[53]

With all due consideration, the first step towards ensuring that the death penalty is not reinstated is making it unconstitutional. If the death penalty had been outlawed in the Liberian Constitution, the new law could not have been passed without a constitutional amendment. Therefore, *de jure* abolitionist status is more reliable when the country has combined international engagement with the prohibition of the death penalty under its constitution. Yet only a few countries choose this option.[54] Countries that have excluded the death penalty in their Constitution 'have … ensured … that the death penalty cannot be reintroduced'.[55] A country that has outlawed the death penalty under its Constitution without joining the Second Optional Protocol qualifies as more solidly *de jure* abolitionist than a country that keeps the death penalty in its Constitution but joins the protocol. In other words, Angola and São Tomé and Príncipe, which have made the death penalty unconstitutional without joining the protocol, have secured their abolitionist status more than Liberia.[56]

It is submitted that Liberia '… is prohibited by its international obligations from imposing the death penalty'.[57] Imposing or not imposing the death penalty, however, will necessarily require a constitutional interpretation of the place of international law in Liberian domestic law. Yet article 2 (2) of the Liberian Constitution provides that '[a]ny laws, treaties, statutes, decrees, customs and regulations found to be inconsistent with [the Constitution] shall, to the extent of inconsistency, be void and of no legal effect'.[58] In this light, the Constitution has primacy over international law and it is most likely that Liberian judges will

53 UN Doc E/2010/10, pp. 30–32 and Amnesty International, *Staying Power: Keeping Up the Fight for Human Rights in 2012 and Beyond*, vol 43, January–February 2013.

54 Article 26 (2) of the Constitution of the Republic of Cape Verde of 1992 as amended in November 1999, article 32 of the Constitution of the Republic of Guinea of 1984 as amended in 1991, *Sabado*, 11 May 1991, article 15 (2) of the Constitution of the Republic of Seychelles of 18 June 1993 as amended by Constitutional Act no14 of 1996, article 40 of the Constitution of the Republic of Mozambique of 16 November 2004, *Mozlegal, Lda* 2004 and section 6 of the Namibian Constitution Second Amendment Act, 2010. Angola, Mauritius and São Tomé and Príncipe are also classified among countries that have outlawed the death penalty in their constitutions. See African Commission on Human and People's Rights, *Study on the Question of the Death Penalty in Africa*, Banjul, November 2011, at pp. 40–42 (unpublished).

55 Roger Hood and Carolyn Hoyle, 'Abolishing the Death Penalty Worldwide: The Impact of a "New Dynamic"' (2009) 38 *Crime and Justice* 1, 11.

56 Article 30 of the Constitutional Law of the Republic of Angola of 2010 and article 22 of Law no 1/ 2003 establishing the Constitution of the Democratic Republic of São Tomé and Prìncipe of 2003.

57 UN Doc E/2010/10, at para 24.

58 Section 2 (2) of the Constitution of the Republic of Liberia of 6 January 1986, ICL Doc Status, 6 January 1986.

uphold the values protected in their domestic constitution. In 2010, Liberia indeed imposed capital punishment on the basis of the 2008 law.[59] To avoid ambiguity, the remaining seven *de jure* abolitionists (Burundi, Cote d'Ivoire, Gabon, Mali, Mauritius, Senegal and Togo) and forthcoming abolitionists should simultaneously amend their constitutions and join the Second Optional Protocol to the Covenant.

Optimistic Perspectives on the Abolitionist Movement in Africa

Despite the concerns outlined thus far, there are further causes for optimism regarding the abolitionist movement in Africa. The resistance to calls to abolish the death penalty in Africa is crumbling. In 1948, when the United Nations General Assembly adopted the Universal Declaration of Human Rights, only Cape Verde would have qualified as a *de facto* abolitionist if it had been independent. In the 1980s nine African countries were either *de jure* or *de facto* abolitionists; in 1997, that number had almost tripled.[60]

In February 2010 Gabon quietly abolished the death penalty in law and in 2012 Benin became the seventeenth full abolitionist African country.[61] The abolition of the death penalty in Gabon, announced one year later, was interpreted as 'an enormous progress regarding human rights' and 'an opportunity for even more progress in Africa'.[62] Thirty-nine countries are now abolitionists, either in law or in practice. There is a strong trend indicating that the death penalty will not be reinstated in abolitionist countries and that most *de facto* abolitionists are on the right path towards *de jure* abolition. Of the 21 *de facto* abolitionists, nine (Algeria, Burkina Faso, Central African Republic, Congo Brazzaville, Ghana, Kenya, Mali, Tunisia and Zambia)[63] declared in 2010 that they were considering abolishing the death penalty in their criminal law or Constitution and have imposed a *de facto* moratorium on the death penalty. In 2013, the Central African Republic and Congo-Brazzaville positively received recommendations from the United Nations Human Rights Council on abolishing the death penalty and joining the Second Optional Protocol on the International Covenant on Civil and Political Rights,

---

59 Amnesty International, *Death Sentences and Executions 2010*, ACT50/001/2011, p. 37.

60 Schabas (n 19) 30–31.

61 Loi no 3/2010 du 15 février 2010 portant Abolition de la Peine de Mort, *Journal Officiel de la République Gabonaise*, 51ème année, no 3, 30 mars 2010. In its 2010 report on capital punishment, Amnesty International mentions 16 countries as it withdrew Liberia from the list of *de jure* abolitionists. See Amnesty International, *Death Sentences and Executions 2010*, ACT50/001/2011, pp. 37 and 44, Annex II. For Benin, see UN Doc A/HRC/24/18, 1 July 2013, para 6.

62 Richard Fielding, *Gabon Quietly Abolishes the Death Penalty*, World Coalition Against the Death Penalty, 4 March 2011.

63 UN Doc E/2010/10, at paras 19 and 20.

aiming at the abolition of the death penalty.[64] In December 2010 Madagascar and Gambia joined the list in voting for the 2010 United Nations moratorium on the use of the death penalty.[65] Whereas Gambia violated its commitment in resuming executions and Kenya extended capital punishment to non-lethal crimes, namely human trafficking, through the Defence Force Act of 2012, Madagascar strengthened its status because in 2012 it signed the Second Optional Protocol that prohibits the use of capital punishment.[66]

Nine of the 10 remaining countries did not vote against the moratorium but significantly chose to abstain or were absent from the session. These were Cameroon, Eritrea, Lesotho, Malawi, Mauritania, Morocco, Niger, Sierra Leone and Tanzania. In 2013, Sierra Leone launched the process of amending its constitution with the view of abolishing the death penalty. In Tanzania, the Minister of Justice declared that his country was also in favour of abolition.[67] In December 2012, the Democratic Republic of Congo and Nigeria abstained as well.[68] Among the *de facto* abolitionists, only Swaziland voted against the United Nations moratorium in 2010. It improved its status by abstaining to vote in 2012.[69] Swaziland's last execution goes back to 1989[70] and it is believed that it will keep its status until the death penalty is legally repealed. The country is waiting for the release of the Constitutional Review Commission report that King Muswati III initiated for, among other things, the study of the appropriate mechanism for abolishing the death penalty. Meanwhile, Prime Minister Sibusiso Dlamini stated in April 2011 that Swaziland will remain retentionist.[71]

In 2011, only 14 of Africa's 54 countries (less than 26 per cent) retained the death penalty. These were Botswana, Chad, the Democratic Republic of Congo, Egypt, Equatorial Guinea, Ethiopia, Guinea Conakry, Libya, Nigeria, Somalia, Sudan, South Sudan, Uganda and Zimbabwe. In 2012, there was a sudden increase in the number of executions. On 23 January 2012, one person was executed by firearm in Somalia. Military courts in Somalia continue to impose the death penalty to non-lethal crimes. The Nuguaal Military Court in Puntland imposed the

64 Amnesty International, *Condamnations à Mort et Exécutions en 2013* (Amnesty International London, 2014), 8.

65 Among *de facto* abolitionists, Algeria, Benin, Burkina Faso and Congo Brazzaville also voted for the 2010 United Nations Moratorium. See UN Doc GA 71/ A 65456 dd2 Part II DRI, 21 December 2010.

66 UN Doc A/HRC/24/18, 1 July 2013, para 13 and Amnesty International, *Staying Power: Keeping Up the Fight for Human Rights in 2012 and Beyond*, vol 43, January–February 2013, at p. 2.

67 Amnesty International (n 64).

68 UN Doc GA 71/ A 65456 dd2 Part II DRI, 21 December 2010 and UN Doc A/67/457/Add.2, 20 December 2012.

69 ibid.

70 UN Doc E/2005/3, at para 33.

71 Bhekie Matsebula, 'Swaziland Stands Firm on Death Penalty', *IOL News*, 11 April 2011.

death penalty on two men accused of possessing explosives under the Puntland Anti-terrorism Act of 2010. In April 2013, the court executed 13 persons accused of links with terrorist organisations. At least 34 people were executed in Somalia in 2013. On 31 January 2012, Botswana also executed another inmate on death row. In 2013, another person convicted of murder was executed in Botswana. On 22 August 2012, the newly independent nation of South Sudan executed two prisoners by hanging at a prison in the capital. By the end of the year South Sudan had already executed five of the more than 200 prisoners on death row. Another four people were executed in 2013. On 26 August 2012, President Yahya Jammeh of Gambia who had repeatedly threatened to execute prisoners on death row sent nine of them to the firing squad. Gambia had spent 27 years as a *de facto* abolitionist. In June 2013, Nigeria executed four inmates that had spent years on death row. It has as well extended the death penalty to a wide range of non-violent crimes by naming them acts of terrorism.[72]

Despite these executions, the overall tendency among retentionist states is towards abolition. The Ugandan proposal to extend the death penalty to same-sex intercourse has been reviewed. A Parliamentarian Committee dropped the death penalty provision for aggravated homosexuality in the Anti-Homosexuality Act and the change is qualified as substantial.[73] In Gambia, international condemnation of the August 2012 executions led the Gambian President to declare a moratorium on executions. The country demonstrated its commitment to stay executions by choosing to be absent from the recent vote on the United Nations moratorium on the use of the death penalty rather than voting against it. It is also expected that Gambian judges will refrain from imposing the death penalty to non-lethal crimes of human trafficking, robbery, rape and drug-related crimes which the government has recently made capital crimes.[74]

Somalia voted for the 2010 and 2012 United Nations moratoria on the use of the death penalty. It was thought that Somalia's positive vote in 2010 indicated that it had joined the group of *de facto* abolitionist countries. The execution of inmates in 2012 and 2013 reverses this expectation and proves further the fragility of moratoria mainly for countries that are experiencing political instability. Chad, which had decided not to attend the 2010 session, voted for the moratorium

72 Kayitesi (n 30); UN Doc A/HRC/24/18, 1 July 2013 and Amnesty International, 'Nigeria Executions: "They Almost Executed Him Secretly"', 28 June 2013. See also Amnesty International (n 64).

73 Amnesty International, *Urgent Action: Anti-homosexuality Bill May Be Passed*, UA 134/11, Index: AFR 59/010/2011 and *New Times*, 24 November 2012.

74 African Commission for Human and Peoples' Rights, *Combined Report of Commissioner Zainabo Sylvie Kayitesi*, Banjul, 28 April–12 May 2011, p. 5, at http://www.achpr.org/English (accessed 13 May 2011) and Amnesty International, *Gambia's Conditional Moratorium on Executions Not Good Enough*, 17 September 2012, at www.http://www2.amnesty.org.uk (accessed 4 January 2013) and UN Doc A/67/457/Add.2, 20 December 2012.

in 2012. During the 2012 vote, Equatorial Guinea maintained its previous status of an absent state.[75]

It is worth noting that both the Democratic Republic of Congo and Nigeria previously declared self-imposed moratoria. In Ethiopia, the June 2011 commutation of death sentences for 23 former officials convicted of genocide and crimes against humanity is expected to lay the basis of a continuing positive attitude towards abolition.[76] South Sudan, which executed five persons in August 2012 on the grounds that criminal statistics and especially the rate of murder called for capital punishment, voted for the United Nations moratorium on the use of the death penalty in December 2012. The vote was believed to be salutary news to the more than 200 inmates on death row.[77] The country, however, further executed four people in 2013.[78] The recurrence of political instability has certainly increased the likelihood of executions for prisoners on death row. Autocratic leaders tend to rely on the death penalty to maintain their fragile regimes.

Furthermore, seven of the fully retentionist countries (Botswana, Chad, the Democratic Republic of Congo, the Gambia, Guinea, Nigeria and Uganda) are party to the Rome Statute of the International Criminal Court. Although audacious, Congolese military judges have put their country on the right track in substituting the death penalty by the penalties listed in article 77 of the Rome Statute. The remaining countries cannot also ignore that, in ratifying the Rome Statute, they joined the community of states that excluded the death penalty for the most dreadful crimes before the world's highest court in criminal matters. It is therefore expected that they react positively to Roger Hood and Carolyn Hoyle's question: 'if … the most serious of all crimes … [are] not punishable by death, why should lesser offenses be so punished?'[79] The African Commission has officially called African retentionist countries that have ratified the Rome Statute of the International Criminal Court to observe article 77 of the statute rather than applying the exception contained in article 80.[80] There is no doubt that despite the provision of article 80 under which states may apply the death penalty, the Rome Statute has laid the basis of a soon-to-come worldwide abolition of capital punishment.[81]

It was anticipated that the Arab Revolution in Maghreb will increase the chances that Egypt and possibly Libya may take more courageous action towards

75 UN Doc GA 71/ A 65456 dd2 Part II DRI, 21 December 2010 and UN Doc A/67/457/Add.2, 20 December 2012. See also Amnesty International (n 64).

76 'Ethiopia Commutes Death Sentences for Top Junta Men', *AFP*, 1 June 2011.

77 *Daily Nation*, 2 November 2012, *Daily Nation*, 15 November 2012 and UN Doc A/67/457/Add.2, 20 December 2012.

78 Amnesty International (n 64).

79 Hood and Hoyle (n 55) 22.

80 Kayitesi (n 30) 6.

81 William A Schabas, *The International Criminal Court: A Commentary on the Rome Statute* (Oxford University Press, New York 2010) 925–926.

the abolition of the death penalty. That alone would have marginalised the seven remaining fully retentionist countries on the continent.[82] Although it is likely that the practice of other countries in their neighbourhood has often had a positive impact on the attitudes of retentionist countries leading the abolitionist movement to be interpreted as having a contaminating effect that states can hardly resist, the turn of events in Egypt and Libya might prove us wrong. These two countries have already shown trends of a fanatic use of the death penalty. This is surely against the ideal of revolutionaries. Amnesty International has for example described the 500 death sentences that Minya Criminal Court handed down against supporters of the former President Mohamed Morsi in March 2014 as 'grotesque rulings'.[83] The ruling wiped out the hope of seeing Egypt returning soon to democracy and respect for the rule of law.[84]

Abolition in Africa remains a matter of national initiative. So far the African Union has not established a clear roadmap towards the abolition of the death penalty. The Working Group on Capital Punishment, established in 2005, is still striving to reach a common position on strategies for abolition. Raising public awareness is the sole strategy that member states have in common.[85] Libya, Egypt, Tunisia and Algeria have rejected the idea of a Second Additional Protocol[86] to the African Charter for Human and Peoples' Rights,[87] and alternative punishments to the death penalty are relegated to general recommendations.[88]

However, of all the strategies, Peter Hodgkinson argues that a remedy to the expressed fears and concerns of the victims and the public in general and to the dilemmas of the politician as regard sentences alternative to death is of paramount relevance.[89] Alternative punishments are those imposed in lieu of the death penalty. There is no consensus on what is an appropriate sentence to replace the death

82 Botswana, Ethiopia, Gambia, Guinea Conakry, Sudan, South Sudan, Uganda and Zimbabwe.

83 Amnesty International, *More than 500 Sentenced to Death in 'Grotesque Ruling'*, available at www.amnesty.org/en/news/egypt-more-500-sentced-death-grotesque-ruling-2014-03-24 [accessed 2 April 2014].

84 Haitham El-Tabei, 'Egypt Sets Presidential Election date as Brotherhood Rejects Sisi', *Daily Nation,* 1 April 2014.

85 'The Kigali Framework: Document on the Abolition of the Death Penalty in Africa', 25 September 2009 (unpublished) and 'The Cotonou Framework: Document on the Abolition of the Death Penalty in Africa', 15 April 2010 (unpublished).

86 Lilian Chenwi, *Towards the Abolition of the Death Penalty in Africa: A Human Rights Perspective* (Pretoria University Law Press, Pretoria 2007) 18–20.

87 'The Cotonou Framework: Document on the Abolition of the Death Penalty in Africa', 15 April 2010 (unpublished).

88 ibid.

89 Peter Hodgkinson, 'Capital Punishment: Improve It or Remove It?' in Peter Hodgkinson and William A Schabas (eds), *Capital Punishment: Strategies for Abolition* (Cambridge University Press, Cambridge 2004) 2.

penalty.[90] In most countries the death penalty is replaced by a severe deprivation of liberty, which often takes the form of life imprisonment.[91]

The broad expression 'life imprisonment' is understood to be hard labour for life, rigorous life imprisonment or forced labour for life in Burkina Faso.[92] The absence of a definition of life imprisonment and guidelines on alternative sentences to the death penalty have led countries to initiate alternative sentences whose cruel, degrading and inhuman nature only differs from the death penalty in that they do not take the offender's life immediately.

Indeterminate imprisonment without the possibility of early release is perceived as a violation of human dignity. It nullifies also hopes of rehabilitation and self-improvement in the person of the offender.[93] Others have said that it is a death penalty by instalments. Bearing in mind the state of African prisons, such a sentence can be worse than the death penalty.[94] This has resulted in release after a certain period of imprisonment or simply provision for a term imprisonment.[95] However, temporary detention during which the prisoner is subjected to unnecessary pain is no less cruel, inhuman and degrading.

The replacement of the death penalty by life imprisonment in confinement in Rwanda provoked strong protest within and outside the country on the grounds that the death penalty had simply been substituted with, among other things, another cruel, inhuman and degrading punishment.[96] Criticism from the International Criminal Tribunal for Rwanda (ICTR) (which stated that it would not transfer its files to Rwanda until the law was reviewed)[97] and human rights activists led the Rwandan government to reconsider its position. It first satisfied the ICTR's claim regarding detainees' transfer but maintained the punishment for offenders within the country.[98] However, criticism continued on the basis of inequality and a double standard of justice that this established.

---

90 UN Doc E/1985/43, at paras 67–69, UN Doc E/C.N.15/1996/19, at para 50 and UN Doc E/2010/10, at para 10.

91 UN Doc E/67 IV.15, 1968, p. 108 at 103.

92 ibid 102.

93 Schabas (n 81) 893.

94 Dirk Van Zyl Smit, 'The Death Penalty in Africa' (2004) 4 *African Human Rights Law Journal* 13.

95 Andrew Coyle, 'Replacing the Death Penalty: The Vexed Issue of Alternative Sanctions' in Peter Hodgkinson and William A Schabas (eds), *Capital Punishment: Strategies for Abolition* (Cambridge University Press, Cambridge 2004) 104.

96 Jamil Dlamulira Mujuzi, 'Issues Surrounding Life Imprisonment after the Abolition of the Death Penalty in Rwanda' (2009) 9 *Human Rights Law Review* 335.

97 *Prosecutor v. Yussuf Munyakazi*, ICTR-97-36-R11bis, paras 22–32.

98 Article 1 of Organic Law no 66/2008 of 21 November 2008 modifying and completing the Organic Law no 31/2007 of 25 July 2007 relating to the Abolition of the Death Penalty, *Official Gazette*, no 23, 1 December 2008.

In 2008, the Supreme Court was called to decide on the constitutionality of life imprisonment in confinement in the *Tubarimo Aloys* case.[99] The court erred in systematically dismissing the defence lawyer's arguments based on inconsistencies between confinement and the constitutional right to not to be subjected to torture, physical abuse or cruel, inhuman or degrading treatment.[100] In 2010, an Organic law[101] came to interpret life imprisonment in confinement in the line of article 15 of the Rwandan Constitution that prohibits torture. Following this development, the ICTR has decided to refer its cases to Rwanda. The tribunal has noted that as regards punishments, 'the ambiguities which existed … have been adequately addressed by Rwanda'.[102]

Most retentionist countries argue that there is currently no valuable alternative to the death penalty. It is thus necessary to present alternative punishments to countries that may be reluctant to abolish the death penalty in the absence of such alternatives and to ensure that the abolition of the death penalty does not result in the creation of worse punishments. So far, a reasonable term of imprisonment with the possibility of early release is generally accepted.

Conclusion

The five steps that generally lead to a progressive abolition are: declaration of a moratorium, *de facto* abolition, *de jure* abolition for ordinary crimes, *de jure* abolition for all crimes and joining the Second Optional Protocol to the International Covenant on Civil and Political Rights, aiming at the abolition of the death penalty. A moratorium on the use of the death penalty whether self-imposed or official, remains an unguaranteed promise that can be broken at a politician's discretion. If the country keeps its commitment then it moves to *de facto* abolitionist status.

Although sometimes revoked, it is believed that *de facto* abolitionist status creates an international obligation under article 6 (2) of the International Covenant on Civil and Political Rights[103] to not reinstate the death penalty. Professor William Schabas argues that international law is clear that 'once a State has abolished the death penalty, it cannot reinstate it'.[104] Article 6 (6) is even more clear on calling *de facto* abolitionists to get rid of capital punishment. States are expected to report on measures that they have undertaken to limit the use or abolish the death penalty.

---

99 *Re Tubarimo Aloys*, RS/Inconst/Pén.0002/08/CS of 29 August 2008.

100 ibid paras 28, 31 and 33.

101 Organic Law no 32/2010 of 22 September 2010 relating to Serving Life Imprisonment with Special Provisions, *Official Gazette*, no special, 14 October 2010.

102 *Prosecutor v. Jean Uwinkindi*, ICTR-2001-75-R11bis, at para 51.

103 The International Covenant on Civil and Political Rights (1966) entered into force 23 March 1976, 999 UNTS 171.

104 William A Schabas, *The Abolition of the Death Penalty in International Law* (3rd edn, Cambridge University Press, Cambridge 2002) 101.

The public embarrassment of reporting has incited some countries to move from the status of *de facto* abolitionist to that of *de jure* abolitionist.[105] Abolition in practice can therefore be genuinely considered as a transitional step towards legal abolition.

Obligations under article 6 (2) of the International Covenant on Civil and Political Rights apply *a fortiori* to *de jure* abolitionists. Their status is confirmed by joining the Second Optional Protocol, which prohibits the reintroduction of the death penalty once it is abolished. However, Liberia's situation indicates that states can still defy international law and create unstable situations. It is for this same reason that Benin was urged to abolish the death penalty under its domestic law. States should thus be reminded or even encouraged to outlaw the death penalty in their respective constitutions before ascending to the international level. Constitutional abolition and accession to international norms prohibiting the death penalty would potentially further reassure Africans that they are not at their politicians' mercy.

105 ibid 138–139.

Appendix

Appendix Table I *De facto* abolitionists in Africa and the date of last execution

No	Countries	Last execution
1	Algeria	1993
2	Burkina Faso	1989
3	Cameroon	1997
4	Central African Republic	1981
5	Congo Brazzaville	1982
6	Eritrea	1989
7	Ghana	1993
8	Kenya	1987
9	Lesotho	1995
10	Madagascar	1958
11	Malawi	1992
12	Mali	1979
13	Mauritania	1989
14	Morocco	1993
15	Niger	1976
16	Sierra Leone	1998
17	Swaziland	1989
18	Tunisia	1981
19	United Republic of Tanzania	1994
20	Zambia	1997

Source: E/2010/10, p. 64, Table 4.

Appendix Table II *De jure* abolitionists in Africa

No	Country	Last execution	Date of *de jure* abolition
1	Angola	1987	1992
2	Benin	1987	2012
3	Burundi	1997	2009
4	Cape Verde	1835	1981
5	Cote d'Ivoire	Never since colonial time	2000
6	Djibouti	Never since colonial time	1995
7	Gabon	1989	2010
8	Guinea Bissau	1986	1993
9	Liberia*	2000	2005
10	Mauritius	1987	1995
11	Mozambique	1986	1990
12	Namibia	1988	1990
13	Rwanda	1998	2007
14	São Tomé and Príncipe	Never since colonial time	1990
15	Senegal	1967	2004
16	Seychelles	Never since colonial time	1993
17	South Africa	1989	1995
18	Togo	1978	2009

Note: * Liberia became *de jure* abolitionist through its accession to the Second Optional Protocol to the International Covenant on Civil and Political Rights, aiming at abolishing the death penalty. However, it still has death penalty provisions under its domestic law.

Source: UN Doc E/2010/10, p. 60, Table 2 and UN Doc A/HRC/24/18, 1 July 2013.

Bibliography

Monographs

Amnesty International, *When the State Kills ... the Death Penalty v. Human Rights* (Amnesty International Publications, London 1989)

Ancel M and Marx Y, *Les codes pénaux Européens* (Centre Français de Droit Comparé, Paris 1958)

Anderson D, *Histories of the Hanged: Britain's Dirty War in Kenya and the End of the Empire* (Weidenfeld and Nicolson, London 2005)

Ayittey GBN, *Indigenous African Institutions* (Transnational Publisher, New York 2006)

Beccaria C, *On Crimes and Punishments* (Richard Bellamy ed, Cambridge University Press, Cambridge 1995)

Bernaz N, *Le droit international et la peine de mort* (La Documentation Française, Paris 2008)

Bidwell R, *Morocco under Colonial Rule: French Administration of Tribal Areas 1912–1956* (Frank Cass, London 1973)

Bolongo L, *Droit pénal spécial Zaïrois* (L.G.D.J., Paris 1985)

Bourgeois R, *Banyarwanda et Barundi, La coutume* (Institut Royal Colonial Belge, Brussels 1954)

—— *Banyarwanda et Barundi: Ethnographie* (Académie Royale des Sciences Coloniales, Brussels 1957)

Bouzaher H, *La justice répressive dans l'Algérie coloniale 1830–1962* (Houma, Algiers 2004)

Bouzat P, *Traité de droit pénal et de criminologie, Tome I: Droit pénal general* (Dalloz, Paris 1970)

Brems E, *Human Rights: Universality and Diversity* (Martinus Nijhoff Publishers, The Hague 2001)

Burchell EM and Hunt PMA, *South African Criminal Law and Procedure* (Juta, Cape Town 1970)

Buzora A, *La peine de mort en droit Rwandais* (Mémoire de licence, Université Nationale du Rwanda, Butare 1990)

Chenwi L, *Towards the Abolition of the Death Penalty in Africa: A Human Rights Perspective* (Pretoria University Law Press, Pretoria 2007)

Cherifi R, *Le makhzen politique au Maroc: hier et aujourd'hui* (Afrique-Orient, Casablanca 1988)

Church HRJ, *West Africa: A Study of the Environment and of Man's Use of It* (Longman, London 1963)

Clifford W, *An Introduction to African Criminology* (Oxford University Press, Nairobi 1974)

Collingwood JJR, *Criminal Law of East and Central Africa* (Sweet and Maxwell, London 1967)

Comité de Législation Etrangère et de Droit International, *Le code pénal de l'empire d'Ethiopie (du 23 juillet 1957)* (Centre Français de Droit Comparé, Paris 1959)

Crabb J, *The Legal System of Congo-Kinshasa* (The Michie Company, Charlottesville 1970)

Crowder M, *Colonial West Africa* (Frank Cass, London 1978)

Cuba L and Cocking J, *How to Write about the Social Sciences* (Longman, Harlow 1997)

Decay R, *Mœurs et coutumes des Malgaches* (Payot, Paris 1951)

Detry A, *Contribution à la reforme de la législation criminelle du Congo Belge* (La Meuse, Liège 1909)

Donnelly J, *Universal Human Rights in Theory and Practice* (Cornell University Press, London 2003)

Drumbl MA, *Atrocity, Punishment and International Law* (Cambridge University Press, New York 2007)

Dyzenhaus D, *Hard Cases in Wicked Legal Systems: South African Law in the Perspective of Legal Philosophy* (Clarendon Press, Oxford 1991)

Elkins C, *Imperial Reckoning: The Untold Story of Britain's Gulag in Kenya* (Henry Holt and Company, New York 2005)

Elliot C, *French Criminal Law* (Willan Publishing, Devon 2001)

Fallers LA, *Law without Precedent: Legal Ideas in Action in the Courts of Colonial Busoga* (University of Chicago Press, Chicago 1969)

Franck HG, *The Barbaric Punishment: Abolishing the Death Penalty* (Martinus Nijhoff Publishers, The Hague 2003)

Friedman LM, *American Law: An Introduction* (Norton and Company, New York 1984)

Furedi F, *Colonial Wars and the Politics of Third World Nationalism* (I.B. Tauris, London 1994)

Garçon M, *Commentaire du code pénal Congolais* (Larcier, Brussels 1947)

Germain R, *La politique indigène du Bugeaud* (Larose, Paris 1955)

Glazier J, *Land and the Use of Tradition among the Mbeere of Kenya* (University Press of America, Lanham 1985)

Gledhil A, *The Penal Codes of Northern Nigeria and Sudan* (Sweet and Maxwell, London 1963)

Gluckman M et al. (eds), *Ideas and Procedures in African Customary Law* (Oxford University Press, London 1969)

Griggs CW, *Early Egyptian Christianity: From its Origin to 451 CE* (E.J. Brill, Leiden 1991)

Grundlingh A, *Boer Collaboration in the South African War of 1899–1902: The Dynamics of Treason* (Protea, Pretoria 2006)

Gulliver PH, *Social Control in African Society: A Study of the Arusha: Agricultural Masai of Northern Tanganyika* (Routledge and Kegan Paul, London 1963)

Harrison D, *The White Tribe of Africa: South Africa in Perspective* (Ariel Books, London 1985)

Harvey WB, *Introduction to the Legal System in East Africa* (East African Literature Bureau, Kampala 1975)

Hassan AS, *Islamic Law in the Contemporary World* (Royston, Glasgow 1985)

Heeren AHL (tr), *Historical Researches into the Politics, Intercourse, and the Trade of the Carthaginians, Ethiopians and Egyptians*, vol 1 (D.A. Talboys, Oxford 1832)

Hild E, *L'organisation judiciaire en Afrique Occidentale Française* (Emile Larousse, Paris 1912)

Hodges T, *Sahara occidental: origines et enjeux d'une guerre du désert* (L'Harmattan, Paris 1987)

Hood R, *The Death Penalty: A Worldwide Perspective* (3rd edn Oxford University Press, New York 2002)

—— and Hoyle C, *The Death Penalty: A Worldwide Perspective* (4th edn, Oxford University Press, New York 2008)

Iliffe J, *Africans: The History of a Continent* (Cambridge University Press, New York 1995)

Irstam T, *The King of Ganda* (Hakan Ohlsssons Boktryckeri, Stockholm 1944)

Jembere A, 'Legal History of Ethiopia 1434–1974: Some Aspects of Substantive and Procedural Laws' (PhD Thesis, Erasmus Universiteit, Rotterdam 1998)

Jensen Krige E, *The Social System of the Zulus* (Shuter and Shooter, Pietermaritzburg 1936)

Jeol M, *Droit public Africain* (Berger-Levrault, Paris 1967)

Junod HA, *The Life of a South African Tribe* (University Book Inc, New York 1962)

Kagame A, *Les organisations socio-familiales de l'ancien Rwanda* (Académie Royale des Sciences Coloniales, Brussels 1954)

—— *La philosophie Bantu comparée* (Présence Africaine, Paris 1976)

Kinemo REJ, *Contemporary Tanzanian Penal Policy: A Critical Analysis* (British Institute in East Africa) http://www.tzonline.org/pdf/contemporarytanzanianpenalpolicy.pdf (accessed 18 April 2007)

Kingsley MH, *Travel in West Africa (Congo Français, Corisco and Cameroons)* (Macmillan, London 1897)

Ki-Zerbo J, *Histoire de l'Afrique noire* (Hatier, Paris 1972)

Kludze KAP, *Chieftaincy in Ghana* (Austin and Winfield, Lanham 2000)

Leibbrandt HCV, *Precis of the Archives of the Cape of Good Hope: The Defence of Willem Adriaan Van Der Stel* (W.A. Richards & Son, Cape Town 1897)

—— *Precis of the Archives of the Cape of Good Hope: Letters Received 1695–1696 by Governor S Van Der Stel* (Cape Times, Cape Town and London 1900)

—— *Precis of the Archive of the Cape of Good Hope, Requesten (Memorials) 1715–1806*, vol 2 (Cape Times, Cape Town and London 1905)

Lepard BD, *Customary International Law: A New Theory with Practical Applications* (Cambridge University Press, New York 2010)
Lepsius R, *Letters from Egypt, Ethiopia and the Peninsula of Sinai* (Henry G. Bohn, London 1858)
Lev Y, *Saladin in Egypt* (E.J. Brill, Leiden 1999)
Lockhart DM (tr), *The Itinerario of Jeronimo Lobo* (The Hakluyt Society, London 1984)
Macaulay T, *Indian Penal Code* (Lawbook Exchange, New Jersey 2002)
MacDermot V, *The Cult of the Seer in the Ancient Middle East: A Contribution to Current Research on Hallucinations Drawn from Coptic and Other Texts* (Welcome Institute of the History of Medicine, London 1971)
Maine HS, *Dissertations on Early Law and Custom: Chiefly Selected from Lectures Delivered at Oxford* (John Murray, London 1883)
Mann K and Roberts R (eds), *Law in Colonial Africa* (Heinmann and James Currey, Portsmouth and London 1991)
Merle R and Vitu A, *Traité de droit criminel: problèmes généraux de la conscience criminelle, droit pénal général* (7th edn, Cujas, Paris 1997)
Miège J-L, *Le Maroc* (PUF, Paris 1994)
Mittlebeeler EV, *African Custom and Western Law: The Development of the Rhodesian Criminal Law for Africans* (Africana, New York and London 1976)
Morgan W and Macpherson AG, *The Indian Penal Code Act XLV of 1860 with Notes* (G.C. Hay and Co, London 1861)
Moses WJ, *Liberian Dreams: Back-to-Africa Narratives from the 1850s* (Pennsylvania State University Press, Pennsylvania 1998)
Nugent P, *Africa since Independence: A Comparative History* (Palgrave Macmillan, New York 2004)
Nyabirungu MS, *Droit pénal général Zaïrois* (DES, Kinshasa 1995)
—— *Traité du droit pénal général Congolais* (Editions Universitaires Africaines, Kinshasa 2007)
Olewale ET, *The Nature of African Customary Law* (Manchester University Press, London 1954)
—— *Ghana and Sierra Leone: The Development of their Laws and Constitution* (Stevens and Sons, London 1962)
Ottenberg S and Ottenberg P, *Cultures and Societies of Africa* (Random House, New York 1960)
Prunier G, *The Rwanda Crisis 1959–1994: History of a Genocide* (Columbia University Press, New York 1995)
Radzinowicz L, *A History of English Criminal Law and its Administration from 1750*, vol 1 (Stevens and Sons, London 1948)
Roberts CC, *Tangled Justice: Some Reasons for a Change of Policy in Africa* (Macmillan, London 1937)
Roberts-Wray K, *Commonwealth and Colonial Law* (Stevens and Sons, London 1966)

Salacuse JW, *An Introduction to Law in French-Speaking Africa, vol I: Africa South of the Sahara* (The Michie Company, Charlottesville 1969)

—— *An Introduction to Law in French-Speaking Africa, vol II: North Africa* (The Michie Company, Charlottesville 1975)

Sandrat G, *Cours de droit coutumier*, Partie II (Groupe Scolaire d'Astrida, Butare 1951)

Sarrat A, *Grandeur et servitude coloniales* (Sagitaire, Paris 1931)

Schabas WA, *The Abolition of the Death Penalty in International Law* (3rd edn, Cambridge University Press, Cambridge 2002)

—— *The International Criminal Court: A Commentary on the Rome Statute* (Oxford University Press, New York 2010)

Schapera I, *The Bantu-Speaking Tribes of South Africa* (George Routledge and Sons, London 1937)

Sharp A, *The Versailles Settlement: Peacekeeping after the First World War, 1919–1923* (Palgrave Macmillan, New York 2008)

Snell GS, *Nandi Customary Law* (East African Literature Bureau, Nairobi 1954)

Snyman CR, *Criminal Law* (4th edn, Butterworths, Durban 2002)

Soga JH, *The Ama-Xosa: Life and Customs* (Lovedale Press, Lovedale 1932)

Sohier J, *Répertoire général de la jurisprudence et de la doctrine coutumière du Congo et du Ruanda-Urundi jusqu'au 31 décembre 1953* (Larcier, Brussels 1957)

—— *Essai sur la criminalité dans la province de Léopoldville* (Académie Royale des Sciences Coloniales, Brussels 1959)

Soret M, *Les Kongo nord occidentaux* (PUF, Paris 1959)

Tamm D, *Roman Law and European Legal History* (Djof Publishing, Copenhagen 1997)

Tardits C, *Le royaume Bamoum* (Armand Colin, Paris 1980)

Terblanche SS, *The Guide to Sentencing in South Africa* (Butterworths, Durban 1999)

Torday E, *On the Trail of the Bushongo* (Seeley, Service and Co, London 1925)

Tredgold CH, *Handbook of Colonial Criminal Law* (Juta, Cape Town 1904)

Turell R, *White Mercy: A Study of the Death Penalty in South Africa* (Praeger, London 2004)

Van Geluwe H, *Les Bira et les peuplades limitrophes* (International African Institute, London 1957)

—— *Mamvu-Mangutu et Balese-Mvuba* (International African Institute, London 1957)

—— *Les Bali et les peuplades apparentées (Ndaka, Mbo, Beke, Lika, Budu, Nyari)* (International African Institute, London 1960)

Van Overbergh C, *Les Mangbetu (Congo Belge)* (Institut International de Bibliographie, Brussels 1909)

Vanderlinden J, *Les systèmes juridiques Africains* (PUF, Paris 1983)

Vansina J, *Les tribus Ba-Kuba et les peuplades apparentées* (International African Institute, London 1954)

Vincent MB, *Etudes sur la loi musulmane (Rit de Malek): législation criminelle* (Joubert, Paris 1842)

Wahba al-Mawardi WH (tr), *The Ordinances of Government* (Garnet Publishing, London 1996)

Yusuf Ali A, *The Glorious Koran* (JM Dent & Sons, London 1909)

Book Chapters and Journal Articles

—— 'Cape Treason Trials' (1901) 18 *South African Law Journal* 164

—— 'Capital Punishment' (1897) 14 *South African Law Journal* 122

—— 'Capital Punishment under the Common Law' (1891) 8 *South African Law Journal* 232

—— 'Death Penalty in South Africa, the Statistics' (1989) 2 *South African Journal of Criminal Justice* 252

—— 'Early Law and Custom' (1885) 2 *Cape Law Journal* 28

—— 'Hangings: Last Ten Years' (1985) 1 *South African Journal on Human Rights* 180

—— 'Legislation-Ghana' (1961) 5 *Journal of African Law* 157

—— 'Notes and News, Customary Criminal Law in Kenya' (1963) 7 *Journal of African Law* 1

—— 'Roman Dutch Law in the Transvaal and Orange River Colony' (1901) 18 *South African Law Journal* 398

—— 'Statistics' (1992) 2 *South African Journal of Criminal Justice* 251

—— 'The Crime of Treason, etc., in the Transvaal' (1896) 13 *South African Law Journal* 182

Agwuele AO, 'Military Occupation, the National Question and the Rise of Ethnic Nationalism' in Toyin Falola (ed), *Nigeria in the Twentieth Century* (Carolina Academy Press, Durham 2002) 349–358

Akpan MB, 'Black Imperialism: Americo-Liberian Rule over the African Peoples of Liberia, 1841–1964' (1973) 7 *Canadian Journal of African Studies* 217

Allam S, 'Un droit pénal existait-il "stricto sensu" en Egypte Pharaonique?' (1978) 64 *Journal of Egyptian Archaeology* 65

Anderson JND, 'Homicide in Islamic Law' (1951) 13 *Bulletin of Oriental and African Studies* 811

Asiwaju AI, 'Law in African Borderlands: The Lived Experience of the Yoruba Astride the Nigeria-Dahomey Border' in Kristin Mann and Richard Roberts (eds), *Law in Colonial Africa* (Heinmann, Portsmouth 1991) 224–238

Auwalu YH, 'Colonialism and the Transformation of Islamic Law in the Northern States of Nigeria' (1992) 32 *Journal of Legal Pluralism* 103

Awe B, 'Conflict and Divergence: Government and Society in Nigeria' (1999) 42 *African Studies Review* 1

Badinter R, 'Moving towards Universal Abolition of the Death Penalty' in *Death Penalty: Beyond Abolition* (Council of Europe Publishing, Strasbourg 2004) 7–11

Bassiouni MC, 'Death as a Penalty in the Shari'a' in Peter Hodgkinson and William A Schabas (eds), *Capital Punishment: Strategies for Abolition* (Cambridge University Press, Cambridge 2004) 169–185

Blundell WH, 'History of King Theodore' (1906) 21 *Journal of the Royal African Society* 12

Braithwaite WC, 'Tribal Laws of the Mendi' (1921) 3 *Journal of Comparative Legislation and International Law* 228

Brett M, 'The Mīm, the 'Ayn, and the Making of Ismā'īlism' (1994) 57 *Bulletin of the School of Oriental and African Studies* 25

Brunschvig R, 'Justice religieuse et justice laïque dans la Tunisie des Deys et des Beys: jusqu'au milieu du XIXème siècle' (1965) 23 *Studia Islamica* 27

Burchell J, 'Criminal Law' in Cornie G Van Der Merwe and Jacques E Du Plessis (eds), *Introduction to the Law of South Africa* (Kluwer Law International, The Hague 2004) 447–491

Centre des Etudes de Sécurité (Arabie Saoudite), 'Légalité et commodité de la peine de mort en droit Musulman' (1987) 58 *Revue international de droit pénal* 431

Chabas J, 'La sanction pénale des actes réglementaires pris par les représentants du gouvernement dans les départements et les territoires d'outre-mer' (1948) 2 *Revue juridique et politique de l'union française* 29

Châtelain J, 'Le régime disciplinaire et pénal des populations indigènes' (1947) 1 *Revue juridique et politique de l'union française* 84

Chenwi L, 'Breaking New Ground: The Need for a Protocol to the African Charter on the Abolition of the Death Penalty in Africa' (2005) 5 *African Human Rights Law Journal* 89

—— 'Initiating Constructive Debate: A Critical Reflection on the Death Penalty in Africa' (2005) 38 *Comparative and International Law of Southern Africa* 474

—— 'Fair Trial Rights and their Relation to the Death Penalty in Africa' (2006) 55 *International and Comparative Law Quarterly* 609

Christelow A, 'Theft, Homicide and Oath in Early Twentieth Century Kano' in Kristin Mann and Richard Roberts (eds), *Law in Colonial Africa* (James Currey, London 1991) 205–223

Chukwuemeka E, 'Indigenous Law and Justice: Some Major Concepts and Practices' in Gordon R Woodman and Akintunde O Obilade, *African Law and Legal Theory* (Dartmouth, Aldershot, Singapore and Sidney 1995) 33–42

Contini P, 'The Evolution of Blood-Money for Homicide in Somalia' (1971) 15 *Journal of African Law* 78

Cooper AD, 'Reparations for the Herero Genocide: Defining the Limits of International Litigation' (2006) 106 *African Affairs* 113

Cotran E, 'The Position of Customary Criminal Law in African Countries' in Akilagpa Sawyerr (ed), *East African Law and Social Change* (The East African Institute of Social and Cultural Affairs, Nairobi 1967) 14–25

Coyle A, 'Replacing the Death Penalty: The Vexed Issue of Alternative Sanctions' in Peter Hodgkinson and William A Schabas (eds), *Capital Punishment: Strategies for Abolition* (Cambridge University Press, Cambridge 2004) 92–115

Crawford JR, 'The History and Nature of the Judicial System of Botswana, Lesotho and Swaziland: Introduction and the Superior Courts' (1969) 86 *South African Law Journal* 476

Daly MW, 'The Development of the Governor-Generalship of the Sudan, 1899–1934' (1983) 24 *Journal of African History* 77

De Smith SA, 'Fundamental Rights in the New Commonwealth-II' (1961) 10 *International Comparative Law Quarterly* 215

Devenish G, 'South Africa from Pre-colonial Times to Democracy: A Constitutional and Jurisprudential Odyssey' (2005) 1 *Journal of South African Law* 457

Donavan DA and Assefa G, 'Homicide in Ethiopia: Human Rights, Federalism and Legal Pluralism' (2003) 52 *American Journal of Comparative Law* 505

Du Bois F, 'Introduction: History, System and Sources' in Cornie G Van Der Merwe and Jacques E Du Plessis (eds), *Introduction to the Law of South Africa* (Kluwer Law International, The Hague 2004) 1–53

Du Plessis LM, 'Capital Punishment: A Legal Philosophical Appraisal' (1989) 2 *South African Journal of Criminal Justice* 181

Fagan E, 'Roman Dutch Law in its South African Historical Context' in Reinhard Zimmermann and Daniel Visser (eds), *Southern Cross: Civil and Common Law in South Africa* (Oxford University Press, London 1996) 33–64

Fatula O, 'Capital Punishment: To Be or not To Be in Nigeria' (2001–2004) 14 *Lesotho Law Journal* 97

Fisher SZ, 'Traditional Criminal Procedure in Ethiopia' (1971) 19 *American Journal of Comparative Law* 709

Fluehr-Lobban C, 'Islamization in Sudan: A Critical Assessment' (1990) 4 *Middle East Journal* 614

Forst M, 'The Abolition of the Death Penalty in France' in *The Abolition of the Death Penalty in Europe* (Council of Europe Publishing, Strasbourg 1999) 105–116

Gardiner FG, 'Notes on the Law of Treason' (1901) 18 *South African Law Journal* 142

Girvin SD, 'The Architects of the Mixed Legal System' in Reinhard Zimmermann and Daniel Visser (eds), *Southern Cross: Civil and Common Law in South Africa* (Oxford University Press, London 1996) 95–140

Gluckman M, 'Limitations of the Case Method in the Study of Tribal Law' in Gordon R Woodman and Akintunde O Obilade (eds), *African Law and Legal Theory* (Dartmouth, Aldershot, Singapore and Sidney 1995) 87–117

Gollan HC, 'Modes of Legislation in the British Colonies: Northern Nigeria' (1905) 6 *Journal of Comparative Legislation* 129

Goodwin MF, 'A Liberian Packet' (1951) 59 *Virginia Magazine of History and Biography* 77

Gouveia Da Veiga FO, 'Portuguese Africa' in Alan Milner (ed), *African Penal Systems* (Routledge and Kegan Paul, London 1969) 213–224

Grove DL, 'The "Sentinels" of Liberty? The Nigerian Judiciary and Fundamental Rights' (1963) 7 *Journal of African Law* 152

Hansungule M, 'The Historical Development of International Human Rights' in Azizur Rahman Chowdhury and Jahid Hossain Bhuiyan (eds), *An Introduction to International Human Rights Law* (Martinus Nijhoff Publishers, The Hague 2010) 1–30

Hart DM, 'Murder in the Market: Penal Aspects of Berber Customary Law in the Pre-colonial Moroccan Rif' (1996) 3 *Islamic Law and Society* 343

Hodgkinson P, 'Capital Punishment: Improve It or Remove It?' in Peter Hodgkinson and William A Schabas (eds), *Capital Punishment: Strategies for Abolition* (Cambridge University Press, Cambridge 2004) 1–35

Holleman JF, 'An Anthropological Approach to Bantu Law (with Special Reference to Shona Law)' in Gordon R Woodman and Akintunde O Obilade (eds), *African Law and Legal Theory* (Dartmouth, Aldershot, Singapore and Sidney 1995) 5–18

Holt PM, 'Egypt, the Funj and Darfur' in Richard Gray (ed), *The Cambridge History of Africa: From c.1600 to c.1790* (Cambridge University Press, London, New York and Melbourne 1975) 14–58

Hone HR, 'The Native of Uganda and the Criminal Law' (1939) 21 *Journal of Comparative Legislation and International Law* 179

Hood R and Hoyle C, 'Abolishing the Death Penalty Worldwide: The Impact of a "New Dynamic"' (2009) 38 *Crime and Justice* 1

Hrbek I, 'Egypt, Nubia and the Eastern Desert' in Roland Oliver (ed), *The Cambridge History of Africa: From c.1050 to c.1600* (Cambridge University Press, London, New York and Melbourne 1975) 10–98

Hunwick J, 'An African Case Study of Political Islam: Nigeria' (1992) 524 *Annals of the American Academy of Political and Social Sciences* 143

Hyams P, 'Due Process versus the Maintenance of Order in European Law: The Contribution of the *Ius Commune*' in Peter Coss (ed), *The Moral World of the Law* (Cambridge University Press, London 2000) 62–90

Hynd S, 'Killing the Condemned: The Practice and Process of Capital Punishment in British Africa, 1900–1950s' (2008) 49 *Journal of African History* 403

Imbert J, 'La peine de mort et l'opinion au XVIIIème siècle' (1964) 19 *Revue de science criminelle et de droit pénal comparé* 509

Iwobi AU, 'Tiptoeing through a Constitutional Minefield: The Great Shari'a Controversy in Nigeria' (2004) 48 *Journal of African Law* 111

Jackson W, 'White Man's Country: Kenya Colony and the Making of a Myth' (2011) 5 *Journal of Eastern African Studies* 344

Jeater D, '"Their Idea of Justice is so Peculiar": Southern Rhodesia 1890–1910' in Peter Coss (ed), *The Moral World of the Law* (Cambridge University Press, London 2000) 178–195

Joireman SF, 'Inherited Legal Systems and Effective Rule of Law: Africa and the Colonial Legacy' (2001) 4 *Journal of Modern African Studies* 571

Kahn E, 'Crime and Punishment 1910–1960: Reflections on Changes since Union in the Law of Criminal Law and its Application' (1960) 191 *Acta Juridica* 191

—— 'Death Penalty Statistics' (1981) 98 *South African Law Journal* 421

—— 'What Is Happening to the Death Penalty?' (1981) 98 *South African Law Journal* 103

—— 'How Did We Get our Lopsided Law on the Imposition of the Death Penalty for Common Law Crimes? And What Should We Do about It?' (1989) 2 *South African Journal of Criminal Justice* 137 and 137

Kerr AJ, 'The Reception and Codification of Systems of Law in Southern Africa' (1958) 2 *Journal of African Law* 82

Kieh GK and Ogaba Agbese P, 'From Politics Back to the Barracks in Nigeria: A Theoretical Exploration' (1993) 30 *Journal of Peace Research* 409

Le Cour Grandmaison O, 'The Exception and the Rule: On French Colonial Law' (2006) 212 *Diogenes* 34

Le Roux J and Bekink B, 'The Abrogation of the Death Penalty in South Africa: Participating in the Ongoing Debate' (2006) 62 *Journal for Contemporary Roman Dutch Law* 201

Lenman B and Parker G, 'The State, the Community and the Criminal Law in Early Modern Europe' in Vic AC Gatrell et al. (eds), *Crime and the Law: The Social History of Crime in Western Europe since 1500* (Europa Publications Limited, London 1980) 11–48

Leslie RD, 'Lesotho, Botswana and Swaziland' in Alan Milner (ed), *African Penal Systems* (Routledge and Kegan Paul, London 1969) 165–189

Lonsdale J, 'Kenyatta's Trials: Breaking and Making an African Nationalist' in Peter Coss (ed), *The Moral World of the Law* (Cambridge University Press, London 2000) 196–239

Lowenstein S, 'Ethiopia' in Alan Milner (ed), *African Penal Systems* (Routledge and Kegan Paul, London 1969) 33–57

Matson JN, 'The Common Law Abroad: English and Indigenous Law in the British Commonwealth' (1993) 42 *International and Comparative Law Quarterly* 753

McClain WT, 'Lesotho's Criminal Law: South African Common Law or a Lesotho Penal Code' (1985) 1 *Lesotho Law Journal* 239

Mediano FR, 'Les pratiques de la justice au 16e-19e siècles: justice, crime et châtiment au Maroc au 16e siècle' (1996) 3 *Annales, histoire des sciences sociales* 613

Mensa-Bonsu HJAN, '"Political Crimes" in the Political History of Ghana: 1948–1993' in Henrietta Mensa-Bonsu et al., *Ghana Law since Independence: History, Development and Prospects* (Black Mask, Accra 2007) 239–307

Milner A, 'Sentencing Patterns in Nigeria' in Alan Milner (ed), *African Penal Systems* (Routledge and Kegan Paul, London 1969) 261–292

Morice G, 'The Administration of Criminal Law in South Africa' (1920) 37 *South African Law Journal* 131

Morris HF, 'How Nigeria Got its Criminal Code' (1970) 14 *Journal of African Law* 137

——, 'A History of the Adoption of Codes of Criminal Law and Procedure in British Colonial Africa, 1876–1935' (1974) 18 *Journal of African Law* 6

Mugerwa NPJ, 'Status, Responsibility, and Liability: A Comparative Study of Two Types of Society in Uganda' in Max Gluckman et al. (eds), *Ideas and Procedures in African Customary Law* (Oxford University Press, London 1969) 279–91

Mujuzi JD, 'Issues Surrounding Life Imprisonment after the Abolition of the Death Penalty in Rwanda' (2009) 9 *Human Rights Law Review* 335

Murray C, 'Hangings in Southern Africa: The Last Ten Years' (1986) 2 *South African Journal on Human Rights* 349

Nathan M, 'The Roman Dutch Law of Homicide' (1902) 19 *South African Law Journal* 115

Nduka O, 'The Traditional Concept of Justice Among the Ibo of South-Eastern Nigeria' in Gordon R Woodman and Akintunde O Obilade (eds), *African Law and Legal Theory* (Dartmouth, Aldershot, Singapore and Sidney 1995) 19–29

Ngondji O L, ' L'impact de le peine de mort dans le processus de l'adoption de la loi de mise en oeuvre du statut de Rome en République Démocratique du Congo", in Kai Ambos and Ottilia A. Maunganidze (eds), Pouvoir et Poursuites : Défis et Opportunités pour la Justice Pénale Internationale en Afrique SubSaharienne (Konrad Adenauer Stiftung, Gottingen, 2012) 73-84.

Obu AA, 'Lawyers, Legal Education and *Shari'a* Courts in Nigeria' (2004) 49 *Journal of Legal Pluralism and Unofficial Law* 113

Ollenu NM, 'The Influence of English Law on West Africa' (1961) 5 *Journal of African Law* 21

Onwekwe CB, 'Militarism versus Democratic Governance' in Toyin Falola (ed), *Nigeria in the Twentieth Century* (Carolina Academy Press, Durham 2002) 385–404

Patrick CH, 'The Status of Capital Punishment: A Worldwide Perspective' (1965) 56 *Journal of Criminal Law, Criminology and Police Science* 397

Peters R, 'Islamic and Secular Criminal Law in Nineteenth Century Egypt: The Role and Function of the Qadi' (1997) 4 *Islamic Law and Society* 70

Rannat SMA, 'The Relationship Between Islamic and Customary Law in Sudan' (1960) 4 *Journal of African Law* 9

Read JS, 'Criminal Law in the Africa of Today and Tomorrow' (1963) 7 *Journal of African Law* 5

——, 'Kenya, Tanzania and Uganda' in Alan Milner (ed), *African Penal Systems* (Routledge and Kegan Paul, London 1969) 89–164

Richard AL, 'Customary Laws of Wrongs in Kenya: An Essay in Research Method' (1969) 17 *American Journal of Comparative Law* 573

Roberts CC, 'African Natives under the English System of Penal Law' (1933) 15 *Journal of Comparative Legislation* 169

Rubbens A, 'The Congo Democratic Republic' in Alan Milner (ed), *African Penal Systems* (Routledge and Kegan Paul, London 1969) 13–32

Russell FF, 'Eritrean Customary Law' (1959) 3 *Journal of African Law* 100–101

Safwat S, 'Islamic Law in the Sudan' in Aziz Al-Azmeh, *Islamic Law: Social and Historical Context* (Routledge, London 1988) 231–249

Schabas WA, 'African Perspectives on Abolition of the Death Penalty' in William A Schabas (ed), *The International Sourcebook on Capital Punishment* (Northeastern University Press, Boston 1997) 30–65

—— 'Islam and the Death Penalty' (2000) 9 *William and Mary Bill of Rights Journal* 223

—— 'International Law and the Death Penalty: Reflecting or Promoting Change?' in Peter Hodgkinson and William A Schabas (eds), *Capital Punishment: Strategies for Abolition* (Cambridge University Press, Cambridge 2004) 36–62

Schacht J, 'Islamic Law in Contemporary States' (1959) 8 *American Journal of Comparative Law* 133

Seidman RB and Eyison JDA, 'Ghana' in Alan Milner (ed), *African Penal Systems* (Routledge and Kegan Paul, London 1969) 59–88

Shadle B, 'White Settlers and the Law in Early Colonial Kenya' (2010) 4 *Journal of Eastern African Studies* 510

Shack WA, 'Guilt and Innocence: Problem and Method in the Gurage Judicial System' in Max Gluckman et al. (eds), *Ideas and Procedures in African Customary Law* (Oxford University Press, London 1969) 153–168

Simiyu VG, 'The Democratic Myth in the African Traditional Societies' in Walter O Oyugi and Afrifa K Gitonga (eds), *Democratic Theory and Practice in Africa* (Heinemann, Portsmouth 1988) 49–70

Siwundhla HT, 'White Ideologies and Non-European Participation in the Anglo-Boer War 1899–1902' (1984) 15 *Journal of Black Studies* 223

Smart HMJ, 'Place of Islamic Law within the Framework of the Sierra Leone Legal System' (1980) 18 *African Law Studies* 87

Smith GT, 'Violent Crime and the Public Weal in England, 1700–1900' in Richard McMahon (ed), *Crime, Law and Popular Culture in Europe* (Willan Publishing, Devon 2008) 190–218

Stephen HL, 'A Model Criminal Code for the Colonies' (1899) 1 *Journal of Comparative Legislation* 439

Stone D, 'White Men with Low Moral Standards? German Anthropology and the Herero Genocide' (2010) 35(2) *Patterns of Prejudice* 33

Tallack W, 'The Penalty of Death' (1890) 7 *South African Law Journal* 82

Tamrat T, 'Ethiopia, the Red Sea and the Horn' in Roland Oliver (ed), *The Cambridge History of Africa: from c.1050 to c.1600*, vol 3 (Cambridge University Press, London 1977) 99–177

Teixeira M, 'Sorcellerie et contre sorcellerie: un réajustement permanent au monde, les Manjak de Guinée Bissau et du Sénégal' (2008) 189–190 *Cahiers d'etudes africaines* 59

Toscano R, 'The United Nations and the Abolition of the Death Penalty' in *The Death Penalty: Abolition in Europe* (Council of Europe Publishing, Strasbourg 1999) 91–104

Tupper L, 'Customary Law and Other Law in the East Africa Protectorate' (1907) 8 *Journal of Comparative Legislation* 172

Turner T, 'Zaire: Flying High above the Toads: Mobutu and Stalemated Democracy' in John F Clark and David E Gardiner (eds), *Political Reform in Francophone Africa* (Westview Press, Oxford 1997) 246–264

Ubah CN, 'Islamic Legal System and the Westernization Process in the Nigerian Emirates' (1982) 20 *Journal of Legal Pluralism and Unofficial Law* 69

Van Niekerk B, 'Hanged by the Neck until You Are Dead' (1969) 86 *South African Law Journal* 457

Van Zyl CH, 'The Study of Law' (1893) 10 *South African Law Journal* 185

Van Zyl Smit D, 'The Death Penalty in Africa' (2004) 4 *African Human Rights Law Journal* 1

Vansina J, 'A Traditional Legal System: The Kuba' in Hilda Kuper and Leo Kuper (eds), *African Law: Adaptation and Development* (University of California Press, Berkeley 1965) 97–119

Wagner G, 'The Political Organization of the Bantu of Kavirondo' in Meyer Fortes and Edward Evans-Richards (eds), *African Political Systems* (Oxford University Press, London 1970) 197–238

Warioba JS, 'The Role of Assessors in Criminal Trials in Tanganyika' (1966) 1 *Journal of the Denning Law Society* 234

Willems H, 'Crime, Cult and Capital Punishment (Mo'alla Inscription)' (1990) 75 *Journal of Egyptian Archaeology* 27

Williams C, 'Asante: Human Sacrifice or Capital Punishment? An Assessment of the Period 1807–1874' (1988) 21 *International Journal of African Historical Studies* 433

Wilson W, 'Murder and the Structure of Homicide' in Andrew Ashworth and Barry Mitchell (eds), *Rethinking English Homicide Law* (Oxford University Press, New York 2000) 21–54

Woodman GR, 'Some Realism About Customary Law: The West African Experience' in Gordon R Woodman and Akintunde O Obilade (eds), *African Law and Legal Theory* (Dartmouth, Aldershot, Singapore and Sidney 1995) 145–170

Yeplaala K, 'Circular Arguments and Self-Fulfilling Definition: "Statelessness" and the Dagaaba' (1983) 10 *History in Africa* 349

Zarr GH, 'Liberia' in Alan Milner (ed), *African Penal Systems* (Routledge and Kegan Paul, London 1969) 191–212

Index

Page numbers in *italics* refer to figures and tables. DP in headings means 'death penalty'.

For Product Safety Concerns and Information please contact our EU representative GPSR@taylorandfrancis.com
Taylor & Francis Verlag GmbH, Kaufingerstraße 24, 80331 München, Germany

www.ingramcontent.com/pod-product-compliance
Ingram Content Group UK Ltd.
Pitfield, Milton Keynes, MK11 3LW, UK
UKHW011002180926
475701UK00004B/515
9781138279513